D0735207

Read & Pray through the BIBLE in a YEAR

MORNING AND EVENING DEVOTIONS FOR WOMEN

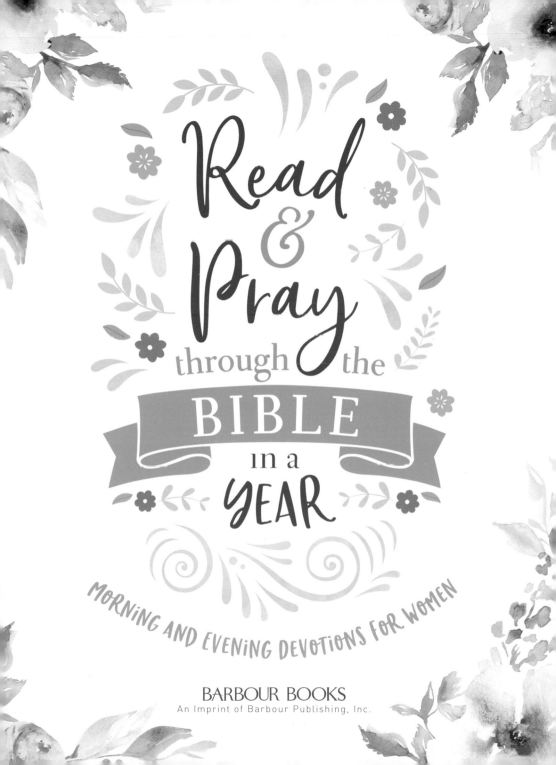

Read & Pray through the BIBLE in a YEAR

MORNING AND EVENING DEVOTIONS FOR WOMEN

BARBOUR BOOKS

An Imprint of Barbour Publishing, Inc.

Read through the Bible in a Year © 2016 by Barbour Publishing, Inc.

Pray through the Bible in a Year © 2018 by Barbour Publishing, Inc.

Written by Emily Marsh and Darlene Franklin.

Print ISBN 978-1-64352-462-7

eBook Editions:
Adobe Digital Edition (.epub) 978-1-64352-589-1
Kindle and MobiPocket Edition (.prc) 978-1-64352-590-7

Published by Barbour Books, an imprint of Barbour Publishing, Inc., 1810 Barbour Drive, Uhrichsville, Ohio 44683, www.barbourbooks.com

Our mission is to inspire the world with the life-changing message of the Bible.

ecpa Member of the
Evangelical Christian
Publishers Association

Printed in China.

Welcome
TO YOUR YEAR IN THE WORD

God's Word is life-giving (Matthew 4:4), true (Psalm 33:4), powerful (Hebrews 4:12), inspired by God (2 Timothy 3:16), profitable to equip and train you (2 Timothy 3:16–17), a light to show you your way (Psalm 119:105), a guide for a pure life (Psalm 119:9), everlasting (Isaiah 40:8; Matthew 24:35), wisdom-giving (Proverbs 2:6), freeing (John 8:32), sustaining (Deuteronomy 8:3), able to save your soul (James 1:21), and something that will give you hope (Psalm 119:114; Psalm 130:5).

God asks you to meditate on this precious gift and to make it a central part of your life. And He promises that if you do, He will make your way prosperous and successful (Joshua 1:8). As one of God's children, you simply cannot ignore His Word. The more intimately you know the Bible, the more fully you will come to know and love the Author. Look forward to how God will change your life as you read through and pray on His Word this year.

All Creation Sings

(GENESIS 1)

>>)))) ❀ <<<<<

MORNING PRAYER·· ·

Creator God, how often You speak to me in the beauty of Your creation. I see Your eternal nature and power in the mountains. I hear Your peace and presence in the sound of waves upon the shore. I feel Your love and delight in the soft fur of a kitten purring against my hand. They prepare my soul for that personal encounter with You in scripture and in Your Son, the Word of God. I pray for those who have deafened themselves to Your voice in creation, that You will open their eyes to the truth by whatever means necessary, before it is too late. Amen.

> *And God saw every thing that he had made, and, behold, it was*
> *very good. And the evening and the morning were the sixth day.*
> GENESIS 1:31

EVENING READING ·

In this first reading of the year, we get a glimpse into the beautiful story that is woven throughout scripture. Genesis 1 speaks of the perfect world that God created. Psalm 1 is written in a fallen world that is marred by sin where we must actively avoid wickedness and seek purity. Matthew 1 is the beginning of God redeeming His people by sending His Son as one of us. Christ's very lineage is strewn with the aroma of redemption. His ancestors include such redeemed sinners as the harlot Rahab, the incestuous Judah and Tamar, the pagan Ruth, and the adulterous David and Bathsheba. God makes it no secret that His business is to redeem sinners and to show His power through the unlikely and the weak.

❧ DAY 2 ❧

Following God's Dreams
(MATTHEW 2)

>>>>>> ❀ <<<<<<

MORNING PRAYER ·

Wonderful Counselor, I confess I have a lot to learn about staying still, emptying my mind of diversions so I'm ready to listen. I thank You that I hear Your voice as I meditate on Your Word. There are times I would like to have clear-cut directions like Joseph received in his dreams. But You know my heart. Would I be afraid? Am I committed to the unwavering, immediate obedience that Joseph practiced? How I thank You that You know the path my life will take and You are already preparing me. Tune my spirit to the frequency You wish me to listen to. Amen.

> *Yet have I set my king upon my holy hill of Zion. I will*
> *declare the decree: the LORD hath said unto me, Thou art my*
> *Son; this day have I begotten thee. Ask of me, and I shall give*
> *thee the heathen for thine inheritance, and the uttermost*
> *parts of the earth for thy possession.*
> PSALM 2:6–8

EVENING READING ·

Genesis 3 presents a grim outlook on the future of humanity. But even in the midst of this chaos, God assures the serpent that one will come to wage war against him. Then in Psalm 2 an anointed King is proclaimed as Ruler over all the earth. And finally in Matthew, we catch a glimpse of this King. Though He was still a young child, the magi recognized Him as the King who was anointed to reign over the nations. A beautiful story of redemption begins to unfold.

As I Awake

(PSALM 3)

❧❧❧❧ ❀ ❧❧❧❧

MORNING PRAYER ·

Oh God who never sleeps, I awake this morning because You sustained me during the night. Today is a gift from Your hand. May I treat it with awe and care, treasuring each moment. May I stay on the path You have laid before me, even when I encounter obstacles. Whatever problems arise today, show me how to glorify You. If I become weak and battle weary, You will lift my head. You are my shield, my deliverer, even when You allow the enemy to assail me. I will lie down tonight, able to rest because You are always with me. Amen.

> *And saying, Repent ye: for the kingdom of heaven is at hand.*
> MATTHEW 3:2

EVENING READING ·

The holiness of God is vividly and frighteningly displayed in the account of the flood. Tragically, God in His holiness could not look on the degradation and sin being practiced by those whom He created. The God we serve today is just as holy and just as incensed by sin, but mercifully, we have been saved from His just wrath through the sacrifice of Christ. Repent of your sins and rest in the knowledge of your forgiveness through Christ.

Speechless Prayer

(GENESIS 8:21–22)

❧❧❧❧❧ ❀ ❦❦❦❦❦

MORNING PRAYER·

Rainbow Covenant God, I read about Noah after the flood and wonder about his prayers. What did he say to You when he offered clean animals on the altar? Only You know, and whatever words he used, You addressed his greatest needs: safety, food, and repopulating the earth. How I thank You that You understand my heart and my greatest needs. You know my every thought, for good or evil; You know the fears that plague me. And You provide for those weaknesses, sometimes before I ask. Oh God, how can I not want to follow a God like that? Amen.

> *I will both lay me down in peace, and sleep: for thou,*
> *LORD, only makest me dwell in safety.*
> PSALM 4:8

EVENING READING

No amount of money, prestige, or security measures can make you truly safe. It is only in Christ that you can find genuine rest, knowing that you are cared for and loved by the Ruler of the universe. Your heavenly Father has secured your future—an eternity with Him. So sleep peacefully, knowing that nothing can touch you outside of His will. God is faithful to His Word and dearly loves His children.

DAY 5

Going Your Way
(PSALM 5)

❯❯❯❯❯ ❀ ❮❮❮❮❮

MORNING PRAYER

Lord God, I look forward to meeting with You every day. I lay my requests before You with full confidence, counting on Your protection. Teach me Your joy in the midst of scary circumstances. Your favor is more than a blessing; it's also a shield against the enemy. Oh, what peace to know that the only harm that comes my way is permitted by You. Lead me on a righteous path. Teach me to love You first and most, and then to love others as I want to be loved. My vision and understanding blur; make Your way straight before me so that I will follow Your path even when the eyes of my heart don't see it. Amen.

My voice shalt thou hear in the morning, O LORD; in the morning will I direct my prayer unto thee, and will look up.
PSALM 5:3

EVENING READING

Just like David, pray with confidence that God will hear you and then eagerly watch for His answer. Start your day off in conversation with your Father. To actively enter into His presence in the morning will make you more aware of Him the rest of the day. Pray for the small things and the big things, knowing that not only will God listen to you, He will also act on your behalf.

Praying Is Loving

(MATTHEW 5:44)

❧❧❧❧❀❧❧❧❧

MORNING PRAYER

Sovereign Lord, I confess I don't like Your command to love my enemies, whether they are personal enemies, nations at war, or religious persecutors. I don't wish them well any more than Jonah wanted good to come to Nineveh. But pray and love are verbs, actions You command I take no matter what I'm feeling. And You know what happens when I pray for my adversaries. My feelings will change. So as I pray for them, I ask for eyes to see them as You see them. And if they walk according to Your will, my life will be better. That's the reconciliation I want. Let me pray in obedience, trusting You with the outcome. Amen.

> *And he brought him forth abroad, and said, Look now toward*
> *heaven, and tell the stars, if thou be able to number them:*
> *and he said unto him, So shall thy seed be. And he believed*
> *in the Lord; and he counted it to him for righteousness.*
> GENESIS 15:5–6

EVENING READING

Do you have faith like Abraham, who believed God that his descendants would be as numerous as the stars of heaven when at the time he had no children? His wife was past the age of childbearing, and they certainly would have been past the point of hoping for such a miracle. He had no earthly evidence that would have made him think that he could have innumerable descendants. But his faith in God caused him to disregard earthly circumstances in favor of heavenly promises.

DAY 7

"What If" Prayer
(Genesis 18:22–32)

>>>>> ❀ <<<<<

MORNING PRAYER

I have to give Abraham credit, Lord. He spoke with You face-to-face and didn't back down. He kept at it, pleading with You to spare Sodom if You could find—in the end—only ten righteous people in the city. He went with a quarter cup–sized request to a gallon-sized, and You kept saying yes. You have done the same for me. I asked for a quarter cup of blessing when You were ready to pour out a gallon. Expand me, prepare me to receive that immeasurable "Yes" when I pray on behalf of others. Amen.

> *Therefore Sarah laughed within herself, saying, After I am waxed old shall I have pleasure, my lord being old also? And the Lord said unto Abraham, Wherefore did Sarah laugh, saying, Shall I of a surety bear a child, which am old? Is any thing too hard for the Lord? At the time appointed I will return unto thee, according to the time of life, and Sarah shall have a son.*
> Genesis 18:12–14

EVENING READING

How often do you fail to take God's promises seriously? Maybe you feel you're not worthy. Maybe deep down you just don't think that God cares enough to keep His promises to you. Or maybe your doubt lies in a lack of faith in His power—that perhaps He can't actually do what He says. Fortunately, our lack of faith does not affect God's faithfulness. God will always keep His promises, whether or not we initially believe it. He will prove Himself to you as He did to Sarah.

☙ DAY 8 ❧

What Is Man?
(Psalm 8)

>⟫⟫⟩ ❀ ⟨⟨⟨⟨⟨

MORNING PRAYER ·

Lord God, this psalm brings the music and lyrics of praise songs to mind. I'm ready to stand with my hands raised to You. At the same time, I'm ready to fall to my knees. *What is man that You are mindful of him? What is woman that You are mindful of* me? When I wait at the foot of the tallest mountain, at the edge of the ocean, on the rim of a volcano creating new land, I feel so insignificant. But the truth is, You made me only a little lower than the angels—crowned with glory and honor, given control over Your creation. I don't understand why or how, but I rejoice in it, praying that all glory will be returned to You. Amen.

> *When I consider thy heavens, the work of thy fingers, the moon*
> *and the stars, which thou hast ordained; what is man, that thou*
> *art mindful of him? and the son of man, that thou visitest him?*
> Psalm 8:3–4

EVENING READING ·

How would it affect your life if you truly understood how important you are to God? God perfectly cares for everything He has created, including sparrows and wildflowers (Matthew 6:26–30). As His child and image bearer, you are much more important to Him than flowers and birds. He, the Creator of every star in the sky, is mindful of you! You can trust that you have and will have all that you need under His protection.

DAY 9

Ask, Seek, Knock

(MATTHEW 7:7–11)

>->>>> ❀ <<<<<

MORNING PRAYER

Oh heavenly Father, I'm the child from the parable; You are the Father who will give good gifts to Your children when we ask You. When I ask for help from You, it's as scary—and as easy—as asking my earthly father. You may not give me what I ask for, but You will give me what is best. I may knock on Your door, asking You to end a specific war. Instead, You give me Yourself, the Prince of Peace, dwelling in me and one day ruling the world. You give me the answer to what I seek, not the means I think is best. And how I thank You that Your wisdom knows the difference. Amen!

> *And Abraham said, My son, God will provide himself a*
> *lamb for a burnt offering: so they went both of them together.*
> GENESIS 22:8

EVENING READING

God spared Isaac, Abraham's son, and blessed Abraham for having the faith to trust God even in the most confusing and heartbreaking of circumstances. God did not spare His own Son and yet blessed us based on no merit of our own. God did indeed provide the sacrificial Lamb. We have every reason to trust God as Abraham did. He's more than proven Himself.

⚘ DAY 10 ⚘

Because I Know Your Name

(PSALM 9:10)

>>>>> ❀ <<<<<

MORNING PRAYER ·

Jesus, Name above all names, I come to You in faith. You will never forsake me, and there is no one more powerful than You. Your names showcase all the ways You supply my every need. Emmanuel—You are with me every second of my day. Prince of Peace—I rely on You because the road is often bumpy. Wonderful Counselor—I seek You when I don't know which way to turn. You are my all in all. You are King of kings and Lord of lords. I bow before You. Strike even more awe into my heart. You are my all in all. Amen.

And they that know thy name will put their trust in thee:
for thou, Lord, hast not forsaken them that seek thee.
PSALM 9:10

EVENING READING ·

Take time to think back over the faithfulness of God in your life. Remember those times when even in the midst of your doubt or fear He showed Himself to you in powerful and visible ways. If you truly know the character and person of God, you will unequivocally, without hesitation, put your trust in Him because you know without a shadow of a doubt that He has never and will never forsake you.

When Men and Women Pray

(GENESIS 25:21–23)

>>>>>> ❀ <<<<<<

MORNING PRAYER ·

Lord, You've heard parents pray for their children since Eve gave birth to Cain. How precious is this record of faith on the part of Isaac *and* Rebekah, the essential link between Abraham and Jacob. How different the prayers of this couple, and what a reminder of the differing roles father and mother bear. Yet You answered their prayers equally. You gave Isaac measurable affirmation—he received a son. You gave Rebekah insight into the twins she carried. Today when I pray, You answer the needs of my mind, soul, and spirit as well as of my body. Amen.

> *And, behold, there came a leper and worshipped him,*
> *saying, Lord, if thou wilt, thou canst make me clean.*
> MATTHEW 8:2

EVENING READING ·

May we have the same attitude as the leper—coming to God with nothing left to give, bowing before Him in full reliance that He is powerful enough to give us strength and make us well. This leper understood that the healing of his infirmity relied completely on the grace of God. Knowing that God *could* heal him, he didn't demand Him to, beg Him to, or even argue with Him about why He should. Instead, he worshipped Christ by humbly acknowledging His power both to heal and to decide whether to heal. Sometimes we doubt God's power simply because He chooses not to display it in the way we wish He would. If only we would approach every prayer with the same humble and worshipful stance as the leper.

≥ DAY 12 ≤

Expecting the Unexpected
(MATTHEW 8:23–27)

>->))) ❀ (((<<

MORNING PRAYER ·

God of the unexpected, how often You surprise me. You always act in accordance with Your character, but not always as I foresee. Often I repeat an ordinary activity, like the disciples crossing the Sea of Galilee in a boat. With You by my side, I expect clear sailing, but a storm arises instead. Like the disciples, I'm tempted to rail at You for not paying attention. But You want my faith. You are with me, therefore I have no need to be afraid. Sunshine or rain, You keep me safe. Amen.

To judge the fatherless and the oppressed,
that the man of the earth may no more oppress.
PSALM 10:18

EVENING READING ·

When the darkness and insidious evil of the world seem so powerful, it is imperative that you remember that the one who calmed the wind and the waves is still the ruler of this earth. He will one day vanquish evil for all eternity. He will judge the earth so that man may no longer oppress His image bearers. He will make all things right. You must hold fast to this truth so you won't lose hope.

Groveling Prayer

(MATTHEW 9:20–22)

>>>>> ❀ <<<<<

MORNING PRAYER

Lord, part of me identifies with the synagogue ruler, his superspiritual position and his worry for his troubled daughter. How many times have I prayed to You about my family, about those dearest to me? But perhaps I relate even more with the woman touching the hem of Your garment. How often have I reached out, feeling unworthy to be in Your company, among Your people, but knowing You cared about me in spite of everything I felt? Oh Lord, what a welcome promise, that You call that desperate plea an act of faith. When You answer my supplication, all praise goes to You. Amen.

But Jesus turned him about, and when he saw her, he said,
Daughter, be of good comfort; thy faith hath made thee whole.
And the woman was made whole from that hour.
MATTHEW 9:22

EVENING READING

Scripture is laden with stories of the compassion of God. Just in today's reading we see that He loves the unloved (Leah), He sees those who feel invisible (the woman with the hemorrhage), He invites the outcasts in (the sinners and tax collectors), and He heals the sick and needy (the synagogue official's daughter and the blind men). You serve a compassionate and loving God who does not overlook any of His children. He cares deeply for you.

GENESIS 30:1–31:21 ❀ MATTHEW 10:1–15 ❀ PSALM 12

When Will God Arise?

(Psalm 12:5)

>>>>> ❀ <<<<<

MORNING PRAYER

Lord Jehovah, I pour out my heart to You, asking for Your favor, to make me more like You. And in Your grace, You answer. But Lord, give me the eyes and the ears to feel Your heartbeat. David knew what things got Your immediate attention: when the poor are plundered and the needy groan. You keep them safe. Make me an instrument of Your love for them. Your words to me are more valuable than silver. Change the priorities in my heart—from things to people to Your Word. Then I will better know how to pray. Amen.

> *For the oppression of the poor, for the sighing of the needy,*
> *now will I arise, saith the LORD; I will set him*
> *in safety from him that puffeth at him.*
> PSALM 12:5

EVENING READING

The Lord sees your struggles and hears your groaning. Your prayers do not fall on deaf ears. God will act in His own perfect timing. God will arise to vindicate the injustices done on His people. If you are oppressed or treated unjustly, recognize that no matter what people may say about you, you are vindicated and justified by the ultimate judge. Doesn't your standing before Him matter infinitely more than your status here on earth?

Words in My Mouth

(MATTHEW 10:18–20)

≈≫≫≫ ❀ ≪≪≪≈

MORNING PRAYER

Jesus, how You must have smiled when I hated speech in high school, knowing the day would come that I would love to speak in front of groups. But I confess I still clam up when I feel uncomfortable. So thank You for this promise. You will give me the words to say when I'm called to account for my love for You—but that doesn't just mean when I face a firing squad. You will give me words when a coworker asks about my faith. You will shield me with Your words if I'm attacked by family and friends dear to me. I pray I will be living in Your words and by Your Word so that they will naturally fall from my lips. Amen.

> *But I have trusted in thy mercy; my heart shall*
> *rejoice in thy salvation. I will sing unto the LORD,*
> *because he hath dealt bountifully with me.*
> PSALM 13:5–6

EVENING READING

Although Jacob's prayer in Genesis 32 was probably inspired more by fear than faith, we can emulate him in that he called to mind God's promises. When you're faced with a fearful situation, remember the promises that God has made to you and pray them back to Him. Although He certainly doesn't need to be reminded of the promises He has made, it will bless you to be reminded of them.

⪢ DAY 16 ⪡

GENESIS 32:22–34:31 ❀ MATTHEW 10:37–11:6 ❀ PSALM 14

Wrestling with God

(Genesis 32:22–30)

⪢⪢⪢ ❀ ⪡⪡⪡

MORNING PRAYER ·

Lord, how often do we talk about wrestling over a problem while forgetting the man who spent a night physically wrestling with You? Jacob had already prayed to You. But You weren't done with him. You came back and wrestled with him all night. He had come so far, but You wanted to help him along. Oh Lord, I don't know if I have ever prayed like that, because I've never been able to stay on my knees for more than an hour (and rarely for an hour). But like Jacob, I have spent vigils when faced with a difficult situation. You battled with me and for me until I was ready for Your blessing—not in making things easier, but in changing me, strengthening me for the task ahead. I need You, Arm-Wrestling God. I won't leave until You bless me. Amen.

And Jacob called the name of the place Peniel: for I
have seen God face to face, and my life is preserved.
Genesis 32:30

EVENING READING ·

It is essential that you remember the times in your life when God has shown Himself to you in special or significant ways. Unlike Jacob, you probably don't have a permanent limp to constantly remind you of your encounter with God. But nevertheless, it is important to remember and celebrate God's faithfulness so that in times of trial, when it can be easy to doubt God, you have something concrete to look back on to remind you of how He always cares for you.

DAY 17

Dwelling with God

(PSALM 15)

≈≈⟩⟩⟩⟩ ✿ ⟨⟨⟨⟨≈

MORNING PRAYER

Lord Jehovah, who wants to dwell in Your sacred tent, never shaken? I do! I want the promise, but the requirements are beyond me. Speaks the truth? Doesn't hurt a neighbor? Keeps an oath even when it hurts? Oh, how grateful I am that righteousness doesn't depend on me. You made me blameless and righteous in Christ. I am holy because of my address, where I dwell in the heavenlies with Christ. You swooped in with one move and carried me off to the ongoing process of making me holy. In fact, I am Your tabernacle. Amen!

> *Lord, who shall abide in thy tabernacle? who shall dwell in thy*
> *holy hill? . . . He that doeth these things shall never be moved.*
> PSALM 15:1, 5

EVENING READING

Psalm 15 gives a list of attributes of one who would be worthy to dwell with God. It concludes in asserting that the one who does these things will never be shaken. This is not to say that struggles and heartbreaks will not reach the righteous. But when you dwell with God, the struggles of this world will be insignificant compared to the beauty and glory of your God. Someone who is anchored to an immovable Rock is hard to shake.

DAY 18

Peaceful Nights

(PSALM 16)

MORNING PRAYER

Dear Lord, how many of Your people struggle with sleepy days and sleepless nights? Why do I keep turning to You at night, pleading for sleep? Because that's my answer. I keep my eyes always on You, putting a lock on my head, that I may not turn to the right or left but only look straight at You. Because You are my Rock, solid, unmoving, I will not be shaken. You make me secure. You provide for my needs. I have no cause to worry. Beyond that, You give me joy and eternal life. In You there is rest. Amen!

Thou wilt shew me the path of life: in thy presence is fulness of joy; at thy right hand there are pleasures for evermore.
PSALM 16:11

EVENING READING

God will show you the path of life. Put Him before you in every decision of your life. If the decision seems too daunting, simply ask Him to reveal the next right step. Make your most urgent desire be to serve Him. You will find that He will guide, protect, and preserve you. The more closely you bind yourself to Him, the more clearly you will experience the fullness of joy available in His presence. He desires to give you pleasures forevermore.

GENESIS 39–40 ❀ **MATTHEW 12:1–29** ❀ **PSALM 17**

Answers Come from God
(GENESIS 40:8)

❧❧❧❧ ❀ ❧❧❧❧

MORNING PRAYER ·

Sovereign God, I looked forward to reading Joseph's prayers, to learn from this man who trusted You in spite of everything that would have driven most of us away. But I haven't found them yet while reading the Bible. Only hints here and there, like when he spoke with Pharaoh's servants. "Do not interpretations belong to God?" Lord, I want to call on You like that. To pray so naturally, for prayer to so permeate my life, that my walk and conversation will breathe with the time I have spent with You. For apart from You, I have nothing of worth to offer. Amen.

> *Keep me as the apple of the eye,*
> *hide me under the shadow of thy wings.*
> PSALM 17:8

EVENING READING ·

You instinctively protect your eyes from harm. When startled, you blink. If something comes flying suddenly in your direction, you immediately shield your face. The apple of your eye is valuable; therefore, you protect it. God's children are like the apple of His eye—something precious that He has taken great pains to protect. He will never fail or cease to protect you. Rest securely in the shadow of His wings.

DAY 20

Heart-Mouth Connection

(MATTHEW 12:34)

>>>>> ❀ <<<<<

MORNING PRAYER

Wonderful Counselor, once again I fall before You, miserable in the way I use my tongue, provoked to self-defense, to anger, ashamed. Oh Lord, it's been a lifelong battle, my default reaction when I feel pressured. I know it's not pleasing to You. I thank You for Your boundless love and provision. I know that You will free me from this sin and that it begins with a heart change. Oh Lord, so fill my heart with Yourself that all that comes from my mouth is the fullness of Your being, Your grace, Your love, Your joy. Only in You. Amen.

> *And Joseph answered Pharaoh, saying, It is not in me:*
> *God shall give Pharaoh an answer of peace.*
> GENESIS 41:16

EVENING READING

When you are honored and glorified on earth, use it as an opportunity to turn the eyes of those praising you to God. May everything that you do on earth be to His glory, for then you will be fulfilling your purpose in this life. True humility is recognizing that your achievements are owed to God and to what others have done to get you where you are. So direct the praise to God and to others—that's where it belongs.

Same as Me

(PSALM 18:25–26)

>-»»» ❀ «««-<

MORNING PRAYER

Oh Living Word, no wonder Your Word cuts the confusing clouds and unveils the real me. Because You come to me where I am. You take the message and frame it with Your faithfulness. You reveal Your blameless character. Your purity shines light on my understanding. If I'm not ready for that spotlight, You will speak to me in Braille until my eyes can see. Oh Lord, how I rejoice because You individualize Your lesson plan, giving me Your strengths and turning my weaknesses into glory for Your name. In all I do, let me honor You. Amen.

> *For thou will light my candle: the LORD*
> *my God will enlighten my darkness.*
> PSALM 18:28

EVENING READING

God knows your future, for He planned it out before you were even born. So ask the one who already knows your path to light your candle and enlighten your darkness. He will give you enough illumination to guide your feet to the next step you should take.

Battle Prayer

(PSALM 18:30–50)

>->>>> ❀ <<<<<

MORNING PRAYER

Oh Lord my Rock, You are not only my place of refuge; You are also my victory. I confess, often I come to You, hoping, pleading for You to head out to battle while I sit on the sidelines. But You call me to put on Your armor and stand beside You in battle. The victory is still all Yours, but You use my hands to beat them, my feet to trample them. You make my arms strong enough to bend bronze. And I shake my head at that one, because with my current health, I couldn't even pick up a bronze bow. I'm standing up for You, Lord, for You are there for me. Amen.

Now therefore, I pray thee, let thy servant abide instead of the lad
a bondman to my lord; and let the lad go up with his brethren.
GENESIS 44:33

EVENING READING

Never assume that someone is unable to be transformed by God's grace. Based upon the remarkably cruel way they treated Joseph, it would be easy to think that his brothers were past saving. And yet, in Judah (one of the brothers who was part of the horrific plan to kill Joseph), we see a dim and imperfect but unmistakable picture of Christ—he was willing to sacrifice his own life for the sake of his younger brother. God can work in any life.

GENESIS 46:1–47:26 ❀ **MATTHEW 13:24–43** ❀ **PSALM 19**

Where the Rubber Hits the Road
(Psalm 19)

>>>>> ❀ <<<<<

MORNING PRAYER ·

God who sees me, Your Word is powerful and beautiful and worthy of study. I desire to imprint it on my heart. But all that means nothing if I don't do what it says. Forgive my sins, both intentional and accidental, and line me up ever more closely with the pleasing path of Your law. May I meditate on Your precepts until the words of my mouth are pleasing in Your sight, reflecting my inner spirit. When I am tired, let me seek rest in Your law. When I need wisdom, may I scan its pages. You have given me all the tools I will ever need. Amen.

> *More to be desired are they than gold, yea, than much fine gold:*
> *sweeter also than honey and the honeycomb. Moreover by them is*
> *thy servant warned: and in keeping of them there is great reward.*
> Psalm 19:10–11

EVENING READING ·

God's Word is perfect, sure, clean, pure, true, and righteous. It enlightens eyes, makes the simple wise, converts souls, brings joy, and is entirely trustworthy because it endures forever. The words of God are far more valuable than gold. It makes sense, then, that great reward is to be found in following His commandments. With such treasure at your fingertips, why would you not immerse yourself in His Word every day?

GENESIS 47:27–49:28 ❀ **MATTHEW 13:44–58** ❀ **PSALM 20**

Praying for Grandchildren

(GENESIS 48)

❧❧❧❧❧ ❀ ❧❧❧❧❧

MORNING PRAYER·

Heavenly Father, thank You for the gift of grandchildren. I can only imagine how excited Jacob was to see Joseph's children and to call down Your blessing on them. I pray that I will be as diligent as Jacob in praying for my grandchildren and now even for the great-granddaughter growing in her mother's womb. I thank You for their unity as a family in worship. I plead they will grow into the beauty of the life You have planned for them, men and women of God. I relinquish their futures to You. More than anything else, I want them to know You. Amen.

> *Now know I that the LORD saveth his anointed; he will hear him*
> *from his holy heaven with the saving strength of his right hand.*
> PSALM 20:6

EVENING READING

Psalm 20 is a beautiful psalm to pray over your life. David's petitions are saturated with the power and knowledge of victory. As someone who has the blessing of living after Christ has conquered death and evil, you can pray with even more confidence in God's victory. You can boast in the name of God for He will save and He will keep you from stumbling. Set up your banners in His name, proclaiming to the world that you are His and that it is His power at work in you.

Walking on Water

(MATTHEW 14)

>>>>>> ❀ <<<<<<

MORNING PRAYER

Lord Jesus, I want to be like Peter, racing to You across the dancing waves. Of course, to do that, I have to get out of the boat. Forgive me for those times when I hear Your call but hesitate, doubting Your voice and climbing back aboard. You know about the times I've taken a few steps before I glance down at the waves massaging my feet, how that good beginning melts into a soggy middle. How thankful I am that You understand my frailties. You reach out Your hand and lift me up, safe, secure, walking again on Your invisible pathway. Oh Jesus, help me to step out onto the water. Amen.

> *But the more they afflicted them,*
> *the more they multiplied and grew.*
> EXODUS 1:12

EVENING READING

As demonstrated in the account of the Hebrews in Egypt, God will often use suffering to increase His people. The very means that man uses as an attempt to snuff out God's children God uses to make them stronger. So when the suffering inflicted on God's people feels overwhelming, rejoice—knowing that through it God will work mightily, thwarting the arrogant plans of man.

❧ DAY 26 ❦

The Burning Bush

(Exodus 3)

>=>>>> ❀ <<<<=

MORNING PRAYER · · · · · · · · · · · · · · · · · · ·

"I am who I am" (Exodus 3:14 niv). Do I dare to say Your name aloud? Yet it's the name You gave to Moses. You are the sum of time and of existence. Apart from You, the world would fall apart. I don't expect to see a burning bush today, but let me feel it with my heart. Fill me with that sense of fear, of awe, of wonder at who You are. So wrap me up in Yourself that I will follow You for the rest of my life, no matter what happens, because the great I Am is always with me. Amen.

And God said unto Moses, I Am That I Am: and he said, Thus shalt thou say unto the children of Israel, I Am hath sent me unto you.
Exodus 3:14

EVENING READING · · · · · · · · · · · · · · · · · · ·

The beautiful, unbreakable thread of God's sovereignty is woven all throughout history. In today's reading, God used an evil Pharaoh, a brutal nationwide infanticide, a "chance" encounter with an Egyptian princess, and a murderer and coward named Moses to accomplish His purposes. Never imagine that a personal besetting sin, weakness, or difficult circumstance is out of God's will or too difficult for Him to use for His glory.

Catching Compassion

(MATTHEW 15:32–38)

>=>>>> ❀ <<<<=<

MORNING PRAYER·

Lord Jesus, You know me. You know I'm the last one eating at the table while everyone else cleans up; You know the blinders I wear when it comes to helping. So I pray that You will speak to me directly, the way You did to the disciples. "I have compassion for these people" (Matthew 15:32 NIV). Point to a specific person at a specific time for a specific need. And when You have called, let me never hesitate. Teach me to act immediately, not worrying about the cost. May my heart beat in time with Yours, and may Your love give sight to my eyes. Amen.

> *Do ye not yet understand, neither remember the five loaves of the five thousand, and how many baskets ye took up? Neither the seven loaves of the four thousand, and how many baskets ye took up?*
> MATTHEW 16:9–10

EVENING READING

How easily we forget God's power and His goodness. In his fear of speaking to the people, Moses failed to remember that it was God who made him and who could easily help him speak. In the pressure of feeding a crowd, the disciples quickly forgot the miracle that Jesus had already performed to feed thousands. What have you forgotten about God? What anxieties have taken root in your heart simply because you have failed to remember that God is powerful and that He loves you and will fulfill His will for your life?

✼ DAY 28 ✼

Journey of Prayer
(EXODUS 6:28–7:6)

>>>>> ❀ <<<<<

MORNING PRAYER ·

Father, I thank You that the Bible shows me the great saints of faith with all their faults. Abraham was able to go years without hearing from You, but not Moses. You even gave him a helper, Aaron. Oh, how I thank You that I don't have to measure up to someone else. You will prepare me uniquely for my calling. If I need repeated instructions, You are happy to guide me. So let me get busy, preparing for the work You have assigned. With the assistants You have given to me, beginning with the Holy Spirit, I will complete the task. Amen.

And I say also unto thee, That thou art Peter,
and upon this rock I will build my church;
and the gates of hell shall not prevail against it.
MATTHEW 16:18

EVENING READING ·

Psalm 23 is such a familiar psalm, yet it is so profound and packed with remarkably comforting and empowering truths. Don't overlook the beauty of this little psalm. Similarly, in Matthew 16, don't discount the power of Jesus' promise "I will build my church"—a remarkably simple phrase that speaks of the power, victory, and sovereign plan of God. No earthly or spiritual power can stand in the way of the inevitable progress of Christ's Gospel. Take courage and find peace in this truth.

The King of Glory

(PSALM 24)

❧❧❧❧ ❀ ❧❧❧❧

MORNING PRAYER·· ·

Heavenly Lord, everything in me and everything in the earth and skies above belongs to You because You are our Creator. I can claim nothing for myself. How I marvel at the miracle of life, from my DNA to the meshing of matter and energy and all the laws You put into place to make them work in an orderly fashion. That is the God I serve, my standard bearer. Of course You are strong and mighty. You could crush all creation with the wave of a single finger, but instead You deal with me in mercy and grace. Come into my life, oh King of Glory. Rule in me. Amen.

The earth is the LORD's, and the fulness thereof;
the world, and they that dwell therein.
PSALM 24:1

EVENING READING ·

God made the world and everything in it. He still sustains and controls the earth and all its inhabitants. He proved His power over His creation in the multiple plagues He brought down on Egypt. This same God with the same amount of power still reigns today. He is to be feared. But, as one of His children, His power ought to give you comfort and courage because there is nothing in your life that He does not have control over.

❧ DAY 30 ❧

My Hope
(PSALM 25)

❧❧❧❧❧ ❀ ❧❧❧❧❧

MORNING PRAYER ·

The reason for my hope: You are God. That says it all, really, because You are all—everything. And Your passion is to be my personal God. Specifically, You are God my Savior. You have saved me. You are sanctifying me now, and one day You will make my salvation complete. With that hope in mind, I pray that You will grant me a teachable spirit. May I check Your GPS before starting on a journey. I depend on You twenty-four hours a day. Thank You that my hope will never fail because You will never fail. So let me carry that hope clutched close to my heart. Amen.

> *And the LORD said unto Moses, Go in unto Pharaoh: for I have hardened his heart, and the heart of his servants, that I might shew these my signs before him: And that thou mayest tell in the ears of thy son, and of thy son's son, what things I have wrought in Egypt, and my signs which I have done among them; that ye may know how that I am the LORD.*
> EXODUS 10:1–2

EVENING READING ·

The process of getting the Israelites out of Egypt was a painful one. God continued to harden Pharaoh's heart, which in turn caused him to oppress the Israelites more and more. In the midst of it all, it would have been difficult not to question what possible purpose God could have for putting His people through this. And yet, we can look back on it now and see that God's purposes were to free His people, to show His power and glory to a heathen nation, and to start His people on a journey to a beautiful land they could call their own. Worship in the midst of confusing and frightening circumstances, relying on God to use your suffering for His glory and for your good.

DAY 31

Behold the Lamb

(EXODUS 12)

≫≫❀≪≪

MORNING PRAYER

Behold the Lamb who takes away the sin of the world. Music swells in my heart and I fall speechless at Your nail-torn feet. My tears are an offering of praise for Your blood, the bleach that cleansed me from my sins. You defend me at Your Father's side. My faith has found a resting place in You, in Your wounds that plead for me. If You didn't pass over me? I shy away in terrified shudders. You painted heaven's doorposts with Your blood that I might enter in. No matter how many times or how many ways I say it, I remain broken, prostrate on the holy ground of Your sacrifice. Amen.

> *Judge me, O LORD; for I have walked in mine integrity:*
> *I have trusted also in the LORD; therefore I shall not slide.*
> PSALM 26:1

EVENING READING

Are you as confident in your integrity as David was in his? Could you ask God to judge you with a clear conscience? This kind of confidence in your own innocence may seem impossible—and on your own, it is. But the blood of the Passover Lamb covers you so that you too can have confidence in the day of judgment.

❯ DAY 32 ❮

Walking the Highway
(PSALM 27)

❯❯❯❯❯ ❀ ❮❮❮❮❮

MORNING PRAYER ·

Teach me Your way, Lord. I'm walking it. I thank You for the confidence of knowing that when I reach my destination, I will see how Your arrow made my way straight from beginning to end. You've put me in an army tank that plows my enemies under as I travel under Your orders. Lord, I seek You. I want to play tag, to sit in Your lap, to watch in awe as You conduct kingdom business. Drum this truth into my soul: I will see Your goodness in the land of the living. Whether my steps today take me through battle or play, I rejoice that You are with me forever. Amen.

> *And Moses said unto the people, Fear ye not, stand still, and see the salvation of the LORD, which he will shew to you to day: for the Egyptians whom ye have seen to day, ye shall see them again no more for ever.*
> EXODUS 14:13

EVENING READING ·

Moses was confident that God would act on behalf of His people. He told the people to watch carefully because he knew that they would see their God's salvation that day. His faith in God's promise to deliver His people from Egypt was so secure that not even six hundred chariots of Egypt could shake his confidence. And God did not let him down. You serve the same promise-keeping, all-powerful God today. May your faith be as strong as the faith of Moses so that you too can stand firm, assured of God's salvation even in the face of overwhelming odds.

≈ DAY 33 ≈

No One Like You

(EXODUS 15:11)

≈≈≫≫≫ ❁ ≪≪≪≈≈

MORNING PRAYER

There is no God like You. In a world that depends on science more than a god, dazzle us with Your majesty. Leave me awestruck with Your glory as I rest in Your Son and as I explore Your creation. Perform wonders to open a crack in the hearts and minds of those who don't believe in You. Thank You for revealing Yourself, for giving me eyes to see. Continue to improve my spiritual vision, that I may see You more clearly. Whatever You teach me, may I faithfully pass it on to others. Amen.

*The LORD is my strength and my shield; my heart
trusted in him, and I am helped: therefore my heart
greatly rejoiceth; and with my song will I praise him.*
PSALM 28:7

EVENING READING

Psalm 28 provides us with a trustworthy equation: trust in God and you will be helped. Sometimes our prescription of the help we want God to provide is different from the help He does provide. But even though it may not feel like it in the moment, what God prescribes for you is infinitely better than anything you could imagine. Take a moment to recall times in your life when this has proven to be true. Then praise Him for His grace and faithfulness to you.

Am I Prepared for Your Answer?

(MATTHEW 19:16–30)

⪼⪼⪼⪼⪼ ❁ ⪻⪻⪻⪻⪻

MORNING PRAYER ·

Lord, I praise You for all the blessings I couldn't have predicted or planned for. You know my heart. I say I want to follow You no matter what, but I fail in completing the task. How precious to You when, like Isaiah, I offer to go. Forgive me when I back down after I count the cost. Let me be gladly willing to give it all, like martyr Jim Elliot. How I rejoice that You give me the strength for today's problems. If the day comes that You ask for my life, I trust You will give me the grace to bear it. Amen.

> *Jesus said unto him, If thou wilt be perfect,*
> *go and sell that thou hast, and give to the poor, and thou*
> *shalt have treasure in heaven: and come and follow me.*
> MATTHEW 19:21

EVENING READING ·

Is there anything in your life that you would refuse to give up for the sake of Christ and His kingdom? The lack of ability to surrender possessions and earthly treasure to God is an indication that you have not fully known your God or the matchless riches that He offers to those who seek after Him. Jesus asks you to be willing to give up earthly comforts because He knows that what He can give is far better than anything this world can offer. It's only in letting go of earthly treasure that you can grab hold of Him.

❧ DAY 35 ☙

Joy in the Morning
(PSALM 30)

═❯❯❯❯ ❀ ❮❮❮❮═

MORNING PRAYER

I exalt You, holy Lord, because You lift me out of the depths and spare me by Your grace. Although I've felt the heat of Your displeasure in the past, and sometimes in my present, Your favor is my future forever. That is why I eagerly await the shout of joy that will follow a night of weeping. Oh, how I wish I could always enjoy Your sunshine, with good weather. But You see my need for rain to bring growth. Through trials, You make me strong. Come foul or fair weather, my joy is in You. Amen.

Is it not lawful for me to do what I will with mine own?
Is thine eye evil, because I am good?
MATTHEW 20:15

EVENING READING

How easily we fall into questioning if God's plan for us is really the best. This doubt is often spurred on when we fall into the dangerous spiral of comparing our lives to the life of someone else. But since God is our Creator and Sustainer, doesn't He have the right to do with us as He pleases? More than that, doesn't He know best what is actually good for us? We must believe wholeheartedly in the goodness of God to protect ourselves from comparing our blessings to the blessings He's given others. There is beautiful freedom in truly accepting that God's treatment of you is perfect.

The First Shall Be Last

(MATTHEW 20:26–28)

>>>>>> ❀ <<<<<

MORNING PRAYER ·

Lord Jesus, I've never asked to sit at Your side in heaven. But I confess I've desired recognition among my peers. How I wonder at Your patience with me. You're God, and You gave up everything for me. Me, who's no taller than Your fingernail. And yet You welcome me as a sister into Your family, a coheir of all the heavenly blessings! Let me draw my sense of self from You. Use me as Your hands and feet and heart, unafraid to abandon my "position." That's what other people need—You in me, not myself. Amen.

> *Ye shall not afflict any widow, or fatherless child. If thou afflict them*
> *in any wise, and they cry at all unto me, I will surely hear their cry;*
> *and my wrath shall wax hot, and I will kill you with the sword;*
> *and your wives shall be widows, and your children fatherless.*
> EXODUS 22:22–24

EVENING READING ·

Though the laws of Exodus can sometimes seem tedious, God's character glimmers through in His instructions of how His people ought to live. His love and stalwart defense of the needy are seen in the recompense that He promises for anyone who dares afflict a widow or orphan. To take advantage of the weak and vulnerable is no small offense in God's eyes. God does not overlook those who are so often overlooked in our world—and, therefore, neither should we.

Moving Mountains

(MATTHEW 21:21–22)

❧❧❧ ✿ ❧❧❧

MORNING PRAYER

Lord Jesus, I tremble at the depth of this promise. You say You'll move mountains if I ask in prayer, believing. My storyteller's brain imagines a rockslide that halts a robbery or opens a road. But what are the mountains in my life? Lord, when I don't get what I ask for, is my faith at fault? Am I asking for the wrong thing? Or am I blind to Your answers? But it's not about me, or my prayer, is it? It's about You! Jump up and down! You, the God of the impossible. You can lift a mountain with a word. Nothing I can ask or imagine is beyond Your capacity to act. Remove the mountain of my disbelief. Amen.

> *My times are in thy hand: deliver me from the hand*
> *of mine enemies, and from them that persecute me.*
> PSALM 31:15

EVENING READING

How would it change your life if you, like David, could truly grasp that your times are in God's hands? Wouldn't that belief foster an unshakable peace in your heart as it banishes fear from your life? You would know that the trials you go through are ordained by God and will be carefully worked out for your good. Why is it that we so often struggle to live our lives firmly planted in this truth?

❧ DAY 38 ❦

Give Me Oil for My Lamp
(Exodus 27:20–21)

≫≫≫ ❀ ≪≪≪

MORNING PRAYER

Lord, I need oil in my lamp. I'm creaky and rusty, my engine complaining when I crank it. I need *You*. Send Your Spirit through my being. Ease the joints to move. May Your light flare up within me. Forgive me for letting my oil supply run dry, like the virgins waiting for the bridegroom. I thank You that Your oil well is bottomless. Fill me, light me, use me to shine Your light to others. Burn away the impurities in my soul so that the light may shine purer. May I come to You daily for renewal. Amen.

> *Jesus saith unto them, Verily I say unto you, That the publicans*
> *and the harlots go into the kingdom of God before you.*
> Matthew 21:31

EVENING READING

There is no deference to earthly status in the kingdom of God. All that matters is belief in the Son of God. Take this as an encouragement that no matter what you have done in this life, you are never past saving. And take it as a warning that no amount of good done in this life will get you into heaven apart from a saving knowledge of Christ.

An Invitation

(MATTHEW 22:8–10)

>>>>>> ❀ <<<<<

MORNING PRAYER

My Lord and King, who am I, that You invited me to the wedding banquet of Your Son? But You not only sent the invitation; You also made me worthy. You saved my soul and gave me new clothes of righteousness to wear. All You ask is that I accept Your gift and come and dine freely at Your table. Oh Lord, with all my being I respond, "Yes, I'm coming!" You've stuffed my hands with invitations to give to others on Your behalf. Litter my path with people You want at Your party, and open my hands to spread the news more heartily than any political campaign. Amen.

> *Many sorrows shall be to the wicked: but he that*
> *trusteth in the LORD, mercy shall compass him about.*
> PSALM 32:10

EVENING READING

Those who trust in God are completely surrounded and encompassed by His mercy. It may be difficult to believe this in times when the hardships of life press so closely that they're almost suffocating. And yet, through all of life's struggles, you have a layer of protection that can't be breached. Your life is completely in God's hands, and He will remain forever by your side.

Make Me an Instrument

(PSALM 33:1–3)

>->>>> ✿ <<<<<

MORNING PRAYER

Heavenly Lord, make me a stringed instrument in the heavenly orchestra. Pluck all ten strings of my heart to resonate with harmonious praise to You. Tune me, that nothing about me will strike a discordant note. Bring our music to a crescendo that will thunder down eternity, Your praise filling every nook and cranny of space and time. May our music dance with the stars and resonate with the waters of the deep. How I rejoice that Your song will never end, the theme never changing, because Your plans stand firm forever. Let me rest on the breath of Your spirit like a leaf floating on the wind. Amen.

> *Rejoice in the LORD, O ye righteous:*
> *for praise is comely for the upright.*
> PSALM 33:1

EVENING READING

Why does God command you to worship Him? Is it because He has some arrogant need to be noticed and praised? Not at all. If you were never to worship Him, it would not affect Him in the least. But it would affect you. Praising God is good, refreshing, and life giving for you. Don't neglect the wonderful gift of worshipping your God.

Your Love, My Hope

(PSALM 33:18–22)

MORNING PRAYER

I hope in Your unfailing love. Even when my hope falters, Your love doesn't. Your eyes are on me because I hope in You. I wait in hope. You help and shield me. Your unfailing love sustains me. In You I rejoice day and night. When Your holiness demanded an answer to my sin, You sent Your Son to the cross. Oh holy Lord! Since You reached out and took hold of me in that pit, how much more can I trust You with the minutiae of my life? I begin every day with that hope filling my heart. Amen.

> *There is no king saved by the multitude of an host: a mighty man*
> *is not delivered by much strength. An horse is a vain thing for safety:*
> *neither shall he deliver any by his great strength. . . . Our soul*
> *waiteth for the Lord: he is our help and our shield.*
> PSALM 33:16–17, 20

EVENING READING

What are you putting your trust in—status, money, health, strength, a good family? Psalm 33 reminds us that security comes from God and God alone. Set your trust on the Rock that will never move or crumble instead of on the shifting sands of the prosperity of this world.

Keeping Watch

(MATTHEW 24:42)

⇒⇒⟩⟩⟩ ❀ ⟨⟨⟨⟨⇐

MORNING PRAYER ·

Lord of lords and coming King, is today the day? Will You bring me up to meet You in the sky as I'm eating a cheeseburger for lunch? In my deepest heart, am I ready? I rest in the assurance of my salvation. I long for the realization of Your kingdom on earth. But I confess there's a big part of me that clings to my life as it is. I want to meet my great-grandchild and see my granddaughter get married. I also confess that I'm not as active as I should be in inviting others to the party, in encouraging them to prepare for Your return. Forgive me; clear my vision and purpose. Amen.

> *O magnify the LORD with me,*
> *and let us exalt his name together.*
> PSALM 34:3

EVENING READING ·

Do you spend more time trying to magnify yourself or striving to magnify God? In magnifying and exalting God, there is great joy as it brings you into closer relationship with Him. The more magnified God, is in your life, the more perspective you will have regarding how small and insignificant you are. This in turn will inspire you to lean on Him, making you more powerful than you ever would be on your own. Surround yourself with people who are passionate about magnifying God as well.

Starting Over

(EXODUS 34)

>>>>> ❀ <<<<<

MORNING PRAYER

You told Moses everything I ever need to know for when You give me a second chance. You are the Lord! You are compassionate and gracious. You are slow to anger and abounding in love and faithfulness. You look for even the smallest sign of faith. You maintain Your love to the thousands—to me. And although You forgive sins, You're also just. How great Your love that Jesus bore the guilt of my sin; how vast the pit for the one who refuses that gift. On the basis of that undeserved favor, I petition You to go with me. Keep me from heading in the wrong direction. Amen.

> *And when Aaron and all the children of Israel saw Moses, behold,*
> *the skin of his face shone; and they were afraid to come nigh him.*
> EXODUS 34:30

EVENING READING

An encounter with God will inevitably change you. Just as the Israelites noticed that the face of Moses shone after meeting with God, so too when you commit to spending valuable time with God each day, you will be changed in a noticeable and beautiful way. His glory will reflect off you, and His love will work through you.

EXODUS 35:30–37:29 ❋ MATTHEW 25:14–30 ❋ PSALM 35:1–8

My Contender

(PSALM 35)

>=>>>> ❋ <<<<=<

MORNING PRAYER

Oh Lord my shield, I come to You, asking for You to rise against my enemies. They seek my life. Don't You see them, Lord, when they plot physical harm? Don't You care when they suck joy from me? Why do You let them fight against me? I run to You. Shine Your light on Your billboard declaring I Am Your Salvation. Take up Your shield and armor. Come to my aid. May Your will blow away those who stand against me, like dust. Oh Lord, how I thank You that You rescue so that I can once again praise Your name. Amen.

And he hath filled him with the spirit of God, in wisdom,
in understanding, and in knowledge, and in all manner of workmanship.
EXODUS 35:31

EVENING READING

Our talents are God given. Therefore, don't derive arrogance from them, but instead humbly thank God for the skills He has given you. Conversely, don't allow yourself to belittle the gifts that God has given you. Joyfully and confidently use them for His service.

Because of Who You Are
(PSALM 35:9–17)

❧❧❧❧❧ ❀ ❧❧❧❧❧

MORNING PRAYER ·

My Lord God, I call on You because You are my God. You're my righteousness. Who is like You? You rescue me from poverty. You hold my life precious in Your sight, God, my Lord. I will give You thanks wherever Your people assemble and will shout hallelujah to You among the throngs. I thank You for friends who stand up for me, who encourage me when I'm down, who praise You and rejoice with me when things are well, who mourn with me when I'm struggling. Your righteousness and greatness will be on my tongue all day long. The more I praise You, the less room I leave for worrying and complaining. Amen.

> *And the King shall answer and say unto them, Verily I say*
> *unto you, Inasmuch as ye have done it unto one of the*
> *least of these my brethren, ye have done it unto me.*
> MATTHEW 25:40

EVENING READING ·

Good deeds are often unnoticed and without thanks in this life. Maybe you even wonder why you still go out of your way to help others. But even if the world doesn't notice, be confident that God notices all the times you reach out to someone in need. God will reward you for your good works. In fact, in doing good for others you will find yourself in a closer relationship with your God, for He says, "Inasmuch as ye have done it unto one of the least of these my brethren, ye have done it unto me."

Anointing at Bethany

(MATTHEW 26:6–13)

>>>>>> ❀ <<<<<<

MORNING PRAYER

Lord, in these few days, You have brought me face-to-face with You, alone, letting the rest of the world fade away. In that hiding place, may I pour out my most prized possessions with tears. May I lavish You with all the love I'm capable of. My gift is a pale reflection of You, for You are Love. Break me, that the ointment of Your Spirit may flow over me and through me and return to You in worship. When I leave the privacy of our quiet time, may I carry the fragrance of that anointing. Tip me this way and that, that I may sprinkle Your love along the way. Amen.

And when the cloud was taken up from over the tabernacle, the children of Israel went onward in all their journeys: but if the cloud were not taken up, then they journeyed not till the day that it was taken up.
EXODUS 40:36–37

EVENING READING

In the desert, the Israelites in a very tangible way had to rely on God for their next step. If the pillar of cloud or fire moved, they moved. If it stayed in place, they waited. We too are on a pilgrimage through this land and must rely on God's guidance for each next step. While we may wish that His presence were as obvious to us as it was to them, we have the greater blessing of having His indwelling Spirit to lead and to guide us. Wait and watch for His movements to guide you into the next phase of your service to Him.

Saltshaker

(LEVITICUS 2:11–13)

❀

MORNING PRAYER

Holy Lord, there's a lot I can learn about prayer from the temple offerings. You have forbidden the leaven of sin in my heart. Search me; show me those hidden places. I don't like the process, but I want to grow more like You. I pray also that the salt of Your righteousness will preserve me from sin. That the flavor of Your will may permeate every request I make of You. That the time we spend together will be food to my soul, a daily party time between two friends. I pray that I will dig from Your salt mine, prepared to season the world around me. Amen.

> *But all this was done, that the scriptures of the prophets*
> *might be fulfilled. Then all the disciples forsook him, and fled.*
> MATTHEW 26:56

EVENING READING

It is uncomfortable and upsetting to read the account of how all of Jesus' disciples abandoned Him to a violent mob that would treat Him, the Son of God, with a callous and shameful arrogance. And yet, don't we often treat Him in the same way? We fail to speak of Him at the first sign of opposition. We continually go back to the same sin as if to say that His sacrifice was not enough to save us. We move our time with Him to the lowest priority as though anything else in our life would be more important than time with our Savior. Repent of the arrogant ways that you have treated the Son of God.

The Case of Peter and Judas

(MATTHEW 26:69–27:6)

>>>>> ❀ <<<<<

MORNING PRAYER· ·

Lord Jesus, on the night You were betrayed, You reached out to the two men who went the furthest in denying You, Peter and Judas. Oh, how my heart grieves with You. How I bathe myself in the wonder of Your love. Too many of our times together hold echoes of Your warnings to Your close friends. Like Peter and like the hymnist, I am prone to wander. Here's my heart—take it, seal it for Your courts above. How I thank You for Your mercy. I pray for those who, like Judas and Peter, lose their way. Correct their steps; lead them back to repentance and right relationship. Starting with me. Amen.

And the chief priests took the silver pieces, and said, It is not lawful for to put them into the treasury, because it is the price of blood. And they took counsel, and bought with them the potter's field, to bury strangers in.
MATTHEW 27:6–7

EVENING READING ·

The tainted money that Judas received for betraying Jesus was used to buy a field in which strangers would be buried. It is a testimony to the all-encompassing love of God that He caused even this filthy money to be used for good. The field bought by Jesus' blood was used to give a final resting place to those who otherwise would have had none. God can truly redeem even the most heinous of acts.

When Words Aren't Enough

(LEVITICUS 6:1–7)

❀

MORNING PRAYER

Holy Lord, how I thank You that You stand ready to forgive my sins. My salvation depends on it as well as my ability to live for You. I thank You for this reminder that my sin doesn't only hurt my relationship with You. When it affects someone else—as it so often does—You call me to reconcile with that person. Oh Lord, I'd rather ignore this part! But Jesus repeated this command, vocalizing in human voice what we had heard from Your written voice. Bring me to obedience. Give me the words to say and the courage to approach anyone I have hurt. Amen.

And about the ninth hour Jesus cried with a loud voice,
saying, Eli, Eli, lama sabachthani? that is to say,
My God, my God, why hast thou forsaken me?
MATTHEW 27:46

EVENING READING

While on the cross, Christ asked why God had forsaken Him. In answer to that question, God could point to each of His children and say that it is for us that Christ was forsaken on the cross. This kind of love is unfathomable to us, that Christ would endure such pain for a people who would so easily abandon Him and spit in His face. He was forsaken so that we never would be. This is the kind of love that we should never take for granted and that should inspire in us worshipful gratefulness.

Preparing for Ministry
(LEVITICUS 8)

❧>>>>> ❀ <<<<❧

MORNING PRAYER· ·

Lord God, You made Aaron's ordination for the priesthood a solemn, holy occasion. Do I expect any less when it comes to preparing for the work You have called me to? You have clothed me in the right uniform by Your Spirit and given me the gifts I need to do the work. I come here, reporting for duty. Before I begin, I wait before You, asking Your forgiveness. Fill me with Yourself and with the skills I need, as You did for the men who built the tabernacle. I ask that all I do will bring glory to You. Amen.

The steps of a good man are ordered by the LORD: and he delighteth in his way. Though he fall, he shall not be utterly cast down: for the LORD upholdeth him with his hand.
PSALM 37:23–24

EVENING READING ·

God orders your steps and then delights to see you walking in them. What peace this affords that God knows and lovingly controls all your decisions. And even when you stumble, you will not fall because the almighty God is by your side to catch and uphold you.

Fellow Seekers

(PSALM 37:27–40)

>>>>> ❀ <<<<<

MORNING PRAYER

Oh Lord, my hope is in You alone, but I am not alone in that hope. I thank You for the company of believers, for those who are blameless and upright. May I focus on what is good and noble and peaceable in their behavior instead of finding fault. Teach me as I watch them. And may they also learn from me. Then we will build one another up and not lead one another astray. Guide me in my choice of companions. Weave us together in holiness and love, that the world will know we belong to You. Amen.

> *And Jesus came and spake unto them, saying, All power is given*
> *unto me in heaven and in earth. Go ye therefore, and teach*
> *all nations, baptizing them in the name of the Father, and of*
> *the Son, and of the Holy Ghost: teaching them to observe all*
> *things whatsoever I have commanded you: and, lo, I am with*
> *you always, even unto the end of the world. Amen.*
> MATTHEW 28:18–20

EVENING READING

The reason that God's people are able to go out into the world to make disciples and bring the Gospel to every nation is because all authority has been given to Christ. This knowledge infuses courage into all evangelism. Christ has already won and sits victoriously on His throne and is with us always, even to the end of the world. He has already chosen out for Himself a people to be His. It is simply our responsibility to faithfully preach His Word. He has already taken care of the hard part.

Something Beautiful

(PSALM 38)

MORNING PRAYER

Oh Lord, You know the depths of my heart, my longings for something powerful and wonderful, my regretful sighing for the realities of daily life. I praise You, the compassionate God, for You will act on my behalf at the right time, in exactly the right way. My life is an open book before You. You know my dreams and my weaknesses. Burn away the evil in me. Line up my longings with Your own. I lift up my hands to You with confidence, knowing I will receive mercy and find the grace to help me. Lord, I call on You, knowing You will answer. Amen.

For in thee, O LORD, do I hope:
thou wilt hear, O Lord my God.
PSALM 38:15

EVENING READING

Do you have the same confidence as David wrote about in this psalm that God will hear when you call to Him? Where is your hope? If it is in your own abilities or merit, then you will find yourself disappointed. Securely fasten your hope to God's love and care for you, and you will never be let down.

Praying for the Sick

(LEVITICUS 13)

>->>>> ❀ <<<<<

MORNING PRAYER

Lord, I thank You for Your concern for the sick. Today I pray for those who are physically, mentally, or emotionally disabled. Open my eyes to see them beyond their labels, as individuals created and loved by You. I lift those with afflictions, STDs like AIDS, that I shy away from. Expand my heart to pray and care and help in any way You lead. I pray also for those whose health limits their activities, who rarely leave home. Use my arms and legs as instruments of Your love. I pray for the necessary support they need, for their health, for their daily activities, and for friendship. Amen.

> LORD, make me to know mine end, and the measure of my days,
> what it is: that I may know how frail I am.
> PSALM 39:4

EVENING READING

Pray that God would give you the eternal perspective of how short this life really is. How would it change your life if you knew how it would end? How differently would you live each day if you really understood how few days you had? We are only pilgrims on this earth. Use the short time here to do the greatest good for God's kingdom and for those around you.

Right Reason, Wrong Choice

(MARK 1:40–45)

❀

MORNING PRAYER

Lord Jesus, how often I disappoint You like the leper in today's reading. Like him, after You do something miraculous in my life, I fail to follow Your instructions for follow-up care. Oh, forgive me! I can't claim I don't know. You made it clear in my spirit. Forgive me for making myself blind and deaf. Oh Lord, I tremble at the role I play in delaying the delivery of Your good news to those who need to hear. Today, let me take each step at Your direction, to unleash the chain of events and blessings You wish to unfold. Amen.

And Jesus, moved with compassion, put forth his hand,
and touched him, and saith unto him, I will; be thou clean.
MARK 1:41

EVENING READING

Notice the beautiful juxtaposition in today's reading. The passage in Leviticus laboriously sets out how a leper ought to be treated and the intense work of cleansing that had to happen. The passage in Mark depicts Christ reaching out and touching a leper to instantly make him well. Touching a leper would have been unheard of in the old Law. But Christ came to usher in a new law in which He touches the unclean and invites the outcast in.

My New Family

(MARK 3:13–34)

❧❧❧❧❧ ❀ ❧❧❧❧❧

MORNING PRAYER

Lord Jesus, from the time You created Adam, You recognized he shouldn't be alone. My mind runs through the list of Your heroes, and I can't think of one without another human to stand by them. How I thank You for my birth family, for placing me with people who prayed and dreamed for me. How grateful I am for my grandmother's legacy of faith. But then You called me away from my family, into a team of believers called to Your purpose. May we go at Your bidding, in Your power, lifting one another up in the power of Your Spirit. Amen.

> *And it came to pass, that, as Jesus sat at meat in his house,*
> *many publicans and sinners sat also together with Jesus and*
> *his disciples: for there were many, and they followed him.*
> MARK 2:15

EVENING READING

What a beautiful God we serve who would rather eat with sinners and outcasts than maintain His social standing in a crowd of hypocrites. If you ever find yourself becoming too concerned about your social image, just remember what kind of Savior you should be emulating.

Watch Where You're Going

(LEVITICUS 16:1–3)

MORNING PRAYER

Lord God, how I relish the freedom to crawl on Your lap and call You Daddy. But the instructions for the Day of Atonement remind me that I shouldn't take that freedom for granted. How great Your love for me that I can approach Your mercy seat without fear. You have opened my sin-blinded eyes and given me glasses tinted by Your blood. I have access to You day and night; the veil is torn. May I always cleanse myself with confession and shower myself in Your Spirit. Teach me Your holiness, Your transcendence, Your majesty and power, that my love will be empowered by a holy fear. Amen.

For on that day shall the priest make an atonement for you,
to cleanse you, that ye may be clean from all your sins before the LORD.
LEVITICUS 16:30

EVENING READING

Once a year the high priest would make atonement for all the people to cleanse them from their sins. But this cleansing would only cover the sins of one year. Now, what beautiful freedom we have that Christ's onetime work on the cross has and will cover all our sins for all time.

This Little Light of Mine

(MARK 4:21–23)

❧>>>>> ❀ <<<<<

MORNING PRAYER

Lord Jesus, I am light and salt, and You want my light to shine. You reminded Your listeners that people don't put lamps under bowls. But how often do I turn out my light? Sometimes I'm scared of putting myself out there. Other times a false sense of humility, a feeling that I have nothing worthy to offer, holds me back. As I say it, I hear Your voice telling me, "By yourself you have nothing. With Me you have everything you need." You are the oil in my lamp, Your Spirit the light that burns within me. Forgive me when I doubt Your calling that will bring it to pass. Stop me from ever covering up that light. Amen.

And he arose, and rebuked the wind, and said unto the sea,
Peace, be still. And the wind ceased, and there was a great calm.
MARK 4:39

EVENING READING

The same God who controls the winds and the sea lives inside you today. Fear has no place and no power against such a formidable opponent. When it seems like the waves of life are threatening to take you under, remember who it is that reigns as King in your heart. Ask Him to still the fear in your life and grant you peace.

❧ DAY 58 ❧

Where Is God?

(PSALM 42)

>>>>> ❀ <<<<<

MORNING PRAYER ·

Oh soul, where is your God? I thirst for You, Lord, more than deer, or athletes running a marathon, thirst for water. I'm running a spiritual race to find You, but the finish line keeps vanishing. The door between us seems to be closed. I go to church, but I don't hear Your voice. I still put my hope in You. Deep calls to deep. In the furthest reaches of my soul, I am soaked in the waterfalls of Your love. At night, when all I see is dark, I sing a prayer to You, my life, my Rock, the God of my salvation. I put my hope in You, for I will yet praise You, my Savior and my God. Amen.

> *And he said unto her, Daughter, thy faith hath made*
> *thee whole; go in peace, and be whole of thy plague.*
> MARK 5:34

EVENING READING ·

Christ radically changed the life of the woman in Mark 5 in more ways than one. First, He healed her bleeding. But perhaps even more importantly, He called her "daughter." This woman would have been an outcast in her society with little human contact because of her condition. So can you imagine the spiritual and emotional healing she must have felt at the hands of her Savior to have been called His daughter—a term of endearment and belonging? You also are called a child of God and forever belong to Him, no matter what happens on this earth.

My Mother's Prayers

(PSALM 44)

>>>))) ❀ ((((<<

MORNING PRAYER ·

Oh Lord, how precious the legacy of my mother's prayers, how deep and consistent they were. Forgive my feelings of superiority, my pride in Bible knowledge and practices. Thank You for Your patience with the shallow things I offer. Teach me to be a living sacrifice, like Mom. May I learn from her how to be faithful in prayer for my expanding family. May I bring my faults to You as openly as she did, begging for Your strength to make me like You. Please, Lord, mold me so that one day my family will look up to me the same way I cherish Mom. Amen.

> *Neither shall ye profane my holy name; but I will be hallowed among*
> *the children of Israel: I am the LORD which hallow you, that brought*
> *you out of the land of Egypt, to be your God: I am the LORD.*
> LEVITICUS 22:32–33

EVENING READING ·

Notice the refrain that often punctuates the end of a point of the Law through Leviticus— "I am the LORD." There didn't need to be any other justification for why the Israelites were to follow the laws set forth. There doesn't need to be any other justification for why we ought to follow the commands and guidance of God today. The fact that the one giving the commands is the perfectly holy almighty God is reason enough to follow Him wholeheartedly.

Celebration

(LEVITICUS 23)

>>>>> ❀ <<<<<

MORNING PRAYER ·

Creator God, I thank You for the gift of time and seasons, for the joy the changing length of days, cycle of plant growth, and differing weather bring. I'm especially thankful to live in an area that enjoys four seasons. And among the seasons, You have sprinkled holy days worthy of special celebration. Let me not neglect those occasions or gathering with Your people to worship each week. How I thank You that every day I can praise You because it is a day You made! Even in the silliness of made-up holidays, like National Frappé Day, I thank You. Daily, may I search for reasons to rejoice in You! Amen!

> *Six days shall work be done: but the seventh day is the sabbath*
> *of rest, an holy convocation; ye shall do no work therein:*
> *it is the sabbath of the LORD in all your dwellings.*
> LEVITICUS 23:3

EVENING READING ·

Though the laws in Leviticus may sometimes seem harsh and tedious, God put them in place for the good of His people. God instituted a Sabbath rest because He knew that as humans it is essential for our well-being to have a day to rest and recuperate. Do you honor this rest that God has given you? Trust God that He knows what is best for you and strive to joyfully keep the Sabbath.

Bread Bowls

(MARK 6:39–44)

❧ ❀ ☙

MORNING PRAYER

Lord Jesus, what a sight that day on the mountain must have been. Did Your disciples feel outnumbered in that crowd? I've often felt alone in a group of fifty, let alone five thousand men. Instead of coming to You, I've left in search of an answer. Have I missed Your miracles by slipping away early? Forgive me. These people hadn't even prayed for Your provision. You saw the need and acted. How I thank You for all the times You see the need before I do, that You provide before I ask. And when I seek, You send messengers with bowls of bread. Amen.

> *And he said unto them, Come ye yourselves apart into a desert place,*
> *and rest a while: for there were many coming and going,*
> *and they had no leisure so much as to eat.*
> MARK 6:31

EVENING READING

If you tend to feel guilty about taking time to rest in a world that demands so much action, take note that Jesus encouraged His disciples to rest from the trying work of evangelism. Seek out time to rest in God and to find rejuvenation in Him. Then go back out into the world refreshed and ready to continue His work.

Reward and Punishment

(LEVITICUS 26)

❧❧❧❧❧ ❀ ❧❧❧❧❧

MORNING PRAYER ··································

Oh God my Father, I confess I'm uncomfortable with the if-then nature of rewards and punishments, because it sounds like it's all up to me. If I can manage to live a perfect life, I'll receive every blessing available on earth. But that will never happen. You know that better than I do. You know my struggles with perfectionism in the past, and You know the secret yearnings of my heart that I am blind to. But reading it again, Lord, I see that You want my heart; You want my focus on You. Open my ears that I may listen and obey. Let me never use my failures as an excuse to avoid You, for that would be the greatest sin of all. Amen.

> *He answered and said unto them, Well hath Esaias prophesied*
> *of you hypocrites, as it is written, This people honoureth*
> *me with their lips, but their heart is far from me.*
> MARK 7:6

EVENING READING ·································

May we not be the kind of people that God could say of, "[They] honoureth me with their lips, but their heart is far from me." Instead, ask God that your heart be so filled with love and adoration of Him that it would overflow into praise and service for His kingdom. May our actions prove our words to be true so that we can be faithful witnesses for Christ.

LEVITICUS 27 ❀ MARK 8 ❀ PSALM 46

Be Still
(PSALM 46:10)

꞊꞊꞊꞊꞊꞊꞊ ❀ ꞊꞊꞊꞊꞊꞊

MORNING PRAYER

Father God, the greatest thing in all my life is knowing You. I hunger for time with You. But I know so little of the art of being still. Teach me the patience of silence so that I may hear You more clearly. Quiet me so that when I speak, others will hear Your voice, not mine. You will be exalted among the nations. You will be exalted in the earth. You will be exalted by the very people who refuse to acknowledge You. I pray that it happens in this age and not when everyone is forced to their knees before You. Amen.

> *Be still, and know that I am God: I will be exalted among*
> *the heathen, I will be exalted in the earth. The LORD of*
> *hosts is with us; the God of Jacob is our refuge. Selah.*
> PSALM 46:10–11

EVENING READING

Psalm 46 is one of the most comforting psalms to meditate on in times of suffering. Even when the whole world seems to be coming apart at the seams, you have no reason to fear because God is with you and will never forsake you. Take a moment in the chaos of life to be still and dwell on the truths in this psalm. Know that He is God, that He is in complete control, and that He is your ever-present refuge and strength in times of trouble.

DAY 64

Dancing before God

(PSALM 47)

❋≫≫ ❀ ≪≪❋

MORNING PRAYER·

Lord Most High, David's psalm makes me want to stand up and shout, sing and dance before You. I want to join hands with people around the world, a global hora before You. The skies would resonate with the sound of clapping hands and joyful cries from all nations. Oh Lord, that's the world I want to see, united in praise of You and not at war with one another! I thank You that one day that will be the reality. It's my birthright as Your daughter. Let me blow Your horn, announcing the good news. You are the King. Of Israel. Of the nations. Of me. Amen.

O clap your hands, all ye people;
shout unto God with the voice of triumph.
PSALM 47:1

EVENING READING

Along with the people in Psalm 47, you too can "shout unto God with the voice of triumph." Why? Because God has secured victory over the world, sin, and death. It may feel like the battle is still raging here on earth and in your own life. But in heaven the victor, Christ, sits on His throne orchestrating all history under His reign. So shout for joy and rejoice in the victory that you have in Christ.

My Firstborn

(NUMBERS 3:13)

>->>>>> ❁ <<<<<<

MORNING PRAYER·· ·

Lord, You couldn't have made it any plainer: "All the firstborn are mine." Open my eyes to understand better what that means. I fall before You in awe that You gave Your own beloved firstborn to save mine. I lift up my child. How grateful I am that he loves You with all his heart. Thank You for Your peace that allows me to release the pains of the past and the concerns of his present and his future to You. Whatever You ask of him—if You ask him to move far away or to serve as a missionary, soldier, police officer, or firefighter—I commit him to You. Give me the courage to let him go in every way. Amen.

And straightway the father of the child cried out, and said
with tears, Lord, I believe; help thou mine unbelief.
MARK 9:24

EVENING READING ·

It's often not until we reach rock bottom in our desperation that we truly understand how much we need God. It's in these moments of candid weakness and vulnerability that we can recognize how small we are and how big God is. God also uses these times to show us how little we really know of Him. Notice how in Mark 9 Jesus doesn't heal the man's son right away. Instead, He waits until the man is entirely sure of his total need of Christ. He even needs help to believe. Don't be ashamed to ask God to help you believe in His love and power. It's through those times of deepest suffering that He lovingly draws you into a more intimate relationship with Him.

❧ DAY 66 ❧

Little Children
(MARK 10:13–16)

❧❧❧❧❧ ❀ ❧❧❧❧❧

MORNING PRAYER ·

Heavenly Father, I've heard that all baby animals are cute, which makes them less vulnerable to attack. Was that Your plan, Lord? I like to think so. I know how precious a newborn baby is, a reminder that You want the world to go on. What a relief, what a joy, to know You had the well-being of my children, of all children, in mind before they were even conceived. You wrote down the days of their lives before the foundation of the world. Keep me from hindering a child's love for You in any way. Use me to lead the little ones to You. Amen.

> *For this God is our God for ever and ever:*
> *he will be our guide even unto death.*
> PSALM 48:14

EVENING READING ·

It is a beautiful thing to serve a God who has lived on this earth as a human, has suffered temptation and loss, has died the death of a mortal, and has risen victorious over it all. There is nowhere you can go and nothing you can do that Christ won't be able to guide you through. Christ has even gone before you in death so that you need not fear that dreaded inevitability. He will hold your hand and walk you through into everlasting glory on the other side. He is your God forever and ever.

What Do You Want?

(MARK 10:46–52)

>>>>>> ❀ <<<<<<

MORNING PRAYER

Lord Jesus, like Bartimaeus, I cry, "Jesus, have mercy on me!" Wonder of wonders, You stop. You call for me. And You don't offer a simple "God be with you." You ask me, "What do you want?" Like Bartimaeus, I want to see! More of You, more in Your Word, more of Your beauty. I want eyes to view other people as You do. I want X-ray vision that uncovers the sin hidden deep in my heart, farsightedness that takes me forward in Your will. Lord, I want to see, that I may live as You have called me to. Amen.

And whosoever of you will be the chiefest, shall be servant of all.
For even the Son of man came not to be ministered unto,
but to minister, and to give his life a ransom for many.
MARK 10:44–45

EVENING READING

Christ turned the values and expectations of His society upside down. Instead of the conquering King that the Jews expected, the Messiah came as a lowly servant whose ultimate act on this earth was a cursed death. Instead of raising up an army of courageous men, Christ sought followers who would humbly serve others. His kingdom is one where the attitude of a child is honored and where weakness is used to greater advantage than strength. His ways are still countercultural and still capable of changing lives and moving mountains.

Benediction

(NUMBERS 6:24–26)

❧❧❧❧ ❀ ❧❧❧❧

MORNING PRAYER ·

Lord God, I offer the Aaronic blessing as a prayer for the people around me: The Lord bless you with plenty, in every circumstance, and with answered prayers. The Lord keep you, in safety, by His faithfulness that will never fail you. The Lord make His face shine upon you, that you may be aware of His glorious presence and respond in worship. The Lord be gracious to you, that you may live in that assurance and extend it to others. The Lord lift up His countenance upon you, revealing what few have seen, exposing sin, filling you with His light. The Lord give you peace in His presence, unlike what the world gives. Amen.

> *Like sheep they are laid in the grave; death shall feed on them; and the upright shall have dominion over them in the morning; and their beauty shall consume in the grave from their dwelling. But God will redeem my soul from the power of the grave: for he shall receive me. Selah.*
> PSALM 49:14–15

EVENING READING ·

For those who don't acknowledge Christ as Lord, there will always be a nagging feeling of meaninglessness and futility to life. They may try to ignore this feeling by building for themselves an empire here on earth or by drowning themselves in pleasure. And yet, that gnawing knowledge will always remain. But for those who are in Christ, a far greater reality awaits us than anything this earth can offer. Once our work here is done, the grave is only an entryway into the matchless glory that will receive us in heaven.

The Listening Ear

(PSALM 50:1–15)

≈>>)))) ❀ (((((≈

MORNING PRAYER ·

Mighty God. The God who will not be silent. Perfect in beauty. God of justice. You are the God who is my God. You have commanded me to listen, for You want to speak uninterrupted. You don't need anything from me. You are entirely self-sufficient. You don't want offerings that are made without thanksgiving and obedience. You want me to call on You because I want You. It's all about relationship. You want me to call on You in trouble so that You may deliver me, so that I may give You thanks and honor. May I learn to live in that state of constant expectation and communication. Clean out my ears; teach me to listen more than speak. Amen.

> *If I were hungry, I would not tell thee: for the world is mine,*
> *and the fulness thereof. . . . Offer unto God thanksgiving;*
> *and pay thy vows unto the most High.*
> PSALM 50:12, 14

EVENING READING ·

The nature of your relationship with God is one that can be hard to comprehend because it is like no other relationship that you have. There is literally nothing that you can offer God that He could not gain on His own. He owns the entire world. So many of our earthly relationships are based on what we can give and get. Our pride and self-sufficiency often leave us feeling uncomfortable if we believe that there is nothing we can give to a relationship. We like to be needed. But with God we have to lay the desire to be needed aside. All we can do is humbly give Him our service and praise.

The Widow's Offering

(MARK 12:41–44)

>>>>>> ❀ <<<<<

MORNING PRAYER· · · · · · · · · · · ·

Lord Jesus, I lay myself before You, ashamed at how little I have given to You. You know my struggles with tithing. And yet, this woman gave everything she had to You. I've been a single mom, but I never gave away those last two pennies. Open my heart, open my hands, to give freely, sacrificially, with joy. You don't ask me to be financially irresponsible. But perhaps You do ask me to give until it's no longer easy or convenient. To give up something I want but don't need. Let me learn from You how to give, even if it means giving the most precious thing in my life. Amen.

> *And so it was, when the cloud abode from even unto the morning, and that the cloud was taken up in the morning, then they journeyed: whether it was by day or by night that the cloud was taken up, they journeyed. Or whether it were two days, or a month, or a year, that the cloud tarried upon the tabernacle, remaining thereon, the children of Israel abode in their tents, and journeyed not: but when it was taken up, they journeyed.*
> NUMBERS 9:21–22

EVENING READING ·

The Israelites had to live day by day, watching and waiting for the cloud or pillar of fire to move from its place. Once the presence of God moved, they had to follow it without delay. Are you as willing to pack up your life and your comforts to follow God wherever He may lead? We would probably grumble and complain to be forced to live in such limbo. And yet, aren't we only sojourners and nomads on this earth? Beware of getting so attached to the things and places of this world that you would grumble to follow the pillar of fire wherever it may lead.

Setting Out
(Numbers 10:35–36)

❀

MORNING PRAYER

Lord God, as I start this new day, I already know You are clearing the trail before me. I punch in, ready to go to work. Do as You promised. Chase my enemies away. Hold my head high so I can walk through their midst confidently and without fear. At day's end, when I come to rest, stay with me. Stand guard over my bed. I pray this not just for myself but for all Your people, the countless thousands across the globe. Let us not move unless You go with us and not stop until You give the signal. Amen.

> *Against thee, thee only, have I sinned, and done this*
> *evil in thy sight: that thou mightest be justified when*
> *thou speakest, and be clear when thou judgest.*
> Psalm 51:4

EVENING READING

In this psalm, David understood the true nature of sin. Every sin is an insult to God and grieves Him deeply. We are often so nonchalant with our sins, imagining that they are pretty much harmless. But Christ didn't die for something inconsequential and harmless. It is important to recognize the weight of each and every sin. Only when we see how abhorrent sin is can we truly come to appreciate the sacrifice Christ made for us.

A Broken Spirit

(PSALM 51:10–19)

>>>>> ❀ <<<<<

MORNING PRAYER

"Create in me a pure heart, O God" (Psalm 51:10 NIV). How many millions have repeated David's prayer? I bow before You in supplication. Oh Lord, forgive me for the times I've sinned! Oh Lord, transform me! I thank You for replacing my heart of stone with a new heart, in the sacrifice of Your Son and by the power of Your Spirit that raised Jesus from the dead. Break me, God, that I may see my sinfulness. Broken and contrite, desperate for a drop of Your mercy, I trust that You will draw near to me when at last I acknowledge I am unworthy to be in Your presence. Amen.

(Now the man Moses was very meek, above all
the men which were upon the face of the earth.)
NUMBERS 12:3

EVENING READING

A fascinating little phrase is tucked into Numbers 12:3—Moses was the meekest man on earth. At first this may seem surprising. Moses was, after all, the leader of a multitude of people, a direct correspondent with God, and someone who had performed miracles. But rather than making him arrogant, the fact that he had seen and spoken with God was the very thing that made him humble. Throughout the Bible an encounter with God never puffs up but inevitably brings people to their knees. Our smallness, inconsequence, and transience is recognized so much more clearly when seen in the radiance of the person of God. No wonder Moses was the meekest man on earth, since he knew his God better than any man on earth.

Olive Tree

(PSALM 52:8–9)

❀

MORNING PRAYER

God, when I'm tempted to make fun of my enemies, may I instead watch them in holy fear, recognizing it could be me making wealth my god like they do, not You, my stronghold. Instead of being uprooted and thrown away, I'm that olive tree flourishing in Your garden. I trust in Your love because I can't outrun it or escape it. For all You have done, are doing, and will do for me, I praise You in the presence of others. I hope in Your name, for You are good. Amen!

> *If the LORD delight in us, then he will bring us into this land,*
> *and give it us; a land which floweth with milk and honey.*
> NUMBERS 14:8

EVENING READING

Joshua and Caleb had remarkable courage and faith. They believed in the power and faithfulness of God in spite of terrifying enemies and faithless, complaining friends. It would have been easy for them to have conformed to the crowd and sided with the majority. But they had enough faith in God to speak up against the majority. How often do we shy away from speaking up for our beliefs because we're scared? Or maybe we're just not fully convinced that He actually is a promise keeper. Fortunately, our faithlessness does not affect His faithfulness.

Troubled Prayer

(MARK 14:32–36)

≈≫≫≫ ❀ ≪≪≪≈

MORNING PRAYER

Lord Jesus, how many times I've come to You feeling "deeply distressed"! And You understand what I'm going through, for You faced Your own prayer battle, overwhelmed with sorrow, to the point of death. My battles with depression, of feeling life isn't worth living, are only a pale reflection of Your sorrow when You sweat drops of blood and knew You were about to die and bear the sin of the world on Your shoulders. If Your heavenly Father would not spare You when You begged for any other way for humankind to be saved, who am I to complain about my trivial travails? In those dark times, may I look to this holy time and lean on You. Amen.

> *The fool hath said in his heart, There is no God. Corrupt are they,*
> *and have done abominable iniquity: there is none that doeth good.*
> PSALM 53:1

EVENING READING

Psalm 53:1 says that they are fools who believe that there is no God. It seems that today's culture is increasingly asserting the belief that those who believe there *is* a God are the foolish ones. And yet, all creation points to a thoughtful, creative engineer. Could it really be that those who find a depth of peace beyond anything this world can offer, those who give their lives for the sake of others and their faith, those whose greatest desire is to please God. . .could it really be that they are the fools? No, those who deprive themselves of a life-giving relationship with God are truly the fools.

Election Times

(NUMBERS 16)

>->>>> ❀ <<<<

MORNING PRAYER ·

Lord, You know how fervently I have prayed during national elections. Sometimes the candidates I voted for won; sometimes they lost. I confess that when the president disappoints me, fulfilling my worst fears, I think, *God? God?* I question Your hand behind our country. Oh Lord, I'm like the people of Israel, talking against Your appointed leader. Tens of thousands of Americans prayed for the elections. Forgive me for second-guessing Your leadership. I rest in the knowledge that Your will for the president, for me personally, and for my country may not match my own vision for our future. Of course I want You to bless America. More than that, I pray that You will teach America to bless You. Amen.

Likewise also the chief priests mocking said among themselves with the scribes, He saved others; himself he cannot save
MARK 15:31

EVENING READING ·

Jesus could have silenced the taunts by coming down off the cross or by calling down legions of angels who would have shocked and awed His murderers. Though doing this would likely have converted much of the watching crowd, the story would have inevitably become legend after a few generations. Instead of saving Himself, Christ bore the shame, insults, and utter humiliation to become so much more than a legend. By keeping silent before His false accusers, He became a Savior to everlasting generations. God so often doesn't use the flashy, eye-catching techniques we might use to accomplish His will. Instead, He uses the relentless endurance of His servants whose greatest desire is to have His will supersede their own. Christ was clearly the ultimate example of this.

Watchful Women

(MARK 15:40–41)

❂⟩⟩⟩⟩ ❀ ⟨⟨⟨⟨⟨

MORNING PRAYER

Lord Jesus, I admit that the woman in me is proud of Mary Magdalene, Mary the mother of James, Salome, and all the other unnamed women who waited at the cross. Would I have had their courage, their stamina, to keep watch publicly? I thank You for their example. I thank You for the faithful service of church women through the years. But mostly I ask that my faith be like theirs—strong, able to endure the most painful test and to keep watch with those going through the hardest times. May I stand up for You even when it isn't popular, when it appears hopeless. Amen.

> *Joseph of Arimathaea, an honourable counsellor, which*
> *also waited for the kingdom of God, came, and went in*
> *boldly unto Pilate, and craved the body of Jesus.*
> MARK 15:43

EVENING READING

Joseph of Arimathaea was bold enough to align himself with the crucified King when he came to take His body for burial. When the majority of Christ's disciples were in hiding, Joseph was publicly honoring Jesus. This was a risky move on his part. He could have easily been ostracized or worse. But the impact that Christ had on him was great enough to overcome the fear of men. Would you be as bold to align yourself with Someone who was just killed by hateful mobs?

Meribah

(NUMBERS 20:12)

᠉᠉᠉᠉᠉ ❀ ᠊᠊᠊᠊᠊

MORNING PRAYER

Heavenly Father, I can't imagine how Moses felt when You said he wouldn't enter the promised land. Of course, instead, he went to *the* promised land—the real Narnia, as C. S. Lewis put it—and how he must have rejoiced in that crossing over. But standing on this side of life's river, I don't quite understand the harshness of Your edict. I accept it by faith, and I pray I will learn from its lessons. And I pray for the times when I face disappointment, everything from losing mobility to having a book deal fall through. I thank You for allowing me to see into the future in the faces of my grandchildren. Amen.

*Now when Jesus was risen early the first day of the
week, he appeared first to Mary Magdalene,
out of whom he had cast seven devils.*
MARK 16:9

EVENING READING

Even in His resurrection, Christ was showing the world His heart for the weak and those without status. The first person He appeared to was not a chief priest or even one of the twelve disciples. He showed Himself first to a woman. In the culture of the day, women were not highly esteemed. But this woman loved her Savior enough to be the first one at the grave very early in the morning. The hearts of those who love Him are so much more precious to Christ than any earthly status.

NUMBERS 21:1–22:20 ❀ LUKE 1:1–25 ❀ PSALM 56:8–13

Under Vows

(PSALM 56:8–13)

❀

MORNING PRAYER

I am under vows to You, my God, vows to bring an offering of thanksgiving before You. And I will thank You not because everything is going well and streams of abundance flow. Although I do give thanks for those times, now I give You thanks for the times that I stumble and You lift me up. That You give me life today. I offer myself as a living sacrifice. I can do nothing else. You are for me. Man can do nothing to me. I trust You and Your Word, and You take away my fear. Oh, give thanks to the Lord, for You are good! Amen.

When I cry unto thee, then shall mine enemies
turn back: this I know; for God is for me.
PSALM 56:9

EVENING READING

Do you believe that God is for you? Or do you believe that maybe He likes you or at least tolerates you when you do what He wants? To believe that God is for you is to have an unshakable confidence that everything that happens in your life is orchestrated by God for your good and His glory. This certainly can be a hard thing to believe during times of personal struggles or heartbreak. But God is for you. And one day, in this life or the next, you'll be able to look back and see the beautiful tapestry that He's woven of your life where each thread of struggle leads to matchless joy.

The Magnificat

(LUKE 1:46–56)

❧❧❧❧❧ ❀ ❦❦❦❦❦

MORNING PRAYER ·

God my Savior, my soul glorifies You; I rejoice in You. Just as You were mindful of Mary, You are mindful of me. You saw me in my humble state and lifted me from the depths. Holy is Your name. May the news of Your mighty deeds on my behalf be told to future generations. May the great- and great-great-grandchildren who won't meet me hear of the God I served. Your mercy extends to me and to a thousand generations. You showed mercy to Mary through her cousin Elizabeth. I thank You for the grace bearers and grace givers in my life. Amen!

> *And the ass saw me, and turned from me these three times:*
> *unless she had turned from me, surely now also*
> *I had slain thee, and saved her alive.*
> NUMBERS 22:33

EVENING READING ·

You never know what seemingly frustrating thing in your life is actually God's way of saving you from harm. In the story of Balaam's donkey in Numbers 22, Balaam was angry at his donkey for continually turning away from the path. Most of us could easily put ourselves in his shoes with his anger building as things continued to not go his way. But the angel of the Lord eventually told him that the very thing he was angry about was what saved his life. An annoying, frustrating, or even very trying situation in life may just be God protecting and guiding you.

Changing Winds

(NUMBERS 24)

⇒⇒⟩⟩⟩ ❀ ⟨⟨⟨⟨⇐

MORNING PRAYER ·

Dear Lord, I confess I'm uncomfortable with this aspect of prayer, that the prayer You place on my heart isn't the one I expect or want. Like when You want me to bless my enemies instead of cursing them. Of course You wanted to bless Israel, but later You sent Jonah to Nineveh, demanding he bless his enemy by sharing Your Word with them. Lord, praying for my enemies is like a wrestling match. Bring my spirit into alignment with Your will. Once You have shown me that will, may I act promptly— even if it means blessing my enemy. I ask especially that You break down any hostility between me and others. Amen.

And she brought forth her firstborn son, and wrapped
him in swaddling clothes, and laid him in a manger;
because there was no room for them in the inn.
LUKE 2:7

EVENING READING ·

God orchestrates history in such an exquisitely unique way. Centuries-old prophecies of a Messiah being born in Bethlehem were fulfilled because of the seemingly mundane act of having to travel for a census. The Savior of the world was born into a world that apparently had no room for Him, forcing Him to be born in a stable. Shepherds, a very lowly class in their culture, were the first to enter the courts of the King. Given the opportunity, it's doubtful that any of us would have written the story of the most important birth in history this way. But in that is the awesome beauty of it all. This is not a man-made story; this is the story of the Creator and Sustainer of the universe.

Adapting

(NUMBERS 27:1–11)

⇝⇉⇉⇉ ❁ ⇇⇇⇇⇇

MORNING PRAYER ⸱ ·

Lord God, how thankful I am that You won't leave me as a second-class citizen without rights any more than You did Zelophehad's daughters. I throw myself on Your mercy, grateful You didn't set me aside because I grew up in a single-parent home or when my marriage failed. You saw *me*, a person created by You and in Your image, and You made me a coheir with Your Son. I pray that I will live as a princess in Your kingdom, endued with Your beauty, clothed in Your salvation, carrying out kingdom duties. Amen.

> *Lord, now lettest thou thy servant depart in peace,*
> *according to thy word: for mine eyes have seen thy salvation,*
> *which thou hast prepared before the face of all people; a light*
> *to lighten the Gentiles, and the glory of thy people Israel.*
> LUKE 2:29–32

EVENING READING ·

God gives His servant Simeon a marvelous blessing to allow him to see the Messiah before he died. Simeon understood the prophecies and plan of God and recognized Jesus for what He was—God's salvation to Israel and the Gentiles. How glorious that he could behold the Savior who would soon bring to fruition all the promises of God that Simeon knew and held to as his hope.

❧ DAY 82 ❧

When I Die

(NUMBERS 27:15–21)

❧❧❧❧❧ ✿ ❧❧❧❧❧

MORNING PRAYER ·

Heavenly Father, how I hope that the prayers I offer when I die are as focused on others as Moses' were, as my mother's were. Mold me in the fashion of elder saints over the centuries. Moses asked for someone to lead Israel, and You appointed Joshua. I pray for my family, as my son and then his children pick up the mantle of spiritual leadership. That Your light will burn as brightly in all four grandchildren down to the youngest as it does in their father. I pray for my church community, my fellow writers, my friends—that You will bring someone to fill the voids I may leave behind. Then take me home. I'm ready. Amen.

> *But I will sing of thy power; yea, I will sing aloud*
> *of thy mercy in the morning: for thou hast been*
> *my defence and refuge in the day of my trouble.*
> PSALM 59:16

EVENING READING ·

How often do you openly praise God for His power and mercy? He sustains us every day of our lives, and yet we sometimes fail to acknowledge that. We often struggle to praise Him privately in our own hearts for all He's done for us, let alone proclaim aloud His praise to others. No matter what happens in your life, you still have ample reason to praise God at the end of the day.

While Jesus Was Praying

(LUKE 3:21–22)

❧❧❧❧❧ ❀ ❧❧❧❧❧

MORNING PRAYER

Lord Jesus, what did You say on the day of Your baptism? You didn't have any sins to confess. Were You celebrating? Asking for Your Father's blessing and strength as You began a public ministry, fully revealing Yourself as Messiah? Thanking God for Your cousin and praying for him? I thank You that You allowed us to see and hear part of that prayer, when the Father spoke for human ears to hear and the Holy Spirit came on You like a dove for all to see. I pray that my time with You will make me transparent, that others can see You in me. Amen.

> *Which was the son of Enos, which was the son of Seth,*
> *which was the son of Adam, which was the son of God.*
> LUKE 3:38

EVENING READING

What a splendid and inexplicable mystery it is that Jesus was both fully man and fully God when He came to earth. He had a traceable genealogy. He came from a line of humans from which He would have inherited strengths, weaknesses, and physical traits. When God chose to come to earth to dwell among men, He didn't show up with a fancy entrance or a doting entourage proclaiming His deity. Instead, He chose to come as part of a family.

You Are Mine

(PSALM 60:6–12)

⟫⟫⟩⟩ ❀ ⟨⟨⟨⟨⟪

MORNING PRAYER

Oh Lord whose name is Holy, how I love this passage, the possessive note in Your voice. "Gilead is mine, and Manasseh is mine; Ephraim is my helmet, Judah is my scepter" (Psalm 60:7 NIV). I hear the echoes. "Darlene is mine!" Before I ask, You are shouting triumph over my enemies, even when they come from my own family. So with confidence I approach You, asking for Your aid. Convict me when I seek human help for something only You can provide. With You I will gain the victory. Not by myself alone, but with all others who belong to You. Amen.

> *Give us help from trouble: for vain is the help of man. Through God*
> *we shall do valiantly: for he it is that shall tread down our enemies.*
> PSALM 60:11–12

EVENING READING

Where do you turn first when you are struggling with something? Have you ever had the experience where you realize hours after anxiously working through a problem that you still haven't asked the Lord for help? In this psalm, we're told that the help of man is vain. Your only completely trustworthy source of help is your heavenly Father. While He can (and does) graciously use the people around you to give you sound wisdom and advice, you should still always turn to Him before anyone else with your troubles.

Lead Me to the Rock

(PSALM 61:2–4)

❧❧❧❧❧ ❀ ❧❧❧❧❧

MORNING PRAYER

Hear my cry, oh Lord; listen to my prayer. When I am under pressure, my heart overwhelmed, when joy and peace are being squeezed out of it, lead me to the rock that is higher than I. Place me where the enemy cannot reach me. You have been my shelter and a strong tower in the past. You will be yet again. I will dwell in Your tabernacle, shielded by Your glory and holiness. In Your presence, clothed in Your righteousness and salvation, I will shine brightly before all who oppose me. I rest as a baby chick under the shelter of those powerful wings. Amen.

When Simon Peter saw it, he fell down at Jesus' knees, saying,
Depart from me; for I am a sinful man, O Lord.
LUKE 5:8

EVENING READING

Peter truly understood his standing before God. In Luke 5:8, he is so aware of his sinfulness and Jesus' holiness that he asks that Jesus would depart from him. Are we as aware of how filthy our sins are in the light of God's perfection? Or do we generally think we have it pretty well together?

You Are My Rock

(PSALM 62)

>>>>> ❀ <<<<<

MORNING PRAYER

Heavenly Father, when I cannot sleep, when I am consumed by worry, let me run to You and cuddle in Your loving arms. My hope comes from You. I will arise with renewed encouragement for the day ahead. You are my rock. You make me strong, unbreakable when I take my stand on You. You are my salvation. You renew my spirit. You are my fortress. I walk in the force field of Your love, protected from harm. Let me take rest on a regular basis, that I will rise with wings like eagles. Amen.

He only is my rock and my salvation:
he is my defence; I shall not be moved.
PSALM 62:6

EVENING READING

David understood that with God as his refuge, he could not be moved. He calls God his rock. This would not have meant a stone or even a boulder but rather a mountain. Just as mountains are unshakably solid, so is God for those who seek refuge in Him. Run to the Rock and hide yourself in His shadow.

DEUTERONOMY 1:1–2:25 ❀ **LUKE 5:33–6:11** ❀ **PSALM 62:7–12**

Do It My Way

(LUKE 6:1–10)

⇒⇒⟩⟩⟩ ❀ ⟨⟨⟨⟨⇐

MORNING PRAYER ·

Living Word, imprint on my heart the principle You gave to the Pharisees: "Which is lawful: to save life or destroy it?" I confess that I sometimes create destruction by being stuck in my way of doing things, that I take away someone else's joy by standing up for my rights. Forgive me, Lord. You have come to free me from rigidity in my thoughts and spirit and life. There is only one way to salvation, but I sometimes get discouraged by theological discord. Let me follow the leading of Your Spirit, informed by Your written Word. Amen.

> *Yet in this thing ye did not believe the LORD your God, Who went in the way*
> *before you, to search you out a place to pitch your tents in, in fire by night,*
> *to shew you by what way ye should go, and in a cloud by day.*
> DEUTERONOMY 1:32–33

EVENING READING ·

Moses rebukes the people for not believing God about the land He had promised them. This was the God who had dwelled with them for the entire journey, showing them the way in a cloud by day and as their light at night. This was the God who had proven Himself over and over again. And yet, they chose fear instead of faith. Is your first reaction to a difficult situation fear or faith? Hasn't God "proven" Himself to you as well?

DEUTERONOMY 2:26–4:14 ❀ LUKE 6:12–35 ❀ PSALM 63:1–5

Slake My Thirst

(PSALM 63:1–5)

>>>>> ❀ <<<<<

MORNING PRAYER ·

God, You are my God. I seek You, thirsting, panting, coughing, unable to swallow or breathe without You. I stumble through the desert where I find myself and remember the days of glory when I saw You in Your sanctuary. In the desert, Your power and glory seem like a mirage. But by faith I cling to them. Your love is better than life. You give me a reason to live. I choose to glorify You with my lips, to praise You today and every day, to lift up my hands in Your name, to sing to You. I know that You will satisfy that hunger and slake that thirst with the best of the land. Amen.

And he lifted up his eyes on his disciples, and said,
Blessed be ye poor: for yours is the kingdom of God.
LUKE 6:20

EVENING READING ·

Earthly success is not at all synonymous with spiritual success. In His sermon, Jesus called those who are poor, hungry, weeping, and hated by men blessed—hardly attributes that we would use to describe a "successful" life. If someone doesn't fit into our nicely defined version of earthly success, it does not in any way mean that God is not blessing that person. So much can be learned from passionate followers of Christ who use their poverty, hunger, sorrow, and persecution for the glory of their God.

Bring Me Back

(DEUTERONOMY 4:29–31)

>>>>>> ❁ <<<<<

MORNING PRAYER

Heavenly Lord, You are not just God; You are my God, and You always treat me with compassion. What I may perceive as ruin is only Your way of guiding me back to renewing my vows. You are my God, always faithful to me, never breaking Your covenant with me even when I've given You grounds. Whatever ruins I perceive in my life are Your gifts, meant to guide me back to the center of Your will. God who fashioned every moment of my life, teach me to follow with ever more of my heart and soul, until I give You my all. Amen.

> *But if from thence thou shalt seek the LORD thy God, thou shalt*
> *find him, if thou seek him with all thy heart and with all thy soul.*
> DEUTERONOMY 4:29

EVENING READING

God is not a God who makes Himself hard to find. He does not try to hide Himself from us or veil Himself so that we can't know Him. In times when God seems far off or it feels like He's abandoned you, maybe you have not been seeking Him as you need to. He promises to be found by those who seek Him—therefore, you have a 100 percent chance of success when searching to know God.

⚡ DAY 90 ⚡

The Lonely Widow

(LUKE 7:11–17)

❁ ❁ ❁

MORNING PRAYER ·

Lord Jesus, how I rejoice because I love You and trust You with all my being. Like the woman in today's passage, I lost my husband, my daughter too, and it seemed I was about to lose my son. But You called him back from the edge of destruction and despair and gave him back to me alive. How I thank You and rejoice in You. I thank You for the gift of my family. I praise You that I can rest, that I can trust You in life and in death. Amen.

> *Now when he came nigh to the gate of the city, behold, there was a dead man carried out, the only son of his mother, and she was a widow: and much people of the city was with her. And when the Lord saw her, he had compassion on her, and said unto her, Weep not.*
> LUKE 7:12–13

EVENING READING ·

Christ's ministry is defined by so much compassion. His actions were inspired not by a people-pleasing, surface-level compassion but a deep-seated love for people, even people that He didn't know. Pray that God would instill in you the same kind of compassion that Christ so beautifully displayed. In this passage, Jesus very dramatically changed the life of this woman, but even a small act of compassion and kindness has the power to turn a life around.

Clothes That Don't Wear Out
(DEUTERONOMY 8:4)

>>>>> ❀ <<<<<

MORNING PRAYER

Lord, how I thank You for the heavenly uniform You have given me. Every day I commune with You, it shines more brightly than the day before. It will never wear out. In my emperor's new clothes, I fade away while You shine ever more brightly in me. From the helmet of salvation on my head to shoes made from the sturdy, soft leather of the Gospel of peace on my feet and the garment of Your righteousness, Your holiness, covering my body, I couldn't ask for better clothing. You have given me forever-wear, all that I need for today and throughout eternity. God—the best couture ever. Thank You, Lord. Amen.

> *And thou shalt remember all the way which the LORD thy*
> *God led thee these forty years in the wilderness, to humble thee,*
> *and to prove thee, to know what was in thine heart,*
> *whether thou wouldest keep his commandments, or no.*
> DEUTERONOMY 8:2

EVENING READING

Moses called the people to remember—to remember their trying journey through the wilderness. They were to remember the humbling times, the proving grounds, and the heart-revealing struggles. They were to remember that God was leading them through those times every step of the way. It is a worthwhile endeavor to record the paths that God has led you down. Remember how faithfully He has led you so that you can boldly step into the future, entrusting yourself to Him as your guide.

❧ DAY 92 ❧

Worshipping with Prisoners
(LUKE 7:36–43)

>>>>> ❀ <<<<<

MORNING PRAYER ·

Loving Lord, I confess I'm more like the Pharisees than the sinful woman in this story. I smell someone with the spiritual odor of sin clinging to them when they come to worship and I judge. Forgive me, Lord! In You there is no male or female, no slave or free—no prisoner or prison guard. Lord, if anything, I ask that You will bring more "sinners" into my life. May I learn from their humility, from their outpouring of love because You have forgiven what I consider the unforgiveable. Break my spirit so that I may accept them as my equals, brothers and sisters in Christ. Amen.

> *Now when the Pharisee which had bidden him saw it,*
> *he spake within himself, saying, This man, if he were*
> *a prophet, would have known who and what manner of*
> *woman this is that toucheth him: for she is a sinner.*
> LUKE 7:39

EVENING READING ·

The irony of Luke 7:39 is almost comic. In his heart the Pharisee was scoffing at Jesus for not knowing that the woman who was showering Him with honor was a sinner. Meanwhile, Jesus not only knew exactly what this woman had done in the past and the repentance that was now in her heart, but He also knew the disrespectful thoughts that the Pharisee was thinking. The Pharisee had grossly underestimated the insight and power of the Man he was dining with.

Testing

(DEUTERONOMY 13:1–4)

⇒⟩⟩⟩⟩ ❁ ⟨⟨⟨⟨⇐

MORNING PRAYER

Lord God, I wonder if I'd be any more prepared for Your tests if I knew about them ahead of time? Instead they show up when least expected, like pop quizzes. I pray that I won't listen to people who offer to help me cheat, that I won't be led astray by false signs and wonders or believe anyone who speaks of a false god. Fan the flames of love in my heart so that passion for You may burn brightly deep within. May its kindling fuel my obedience, light my service, and provide the adhesive that keeps me fast to You. Amen.

They drop upon the pastures of the wilderness: and the little hills rejoice on every side. The pastures are clothed with flocks; the valleys also are covered over with corn; they shout for joy, they also sing.
PSALM 65:12–13

EVENING READING

Have you ever been outside on one of those days where you can almost hear nature praising its Maker? Have you ever seen a sight so heart-wrenchingly gorgeous that you have to start praising Him as well? What a wonderful thing that God has so blessed us by putting His beauty and creativity on full display for our pleasure. May we never take His creation for granted.

Drowning

(LUKE 8:22–25)

❧⟫⟫⟫ ❀ ⟪⟪⟪❧

MORNING PRAYER ·

Master, I'm going to drown! How many times has my cry echoed that of the disciples? How often I've seen the leaping waves and tried to bail out my sinking boat. I know You're there, but sometimes it seems like You're asleep, not paying any attention. Forgive me for trying to solve the problem by myself. Forgive me for my lack of faith, for not coming to You before the situation reached a crisis stage. Oh Lord, how I thank You that You are in the boat with me when the storm is raging. The next time I'm about to capsize, may I turn to You, asking You to speak, "Peace, be still," to my heart. Amen.

And he said unto them, Where is your faith? And they being afraid
wondered, saying one to another, What manner of man is this!
for he commandeth even the winds and water, and they obey him.
LUKE 8:25

EVENING READING ·

Are you ever surprised when God does something amazing in your life? The disciples in today's passage were in fearful awe when Jesus calmed the wind and the waves. Christ rebuked them for this, asking them, "Where is your faith?" Why is it that we are sometimes surprised when we see God's goodness in our lives? Is our faith so weak or our knowledge of God so limited that we doubt His power and love?

DAY 95

DEUTERONOMY 16:9–18:22 ❀ LUKE 8:40–56 ❀ PSALM 66:8–15

Faith vs. Fear

(LUKE 8:50)

≈⸱⟩⟩⟩⟩ ❀ ⟨⟨⟨⟨≈⸱

MORNING PRAYER·

Heavenly Father, I come before You this morning, a heart in despair. My beloved child is dead, and I feel as though my heart has been torn in two. I confess I am listening to inner condemnation that says if I had been a better mother, she wouldn't have died. Oh Lord, forgive me for wrong thinking. Create in me a new mind. You tell me not to be afraid. You command me to turn the loss over to You and to believe in You, not what You will do. When my feet are planted in You, I will sing praises to You, free from fear. Nothing I might lose can compare to what I gain in You. Amen.

And her spirit came again, and she arose straightway:
and he commanded to give her meat.
LUKE 8:55

EVENING READING

Today's passage in Luke is a lovely example of how God uses both miraculous and ordinary means to complete His work. Jesus miraculously healed the girl, but then He instructed her parents to give her something to eat. This seems like an oddly mundane thing to instruct them to do after He just performed the phenomenal feat of bringing her back from the dead. But we shouldn't be surprised when God uses ordinary means to advance His kingdom.

A Time to Stay Home
(DEUTERONOMY 20:5–9)

❧≫≫≫ ❀ ≪≪≪❧

MORNING PRAYER· ·

Compassionate God, how I thank You for these instructions to Moses. You don't call me to a life of constant battle. Your plan tells me to invest time in my family and to take care of what You've given me. I confess I struggle with finding the right balance. At times I shut myself off from others. Other times I keep so busy with activities that I neglect what's important. I pray that Your loving wisdom will guide me as I schedule my days. Show me when to say no. Teach me to handle the unexpected with grace. Amen.

And shall say unto them, Hear, O Israel, ye approach this day unto battle against your enemies: let not your hearts faint, fear not, and do not tremble, neither be ye terrified because of them; for the LORD your God is he that goeth with you, to fight for you against your enemies, to save you.
DEUTERONOMY 20:3–4

EVENING READING ·

Though the majority of us aren't facing enemy armies on a daily basis, we still have battles to fight nearly every day. Some may be more difficult than others, but we all at some point need courage to face the next step in life. Go forward with confidence knowing that it is God who fights for you. Fear not, for the all-powerful God is on your side.

Make Me a Blessing

(PSALM 67:1–2)

❧❧❧❧❧ ❀ ❧❧❧❧❧

MORNING PRAYER

Gracious God, how often have I prayed the first half of this prayer, that You will bless me and cause Your face to shine on me. I praise You for the beauty of the second half of the prayer. When You bless me, make Your ways known upon the earth, Your salvation among all nations. I ask the same for all believers, that Your blessing may be so obvious that others might clamor for the way for themselves, that a single candle will become two then three until whole villages and regions blaze with Your fullness and light. Amen.

God be merciful unto us, and bless us; and cause his face
to shine upon us; Selah. That thy way may be known
upon earth, thy saving health among all nations.
PSALM 67:1–2

EVENING READING

We all certainly want God to bless us. But why do we want Him to bless us? Merely for our own good, comfort, or security? In today's psalm, the author asked to be blessed so that others may know of the greatness of God. Use the blessings that God has bestowed on you to talk of and magnify Him. Strive to always be enthusiastic to speak of God and all that He has done for you so that others may be blessed by Him as well.

Counting the Cost

(LUKE 9:57–62)

❧❧❧❧❧ ❀ ❧❧❧❧❧

MORNING PRAYER ·

Lord, even my dull human spirit can see the contradiction between calling You "Lord" but saying "wait a minute" before I obey. Your standards haven't changed. You'll ask me to let go of whatever I most want to put in Your place. You're a jealous God, and You won't share Your glory with another. I confess, I don't always understand how that works. But do I value Your good gifts more than You, the Giver? May it never be. May I not look to the side, at what others are doing. May I not look back, at what might have been. Instead, may I turn my gaze upon You, the author and finisher of my faith. Amen.

A father of the fatherless, and a judge of the widows, is God in his holy habitation. God setteth the solitary in families: he bringeth out those which are bound with chains: but the rebellious dwell in a dry land.

PSALM 68:5–6

EVENING READING ·

God is a relational God. So much so that even in His own person, He is not one but three. It's no wonder, then, that He feels so strongly for the orphan, the widow, and those who don't belong anywhere. His heart for these people is so apparent throughout all of scripture. He is the Father to those who have none and the protector of the widow. He places those without a home into families. If God is so concerned about these children of His, shouldn't we be as well? And in times when you feel as though you don't belong anywhere, remember that God is always by your side as your loving Father.

DEUTERONOMY 26:1–28:14 ❀ LUKE 10:1–20 ❀ PSALM 68:7–14

Inspection Time

(DEUTERONOMY 26:12–15)

❧❀❧

MORNING PRAYER

Lord God, everything I am and have belongs to You, but within that framework You've given me money to take care of my needs. Thank You for that gift, that trust. Teach me the discipline of setting aside some of those funds, and my time, to give to others who are in need. Make me a living sacrifice of worship. Oh Lord, how I long to say with confidence that I've obeyed *all* Your commands, for that is what You require. You desire more than my offering. You want my obedience. Forgive me when I fail at either. Amen.

> *Notwithstanding in this rejoice not, that the spirits*
> *are subject unto you; but rather rejoice, because*
> *your names are written in heaven.*
> LUKE 10:20

EVENING READING

Jesus presents an interesting challenge in today's passage. He adjured the disciples to rejoice not in the power that they had through Him, but in the fact that their names were written in the book of life. How often do we rejoice in earthly pursuits or successes and forget that the single most important thing for which to be grateful is our salvation? While we absolutely should rejoice in the gifts that God has given us on earth, it would benefit us to think more often on the greatest gift of all that God has given us—eternal life through His Son.

Thinking Like a Child

(LUKE 10:21)

❧❧❧❧❧ ❀ ❧❧❧❧❧

MORNING PRAYER ·

Lord Jesus, make my prayer like Yours. Fill me with Your joy through the Holy Spirit, that I may return praise to Your Father. Joyful, full of praise, I fall in wonder before You, the Lord of heaven and earth. *You* are the Lord, not the wise or rich or powerful of the earth. May I approach You like a child expecting good gifts from my Father. Lord, forgive me if I come like a know-it-all, thinking I only need to ask Your opinion to compare to mine. May I accept Your ways as best without question. You want to bless Your children. How I wonder and rejoice in that. Amen.

Blessed be the Lord, who daily loadeth us with benefits,
even the God of our salvation. Selah.
PSALM 68:19

EVENING READING ·

The Lord "daily loadeth us with benefits." What marvelous imagery that is. It implies that the blessings that God gives us on a daily basis are so bountiful as to almost be too much to carry. Our lives are overflowing with the goodness of God. Take a moment to ponder and write down some of the benefits that God has given you in the past week.

Learning the Lesson

(DEUTERONOMY 29:2–6)

⇒⟩⟩⟩⟩ ✿ ⟨⟨⟨⟨⇐

MORNING PRAYER

Lord, I laugh at Israel for their failure to learn lessons after forty years. But You're reminding me, *"What about the things I've been teaching you during your sixty-plus years?"* Oh Lord, forgive me for ever taking You for granted! As I go about my day, bring to mind the things You've done in my lifetime. Instruct my inner being through what You've done for Your people in the past. May I give thanks for everything as Your gracious provision, instead of treating it as my right. Through it all, open my eyes to see that You are God. You are *my* God. Amen.

I call heaven and earth to record this day against you,
that I have set before you life and death, blessing and cursing:
therefore choose life, that both thou and thy seed may live.
DEUTERONOMY 30:19

EVENING READING

Just like the Israelites, every day we are faced with a choice: Will we choose death and a curse or life and a blessing? The choice seems simple enough—as Moses said, choose life. And yet, don't we often choose death when we continually go back to old patterns of sinful thought or behavior? We purposefully neglect our life-giving time with God for other worthless pursuits. Think about ways in which you can choose life on a daily basis, and then wait for the beautiful ways in which God will pour that abundant life into you.

God on Display

(PSALM 68:28–35)

⤳⟩⟩⟩⟩ ❀ ⟨⟨⟨⟨⟨

MORNING PRAYER· ·

God of the nations, display Your awesome power. Fill the earth with the sound of Your mighty thunder summoning Your strength. I pray that the people of the earth will bring tribute to You, acknowledging Your lordship over them as individuals and nations. Make "in God we trust" more than words on our money. I pray for the people of the earth, especially those who don't know You, that they will submit themselves to You. That they'll sing to You and proclaim Your power. May they fall in worship and accept Your offer of salvation. Amen.

> *Be strong and of a good courage, fear not, nor be afraid of them:*
> *for the LORD thy God, he it is that doth go with thee;*
> *he will not fail thee, nor forsake thee.*
> DEUTERONOMY 31:6

EVENING READING ·

Moses spoke such beautiful words to the Israelites before his death. He encouraged them to be courageous because God would go with them and would never fail or forsake them. You serve the same God today. He will never fail you, forsake you, or leave your side. How can you be confident that this is true? Because He forsook His own Son so that He would never have to turn His face from you. What a humbling and glorious truth. There is no one who can be trusted more fully than a God who has sacrificed so much to redeem you. So be courageous. Your God will never fail or forsake you.

Save Me, Lord

(PSALM 69:1–9)

❀

MORNING PRAYER

Save me, oh God, I cry one more time. Lord, I'm weary of calling for help. I'm floundering. My feet can't find a foothold. Your Spirit must carry my prayers, for my voice is gone. My eyes have failed; I no longer see You. Everything has been stripped from me, and people are demanding I pay for things I never took. Deliver me from the depths I've plunged into out of my own choice. Forgive me both for my own sin and especially for the disgrace I have brought upon people who hope in You. I come to You because You've always been my help before. Amen.

Save me, O God; for the waters
are come in unto my soul.
PSALM 69:1

EVENING READING

The Bible is an incredibly relatable book. It's filled with stories of people we can relate to—it's not filled with stories of perfect human beings whose faith is so strong that they never struggle or doubt God. Psalm 69 is just one example of a child of God in deep, overwhelming turmoil. Don't ever be afraid or ashamed to cry out to God in this way. Your faith or standing with Him is not lessened because you feel like the waters are encompassing you and you desperately need His help. Take courage from these very real humans in the Bible, and speak to God with as much candor as they did.

Joshua's Call

(JOSHUA 1:1–9)

>>>>>> ❁ <<<<<<

MORNING PRAYER ·

Wow, God, what a difference between Joshua and Moses. Moses kept asking You to send someone else, but Joshua went right to work. Make me more like Joshua than like Moses—at least when it comes to what You've called me to do. I'm very thankful You haven't commissioned me to lead an army bent on conquering. But whether I'm a five-star general or a stay-at-home mom, bend my will to obey. *"Don't be afraid. I'm with you wherever you go."* I praise You for the promise. Reveal Your will for this day, as You did for Joshua. Amen.

> *And I say unto you my friends, Be not afraid of them that kill the body, and after that have no more that they can do. But I will forewarn you whom ye shall fear: Fear him, which after he hath killed hath power to cast into hell; yea, I say unto you, Fear him.*
> LUKE 12:4–5

EVENING READING ·

Luke 12:4–5 may sound like a threat at first. But in these words of Christ's is actually glorious comfort. In the whole scheme of eternity, we really have nothing to fear from man. And for those who are in Christ, we have nothing to fear from God because we have already been adopted into His family and redeemed for eternal life in heaven. Therefore, we have nothing to fear at all because, in the end, all man can do is hasten us on to a beautiful eternity with God in glory.

Treasure That Won't Corrupt

(LUKE 12:32–34)

MORNING PRAYER·

Lord of heaven, You've entrusted Your kingdom to me. I tremble at that confidence. Today and every day, may I exchange the treasures of my sharecrop farm for the glory of Your kingdom. Teach me to invest, not in silver and gold, but in the coin of Your realm, which will never be taken away. I'm not sure what the treasure I'm accumulating consists of. A desire to know You? People I've influenced for good? Praise to You? Whatever it is, it's of infinite value. Let me live each day with eternal values in view. Amen.

> *And Joshua said unto the people, Sanctify yourselves:*
> *for to morrow the LORD will do wonders among you.*
> JOSHUA 3:5

EVENING READING

The faith of Joshua in this verse is so inspiring. He didn't tell the people to sanctify themselves just in case God decided to do something amazing. He didn't tell the people to hope and pray that God would show up. No, he told them to sanctify themselves because God will do wonders tomorrow. There is no doubting or second-guessing. Joshua knew His God. He knew Him to be an absolutely faithful promise keeper.

When You Fall

(JOSHUA 7:1–12)

❧❧❧❧❀❧❧❧❧

MORNING PRAYER

Oh Lord, how I know Joshua's feelings after Ai. Just when everything seems to be going well, I rely on myself or hold back something that belongs to You and down I go. Forgive me for using my words to build myself up. Take them, take me, and use me to glorify Your name. Correct my steps so that I follow Your commands, not in selfish pursuits. Forgive me, Lord, when I grab ahold of something that belongs to You and bury it deep, saving it for myself. Forgive me for the harm I bring to my children. Amen.

Blessed is that servant, whom his lord
when he cometh shall find so doing.
LUKE 12:43

EVENING READING

Do you live every day in anticipation of Christ's coming? Or do you put off ministry and service for God's kingdom, reasoning that you'll do that when you have more time in the future? Our time on earth is the only chance we'll get to share Christ with others. It's the only chance we have to serve the needy and hurting. Don't wait for this time to pass. Live for Christ's kingdom and His coming today and every day.

Judging for Myself

(LUKE 12:57)

❧❧❧❧❧ ❀ ❧❧❧❧❧

MORNING PRAYER

Lord, I confess I doubt myself and Your calling far beyond what is reasonable. Not that doubt is reasonable since You're the all-powerful God, but You welcome honest questions. Do spiritual giants struggle with doubt? Did Billy Graham ever question if he had anything worthwhile to share when he preached? Did C. S. Lewis wonder if his books would help anyone? Remind me that any good that comes from my actions, my words, flows from You. It's not whether I'm prepared but whether I trust You to do what You've promised. Whenever I'm questioning You, counsel me to accept Your judgment. Show me when it's a good time to ask for advice and when to trust You without question. Amen.

Suppose ye that I am come to give peace on earth?
I tell you, Nay; but rather division.
LUKE 12:51

EVENING READING

Christ told His disciples that He did not come to bring peace but division. This is not exactly a heartwarming concept. But it can certainly be encouraging for you if you are facing opposition simply because you align yourself with Christ. Christ promised that where He was and where He was proclaimed there would be resistance. Sometimes facing opposition for the sake of Christ is a sign that you are doing exactly what you should be doing and following faithfully in the steps of Jesus who went before you.

DAY 108

Hope Endures

(PSALM 71:1–6)

>>>>> ✿ <<<<<

MORNING PRAYER

Lord God, You've been my hope since my youth. Oh, how my soul rejoices in that confidence. Thank You for saving me at a young age and for leading me. Your sovereign will redirected me when I pursued a false lead. I thank You for the strength that hope gave me with each twist and turn. And I rejoice in hope because of joy. Completion and new beginnings await me when I follow You. Forgive me for the times I let the embers burn low and I allowed myself to wallow in despair. What can I add to Your perfect foresight? Nothing. I rest in that hope. Amen.

> *For thou art my hope, O Lord GOD:*
> *thou art my trust from my youth.*
> PSALM 71:5

EVENING READING

Where is your hope found? In your job? Family? Financial security? Social status? In today's psalm, the author wrote that his hope is grounded firmly in his Lord. Hope and trust in God, and you won't be disappointed. This certainly doesn't mean that hoping in God is a way to avoid hardships and struggles. Instead, God will prove His trustworthiness through those times so that you can learn to hope in Him all the more.

Hope Today and Always

(PSALM 71:7–16)

❧❀❦

MORNING PRAYER ·

My Living Hope, I'll always have hope. It's based on Your character and Your faithfulness. In my short memory, You have never failed me—or anyone who has trusted You. The more I praise You, the more my expectation increases. When I speak today, let me speak of Your righteous deeds, Your saving acts. Fill my mouth with news of Your saving acts—I'll never run out of stories to share. Let me proclaim Your mighty works, and not those of mortal man. As I teach my family, let me lift You up as our Standard. Amen.

> *But I will hope continually,*
> *and will yet praise thee more and more.*
> PSALM 71:14

EVENING READING ·

The resilience of those who truly know God is remarkable. We see examples of this all through the Bible in God's prophets, disciples, apostles, and followers. In today's passage we see it in David. In this psalm, his life situation does not sound like anything to be happy about—even his enemies thought that God had forsaken him. And yet, he continued to hope in God, praise Him, and speak of His righteousness. Only the Lord can grant this kind of strength and perseverance in His children.

Give Me This Mountain

(Joshua 14:6–15)

❧ ❀ ❧

MORNING PRAYER

Heavenly Father, like Caleb, I'm drawing near the end of my life. I'm checking in: What about those dreams and visions You gave me that haven't been fulfilled? I celebrate the mountains You've put me on that I didn't ask for. But I want that mountain before I die. You know my frailty. Unlike Caleb, my vigor isn't what it once was. Clear my vision, increase the acuteness of my mind, give me strength for the day—equip me for the battle for what is yet to be. May all glory be returned to You. Amen.

> *Thou, which hast shewed me great and sore troubles, shalt quicken me again, and shalt bring me up again from the depths of the earth. Thou shalt increase my greatness, and comfort me on every side.*
> Psalm 71:20–21

EVENING READING

At times God may bring you through hard trials and "sore troubles." But you can be as confident as David was in this psalm that God will raise you up again from the depths of despair. David used beautiful imagery of God comforting him on every side— His comfort surrounds and protects His people. Even in (and often *especially* in) the darkest moments, you can feel His comfort and strength sustaining you.

DAY 111

Taking Up My Cross
(LUKE 14:27)

>>>>> ✿ <<<<<

MORNING PRAYER ·

You say I can't be Your disciple if I don't pick up my cross. Do I dare ask—but what is that cross? It's not wood I can buy at a lumberyard or something I wear around my neck. Do You give one to every Christian, along with a new heart? Or is it tailor-made for me? You ask me to pay a price for my cross. It might be letting go of my family or letting go of my life. Following You comes with a price tag, and that scares me. When decision time comes, will I hold back when You demand every penny in my life's wallet? Stamp out my fear of future sacrifice by giving me strength for today. Amen.

So likewise, whosoever he be of you that forsaketh
not all that he hath, he cannot be my disciple.
LUKE 14:33

EVENING READING ·

Would you qualify to be one of Jesus' disciples? It's a sobering question. Jesus said that only those who forsake everything they have can be His disciples. While God is not asking you to all of a sudden give away everything you have, would you be willing to if He did ask? What if your earthly comforts and treasures were taken away? How would you react? If your faith in Jesus is not dependent on earthly possessions and relationships, then you are worthy of being His disciple. Seek to know Him better so that you will have this kind of faith.

❧ DAY 112 ❦

Sanctuary

(JOSHUA 20)

❧ ✿ ❦

MORNING PRAYER

Lord of lords, what a wonder that the God who runs the universe considers the needs of the falsely accused. You arranged for them to have a safe place to await trial. But over the years, we've stretched the concept of Your provision and perhaps even misapplied it. I pray for my country, that its government, its cities and people will align themselves with Your Word in providing places of refuge. I pray for wisdom in handling refugees and prisoners. For the justice system. I pray that You will provide sanctuary for political and persecuted refugees. Reveal to us what that looks like in the twenty-first century. Amen.

> *Likewise, I say unto you, there is joy in the presence*
> *of the angels of God over one sinner that repenteth.*
> LUKE 15:10

EVENING READING

When someone comes to know the Lord, it is no small thing in heaven. In fact, Jesus declared that the angels rejoice when someone prays to receive Christ. What a marvelous thing that heaven rejoiced when you were adopted into God's family. You are a valuable part of His kingdom, worth being celebrated.

The Prodigal Son

(LUKE 15:11–32)

≽≫⟩⟩ ❀ ⟨⟨⟨≼

MORNING PRAYER

Heavenly Father, in the parable of the prodigal son, I'm the angry older brother, aren't I? You know the struggles I had growing up as an only child, when Mom seemed to favor her step-grandchildren. Remove that big ball of feeling entitled and ignored. Correct me, that I may switch the attitude of complaining to one of gratitude. Open my eyes to Your constant love that never changes. I thank You that when I was that prodigal, seeking a way home, You ran to greet me and dressed me in Your new clothes. I thank You for the older brothers and sisters who welcomed me to the family. Amen.

There failed not ought of any good thing which the LORD
had spoken unto the house of Israel; all came to pass.
JOSHUA 21:45

EVENING READING

All of God's promises will come to pass. No good gift from Him will fail. God does not promise us things to manipulate, control, or distract. He promises us good things because He loves us in a way that we can't even comprehend. It is an entirely selfless, self-sacrificing love, the kind that we cannot fully know on earth apart from Him. So cling to His promises as truth, and look forward to their fulfillment. Just as He was faithful to the Israelites, He will be faithful to you.

Choices

(JOSHUA 24)

⧽⧽⧽⧽⧽ ❀ ⧼⧼⧼⧼⧼

MORNING PRAYER ·

Lord God, the challenge Joshua issued at the end of his life rings deep in my heart, cutting and convicting me. I thank You for the people who came before me who said, "We will serve the Lord." I thank You for those who stand with me, that together we affirm, "We will serve the Lord!" I rejoice in my children holding place with our family, repeating the oath. Make that choice real in the give-and-take of my daily life, that I will do as I've promised. You know the truth, that what I promise today I will struggle to fulfill tomorrow and ten years from now. Keep my heart steadfast on You. Amen.

> *If therefore ye have not been faithful in the unrighteous mammon,*
> *who will commit to your trust the true riches?*
> LUKE 16:11

EVENING READING ·

It's easy to compartmentalize our lives into tidy little boxes that separate the spiritual from the everyday and earthly. Today's passage in Luke is an excellent reminder that we need to be faithful in every aspect of our lives, whether or not it seems to directly relate to the kingdom. Honor God in the way you treat your family, perform at your job or school, do your finances, etc. Be faithful in these things so that you can be entrusted with far more precious riches.

Testing Stones

(JUDGES 2:1–3)

>>>>> ✿ <<<<<

MORNING PRAYER ·

Lord of hosts, this passage terrifies me. I love hearing the sweet, gentle voice of Your Wonderful Counselor. I freeze in the presence of Your angel and the pronouncement of guilt and punishment. I confess, I've messed up; I've broken the covenant I made when my children were small. Oh Lord, how am I to contend with the high places I didn't break down in the strength of my youth? You leave them there to test me and, even worse, to test my descendants. Oh Lord, forgive me! Please spare them. In Your strength, those ingrained behaviors can be demolished. Amen.

> *Until I went into the sanctuary of God;*
> *then understood I their end.*
> PSALM 73:17

EVENING READING ·

The first part of Psalm 73 is an anxiety-ridden, somewhat cynical view of the world. David was so overcome with the undeserved prosperity of the wicked that he began to doubt whether following a righteous path was worthwhile. He became so worked up that his thoughts were too painful to even consider. But the turning point of the psalm comes in verse 17—"Until I went into the sanctuary of God..." When you are anxious and overwhelmed, run to God's sanctuary. Don't neglect your time with His people, and savor the times in His courts in your own personal devotions. Being in God's presence fixes cynical perspectives and soothes anxiety.

The Thankful Leper

(LUKE 17:11–17)

>›››› ❀ ‹‹‹‹‹

MORNING PRAYER ·

Jesus, Master and Savior, have pity on me! I'm broken and discarded, spurned by other discards of society. Before I could know what You were about, while I was on my way, You spoke and made me whole. Oh, I never thought I could ever be free of the sin disease, and yet You restored what the foxes have eaten. Let me always be like the one leper who came back to thank You. Too often I take Your gifts for granted. Thank You that You take that tiniest sliver of faith—which You gave to me—and grow it into this miracle! Amen.

> *And one of them, when he saw that he was healed, turned back,*
> *and with a loud voice glorified God, and fell down on his face*
> *at his feet, giving him thanks: and he was a Samaritan.*
> LUKE 17:15–16

EVENING READING ·

Why did the one former leper return? He returned because he knew where he had been and he knew that God was solely responsible for his present state. Are we as aware of who we are without God's grace? If we were, we would probably be as grateful as the man in today's passage. We too would fall at His feet so overcome with what God has done in our lives.

DAY 117

Patience in Prayer

(LUKE 18:1–8)

>>>>>> ❀ <<<<<<

MORNING PRAYER

Heavenly Father, what a thought. Do you teach me about delayed satisfaction in my life, that I will know better how to persist in prayer? Sometimes I pray and the answer comes quickly and clearly. More often, I lift up a concern and wonder why the answer doesn't come. But then it does, in the blink of an eye, in such a way that only You could have done it. Wow, that's it, isn't it? When the answer comes that way, all the glory goes only to You. Oh Lord, may You find me faithful. Amen.

> *And the publican, standing afar off, would not lift*
> *up so much as his eyes unto heaven, but smote upon*
> *his breast, saying, God be merciful to me a sinner.*
> LUKE 18:13

EVENING READING

The publican in today's passage had the right perspective on who he was and who God is. His unworthiness to stand in the presence of a perfectly holy God was painfully apparent to him. All he could do was humbly beg for God's mercy. In our culture that praises the bold, unhindered, and self-sufficient, the publican's behavior may seem weak. But actually, it is through this kind of weakness that we become more powerful than we can imagine. For when we empty ourselves before God, He fills us up fully with His own strength.

Gideon's Fleece

(JUDGES 6:36–40)

≥≥≥≫ ✿ ≪≪≪≤

MORNING PRAYER

Lord God, how I thank You for Your patience with Gideon. I thank You for this example. When You call me to do something that's unexpected and unlikely, if not impossible, I rest, knowing I can ask for confirmation. I pray I will imitate Gideon's faith, that I will demolish idols and magnify Your name. I don't need confirmation to know that's Your will. But when I'm asking You to move the mountains that stand between me and what I believe You want me to do, I want to be sure about what I'm doing. Thank You for the fleeces that either blaze an open road or turn me aside from false trails. Amen.

> *And the LORD said unto Gideon, The people that are with thee are too many for me to give the Midianites into their hands, lest Israel vaunt themselves against me, saying, Mine own hand hath saved me.*
> JUDGES 7:2

EVENING READING

God knows our natures so well. He was fully aware that He had to make Gideon's army absurdly small and weak in order for them to understand that the victory was only from God. How often do we take credit for all our successes in life? When things are going well, we pat ourselves on the back for a job well done. It's often because of our assumed self-sufficiency that God will bring challenges into our lives that force us to realize that we are sustained through Him and Him alone.

Asaph's King

(PSALM 74:12–17)

≥≥≥⟩⟩ ❀ ⟨⟨⟨≤≤

MORNING PRAYER

God my King, You have placed people in authority over my country. But in all the years of my life, You are my only King. You, and You alone, have the right to be sovereign. Forgive me when I create minigods—myself, my family, my work. Knock them down, by whatever means, that You might reign in me. You are not only my Sovereign; You are also ruler of the earth. You are not only my Redeemer; You are also the Savior of the world. I long for the day when all people on earth worship You as Lord of lords. Amen.

And Zacchaeus stood, and said unto the Lord: Behold, Lord,
the half of my goods I give to the poor; and if I have taken any
thing from any man by false accusation, I restore him fourfold.
LUKE 19:8

EVENING READING

Zacchaeus could attest to the fact that encounters with Christ change people. Zacchaeus was a selfish criminal who stole from those he levied taxes on. In the course of his career, he would have hurt many families for his own comfort and leisure. But his heart and lifestyle changed when Christ sought him out and came to his house. Don't ever imagine that such a self-absorbed and cruel sinner is past the saving power of Jesus. Christ came to earth to seek out the lost. He continues on that mission today.

JUDGES 9:24–10:18 ❀ LUKE 19:29–48 ❀ PSALM 74:18–23

Poor and Needy

(PSALM 74:18–23)

❧❧❧❧❧ ❀ ❧❧❧❧❧

MORNING PRAYER

Sovereign Lord, may the poor and needy praise Your name. When I was poverty-stricken and without resources, You answered my prayer. I intercede for those without any form of support. For those who are as defenseless as turtledoves—rescue them. For those who are suffering in spirit, body, or mind—heal them. For those who have been humiliated—remember them. Lift them up. Make the lame walk and the blind see. Free the prisoners. Comfort those who are grieving. Above all, may You satisfy their hunger for righteousness and save them from the depths of sin. How I praise You for all You have done and will do. Amen.

> *And they that were sent went their way,*
> *and found even as he had said unto them.*
> LUKE 19:32

EVENING READING

The Gospel writers recorded this story of finding a donkey right where Christ had told them it would be. It may seem like an insignificant little tidbit to include in the stories of when God walked on earth. But it records a valuable story of how God ordains every detail of our lives. Even the minute details of your life matter to your God.

Cornerstone

(LUKE 20:17–18)

≈≥≥⟩⟩⟩ ❀ ⟨⟨⟨⟨≈≤

MORNING PRAYER

Jesus, You are the cornerstone. I stand on You; I hide in the cleft of Your rock when evil lurks. Your granite surface is the measuring stick for my beliefs and practices. I trust in You, depend on You, and praise You. Woe be to me if I ever stop trusting in You. The rock will become a millstone around my neck, pulling me under. It will break my bones and my spirit when I land on it like a free-fall skydive. It will grind me to fine powder and use my life's wheat. How I thank You that, even then, You can take those broken pieces and make me whole again. Amen.

> *For promotion cometh neither from the east, nor from the west, nor from the south. But God is the judge: he putteth down one, and setteth up another.*
> PSALM 75:6–7

EVENING READING

God is ultimately the one who promotes or demotes. Therefore, work and live as for the Lord. When your job, homework, or housework seems insignificant or thankless, remember that it is God for whom you work. He's the one who sees your efforts. He will reward you. So continue to labor hard for Him.

The Living and the Dead

(LUKE 20:34–38)

❧❧❧❧❧ ❀ ❧❧❧❧❧

MORNING PRAYER

Living God, how final death looms to those of us still living on this earth. We miss our loved ones fiercely. The death of strangers—whether by illness or violence or neglect—troubles us. Too soon, we cry. How I take comfort in these verses. You are the God of the living! Everyone who belongs to You lives forever with You. Oh Lord, say hi to my grandmother, my mother, my daughter, all with You. Teach me to live the life You have given here and now to the full. I trust You that my ever-after will be more glorious and wonderful than anything I have ever known. I join with the living, in heaven and on earth, in praising Your name. Amen.

Beware of the scribes, which desire to walk in long robes,
and love greetings in the markets, and the highest
seats in the synagogues, and the chief rooms at feasts.
LUKE 20:46

EVENING READING

It's a probing question that should be asked: What are your motives for doing good? Do your good works stem from a desire to be praised or a desire for God to be praised? While God can certainly use deeds done for the wrong motives to His glory, you will be abundantly more blessed when your work comes from a humble desire to faithfully and fully serve your God.

Samson's Two Prayers

(JUDGES 15:18, 16:18)

⇒⇒⟩⟩⟩ ❀ ⟨⟨⟨⟨⟪

MORNING PRAYER ·

What a difference between Samson's two prayers, Lord. I confess that my prayers are often like that of the young Samson, arrogant, selfish, shortsighted. Was there a kernel of faith in bringing those requests to You, the Great Giver? And not seeking help elsewhere? May my spirit become more like that of the older Samson. When my life is in tatters, make me humble and penitent, with a sacrificial spirit. Remember me, Lord, not because I'm anyone special, but for Your sake. Restore the strength of my youth one last time, that Your name will be known far and wide and You will be glorified. Amen.

> *And he said, Of a truth I say unto you, that this poor widow*
> *hath cast in more than they all: for all these have of their*
> *abundance cast in unto the offerings of God: but she of her*
> *penury hath cast in all the living that she had.*
> LUKE 21:3–4

EVENING READING ·

Have you ever put kingdom work on hold because you felt like you didn't have enough to offer? Today's story in Luke completely negates that excuse. The poor widow in this passage gave an offering that by the world's standards was worthless. But by God's standards, it was the most valuable offering that she could have given. Fortunately, God's kingdom does not function on the same economy as our worldly kingdom. So bring your offerings of time, talents, and treasure to Him no matter how insignificant they may seem to you.

Everlasting Words

(LUKE 21:33)

>>>>> ❀ <<<<<

MORNING PRAYER ·

First You deliver the bad news—heaven and earth, the universe as I know it, will come to an end. The matter You've created will disappear, and that's scary. But then You give the good news—Your words won't pass away. When I am left alone, in the void, Your words—You Yourself!—are there. They last forever, never disappearing. Nothing can destroy them. They are forever true, never wearing out, always up-to-date. They will always accomplish Your purpose. Oh Lord, may I meditate on Your Word, memorize it, feast on it, for then I shall be eternally satisfied. Amen.

Heaven and earth shall pass away:
but my words shall not pass away.
LUKE 21:33

EVENING READING ·

This world is entirely transitory, unpredictable, and mortal. You may have painfully experienced firsthand how often things in this life change and how quickly lives, relationships, and status can be extinguished. Life can feel very much like an unmoored sailboat in a vast, choppy ocean. But in God you have the firmest foundation possible. He anchors you securely to Himself and to His plans for you. Even if this entire world were to pass away and slip into oblivion, His Word will remain steadfast. And in His Word we have hope for eternal life that is not affected by the fate of this earth.

Who's Listening?

(PSALM 77:1–11)

❧❧❧❀❦❦❦

MORNING PRAYER

Lord God, like Jeduthun, I cry out to You. My spirit shouts. I thank You that it's okay to cry for You when I'm in distress. Sometimes I wonder if You're listening. But Your Spirit is convicting me, asking me, *"Which is more important: for God to listen to you—or for you to listen to God?"* Forgive me for thinking prayer is all about me! Clear the clouds of doubt and fear from my vision, the echoes of despair from my hearing, that I may see and hear You. Perhaps the darkness has come to teach me to truly listen. Amen.

> *Hath God forgotten to be gracious? hath he in anger shut up*
> *his tender mercies? Selah. . . . I will remember the works*
> *of the LORD: surely I will remember thy wonders of old.*
> PSALM 77:9, 11

EVENING READING

We have all (including today's psalmist) been in situations that cause us to question the very goodness and sovereignty of God. But instead of being spiritually nearsighted and writing God off when the here and now isn't going the way you deem it should be, expand your vision to remember His wonders of old. Call to mind the way He has cared for and sustained you (and centuries of His children) in the past. It is likely that the very struggle you're enduring now will later become one that you will look back on to recall God's faithfulness.

Enter Not into Temptation
(LUKE 22:39–46)

❧≫≫≫❀≪≪≪❦

MORNING PRAYER ·

Lord Jesus, bend my heart to obey Your words. I pray that I'll not enter into temptation when I'm feeling pressure because of new problems or everyday stress. May I put on my full armor, from the helmet of salvation to the Gospel-of-peace shoes to the sword of the Spirit. Teach me the discipline of prayer to prepare for battle. I'm absolutely blown away that You wanted Your disciples to pray for their needs when You were facing death. How often do I stand on the edge of an unseen precipice and fail to follow Your preparation instructions? Forgive me. Yet in Your grace You rescue me. Amen.

> *Saying, Father, if thou be willing, remove this cup*
> *from me: nevertheless not my will, but thine, be done.*
> LUKE 22:42

EVENING READING ·

"Not my will, but thine, be done." This is a remarkably difficult attitude to have even in minor everyday struggles. We have no problem abiding with God's will when it lines up perfectly with ours. As soon as God's plan veers away from the course that we've set for our lives, we often begin to doubt that He's really got it right after all. It's only through the power of Christ that we can superhumanly bend our will and desire to rest in God's perfect plan for us.

Ruth's Prayer

(RUTH 1:16–17)

>>)))) ✿ (((((<

MORNING PRAYER

Lord God, how I thank You for the women of the Bible, for their real problems and their astonishing acts of faith. But among them all, Ruth is one of my favorites. How I praise You for the testimony coming from a woman who wasn't from Israel. May You deal with me if I fail in fidelity to those I owe my love, service, and support. When You lead me into strange lands, may I move forward boldly, gleaning in the fields if that's the only work I can find. Open my eyes to the helping community, like Boaz and his fields, that You have prepared for me in that new place. Grant me the humility to accept the task, no matter how humble. Amen.

> *And Peter said, Man, I know not what thou sayest. And immediately, while he yet spake, the cock crew. And the Lord turned, and looked upon Peter. And Peter remembered the word of the Lord, how he had said unto him, Before the cock crow, thou shalt deny me thrice.*
>
> LUKE 22:60–61

EVENING READING

Do we deny God in our daily lives? Maybe without even consciously realizing it? Maybe a better question is, do we feel the kind of remorse that Peter felt over denying our Lord? Our God is so merciful that even when we deny and disappoint Him time and time again, He will forgive us and not alter His love for us. The frightened, overwhelmed Peter became so courageous in his proclamation of Christ that he was willing even to die for the cause of His Savior. You are never too weak to be out of God's love or plans.

RUTH 3–4 ❀ LUKE 23:26–24:12 ❀ PSALM 78:5–8

Dying Prayers

(LUKE 23:32–46)

⋙⟫⟫ ❀ ⟪⟪⋘

MORNING PRAYER

Lord Jesus, Your final words make me uncomfortable because death seems so final and the passage difficult. I pray that when my time approaches, I will reflect the same grace and priorities as You did. That stops me. I pray to my living Savior because You died and yet now You live. There's my hope. You prayed for forgiveness for those who killed You. May I also seek reconciliation with those who have wronged me—whom I have wronged—before I die. You also continued Your mission of bringing people into the kingdom. May I continue to share the good news with my last breath. Let me commit myself as fully to You in death as I have in life. Amen.

And the women her neighbours gave it a name, saying,
There is a son born to Naomi; and they called his name Obed:
he is the father of Jesse, the father of David.
RUTH 4:17

EVENING READING

Ruth beautifully embodied God's pursuit of those outside the nation of Israel and foreshadowed the time when all nations would be included in God's people. Here was this foreigner from a pagan land who ended up as an ancestor of David and, therefore, an ancestor of Christ. The glorious story of God's redemption of people from every tribe and nation was already being threaded into the genealogy of His Son. If you look back at the genealogy of Christ in Matthew 1, you'll notice that only a generation or so before Ruth, Rahab (the harlot from Jericho) was also engrafted into the line of Christ. One can only wonder if Ruth and Rahab may have known each other as foreigners brought into the fold of God's people.

Hannah's Prayer

(1 SAMUEL 1)

≷≷≷❋≶≶≶

MORNING PRAYER ·

Dear Lord, how many parents have followed Hannah's example in giving their children back to You? I did. My precious daughter was a special gift from You, and she knew she was an answer to prayer. I thank You for that testimony, but I also remember the pain that came with it. The fear of losing her in the womb prompted the first prayer, and pain ripped me in half when she died too young. I pray for all those who are childless, for those whose children have died. Comfort our grief. Fill our empty arms with Your fullness and joy. Our disappointment will lead to Your best for us. Let us cling to that in faith. Amen.

> *But Hannah went not up; for she said unto her husband, I will*
> *not go up until the child be weaned, and then I will bring him,*
> *that he may appear before the LORD, and there abide for ever.*
> 1 SAMUEL 1:22

EVENING READING ·

Hannah had an astonishingly selfless understanding of how Samuel was completely a gift from God. She had begged for a child, and then when God granted her wish, she decided to give Samuel to serve in the temple of God his whole life. This is remarkable. We often grip so tightly to what God has given us freely that we forget where it came from in the first place. But Hannah was so grateful to God that she humbly loosened her grip on this good gift to return her son to the Lord.

≈ DAY 130 ≈

You Came to Your Own

(JOHN 1:9–13)

>>>>>> ❀ <<<<<<

MORNING PRAYER· ·

Lord Jesus, when I received You, You also received me. Joy sings in my soul because it's a mutual relationship. You adopted me and gave me legal rights entitling me to everything You have. You did more than take me into Your family. You rebirthed me, re-creating my soul and spirit. I am Your child because I am made new in Your likeness. Your paternity now defines me. Miracle of miracles, You softened my heart to believe in You. Oh Lord, I pray for those who still refuse to accept Your gift of salvation. Convict them; bring them back to You. Amen.

> *In the beginning was the Word, and the Word was with God,*
> *and the Word was God. . . . And the Word was made flesh,*
> *and dwelt among us, (and we beheld his glory, the glory as*
> *of the only begotten of the Father,) full of grace and truth.*
> JOHN 1:1, 14

EVENING READING ·

In the Greek philosophy of the day, the word *Logos* (translated as "Word") carried the connotation of the reason for life. So John very boldly proclaims that the Word, the reason for life, became flesh and dwelled among us. The reason for life is not a philosophy, a job, or a goal that must be attained with effort. Instead, the Logos is a Man. Life finds its deepest fulfillment in relationship with Him. He dwelled with John and now dwells in you.

In Spite of It All

(PSALM 78:25–33)

>>>>>> ❀ <<<<<

MORNING PRAYER· ·

Lord God, when I read these verses, I want to hide under a rock. I confess I'm like the Israelites. I gorge on all Your good gifts until I'm sick, and then I blame You because I'm not doing well. When You correct me, too often I ignore Your conviction and keep on sinning. Can't I see the direction I'm headed in? If I don't pay attention and change my ways, the gifts may stop. I wind up unsatisfied, in utter futility—in terror, in fact. For once I have known Your goodness, Your absence is frightening. Do whatever it takes to bring me to my senses. Bring me to repentance before it's too late. Amen.

> *And when they arose early on the morrow morning, behold,*
> *Dagon was fallen upon his face to the ground before the ark of the*
> *LORD; and the head of Dagon and both the palms of his hands were*
> *cut off upon the threshold; only the stump of Dagon was left to him.*
> 1 SAMUEL 5:4

EVENING READING ·

The story at the start of 1 Samuel 5 is almost comical as time and time again the city's idol is found on its face in front of the ark of God. But what is not comical at all is the truth demonstrated in this story: No other god is a match for our God. No idol that we may cling to today can stand up to the power of God. All will come crashing down at His feet. Stop holding on to things that can't possibly replace God.

Only Flesh
(PSALM 78:34–41)

>>>>>>> ❀ <<<<<

MORNING PRAYER ·

Lord God, living for You is a continual act of faith. It goes against my instinct. I rub against a hard time and stumble and fall. Oh, forgive me when my doubt entices me to test You. Who do I think I am—a mere human, daring to bring a case against God? How rich is Your mercy to me, that You remember I am only flesh, a passing breeze that doesn't return. How great Your mercy, how expansive Your forgiveness. You are my Rock. You are my Redeemer. You will not allow me to wander too far away from You. I thank You for Your loving discipline that brings me back to You. Amen.

> *And Saul answered and said, Am not I a Benjamite, of the smallest*
> *of the tribes of Israel? and my family the least of all the families*
> *of the tribe of Benjamin? wherefore then speakest thou so to me?*
> 1 SAMUEL 9:21

EVENING READING ·

In 1 Samuel 9:21, Saul tried to counter what Samuel was telling him by explaining to Samuel that he was from the smallest tribe and most insignificant family in Israel. He argued that because of this, God couldn't possibly mean to anoint him king. Clearly, God must have made a mistake. Little did Saul know that choosing the most unlikely is God's usual strategy. Time and again, God uses the weak, the small, or the inhibited to do His work. Since power comes solely from Him, He does not need to choose the strong, powerful, or influential to accomplish His will.

Shortsighted

(JOHN 3:1–22)

≈≈⟩⟩⟩⟩ ❀ ⟨⟨⟨⟨≈

MORNING PRAYER

Lord Jesus, I like how Nicodemus acted on what he knew, that You were a teacher, a man sent from God to do miraculous deeds. If only more people would act on what little they know of You. He wanted to hear but didn't understand. If this man, a lifelong student of Your Word, misunderstood You so, what hope is there for me? I come to You, shortsighted and blind, and You offer me a second birth. Oh Lord, how I rejoice that I gain new eyes to see the wonderful things of Your Word, ears to hear Your voice, a heart to beat in time with Yours. Amen.

> *And this is the condemnation, that light is come into the world,*
> *and men loved darkness rather than light, because their*
> *deeds were evil. For every one that doeth evil hateth the light,*
> *neither cometh to the light, lest his deeds should be reproved.*
> JOHN 3:19–20

EVENING READING

Don't be surprised if you encounter opposition for the sake of Christ. Sadly, too many in this world love the darkness more than the life-giving Light. It is tragic that someone would prefer to stumble in the darkness than walk in the brilliant light of God. It is your job to shine that light of God into the darkest corners of the world so that, because of you, others (even if just a few) may learn to bask in the light of the Son.

Far Be It from Me

(1 SAMUEL 12:20–25)

>>>>> ❀ <<<<<

MORNING PRAYER

Lord God, make Samuel's promise my own. Far be it from me that I should sin against You by failing to pray for the people You've placed in my circle. Forgive me for my lapses in that area. Samuel made praying for Israel his life's work. I do pray for others—kind of. I phrase my thoughts of them as prayers. I hear their needs and my heart sends up a cry. I clasp their hands and pray right then and there. But do I follow through, pray until I know the answer? Ah, Lord. There is so much I still need to learn. Make me an instrument of prayer. Amen.

He gave his people over also unto the sword;
and was wroth with his inheritance.
PSALM 78:62

EVENING READING

How could a loving God give His people over to nations that hate them? God is a jealous God. He so desires us to follow Him that He will go to great lengths to make that happen. This is an incredibly good thing for us. Ease and prosperity have a way of making us forget God. Sometimes He has to remind us that our true life source can only be found in Him. And sometimes He must use hard circumstances to actually get through to us. It is, in fact, a sure sign of His love when He rebukes His people. For Him to not care and to allow you to fill your existence with deadening activities devoid of Him would be far, far worse than any trial He will lead you through.

Rejecting Joseph

(PSALM 78:67–68)

>>>>>> ❀ <<<<<<

MORNING PRAYER ·

Lord God, did I read that right? You *rejected* the tents of Joseph? Sure, You chose Judah, David's tribe, the Messiah's tribe. But I've never thought of it as actively rejecting Joseph. Why Judah and not godly Joseph? Joseph never slept with his dead son's widow. He never strayed from You that we know of. In the end Judah changed, offering himself in place of Benjamin. I take comfort that Joseph was a vital part of Israel, just not its designated leader. Ultimately, it's all about Your sovereignty. Jacob You loved; Esau You hated. Wonder of wonders: You chose me. Amen.

> *Jesus saith unto them, My meat is to do the*
> *will of him that sent me, and to finish his work.*
> JOHN 4:34

EVENING READING ·

Food is essential to life. Without it we die. In John 4:34, Christ declared that His food was to do the will of His Father. Fulfilling God's will for His life was His very sustenance. Is doing God's will as important to you as your daily food? You would notice if you went a day without food. Would you notice if you went a day without seeking God? Don't starve yourself of the necessary spiritual nourishment of seeking after God and doing His will.

≥ DAY 136 ≤

Appearances
(1 Samuel 16:6–7)

>>>>> ❀ <<<<<

MORNING PRAYER · •

Lord, this morning, I worried about fixing my hair for a picture. Did any of Jesse's sons primp before they appeared before Samuel? The prophet showed his feet of clay here, looking at the striking appearance of Jesse's oldest son. Thanks for the reminder that I don't have to be perfect to follow You. But Samuel waited for Your leading as the father paraded healthy son after healthy son, all six of them, until only the youngest was left. Lord, when You bring someone into my life, forgive me if I reject them because of their appearance. May I train my eyes to see the true person beneath the externals. Amen.

*And it came to pass, when they were come, that he looked on Eliab,
and said, Surely the Lord's anointed is before him. But the Lord said
unto Samuel, Look not on his countenance, or on the height of his stature;
because I have refused him: for the Lord seeth not as man seeth; for man
looketh on the outward appearance, but the Lord looketh on the heart.*
1 Samuel 16:6–7

EVENING READING · •

Our human perspectives and mind-sets so often blind us to an eternal and God-given perspective. We see examples of this in today's passage. The fear of the opinion of his fellow man was more powerful to Saul than his fear of God. Samuel looked at the impressive outward appearance of David's brothers and had to be reminded by God that his earthly perspective was limited. Ask God for an eternal perspective. It will certainly change the way you see things.

The Battle Is the Lord's

(1 SAMUEL 17)

>->>>> ❀ <<<<<-

MORNING PRAYER

Lord God, I've faced some scary enemies, but I've never fought someone as physically imposing as Goliath. It would be like trying to stop a nuclear attack armed with only muskets. Did David's youth help him to have that single-minded confidence? Oh, to have that vision. Forgive me when I allow spears and javelins to eclipse the complete sovereign power of Your name. When Your enemies defy You, may I take up the battle. It belongs to You, and You will give the victory, whatever the weapons of my battlefield. In fact, I rejoice in my poor weapons because they show that You have saved, and You alone. Amen.

> *Then said David to the Philistine, Thou comest to me with a sword, and with*
> *a spear, and with a shield: but I come to thee in the name of the LORD*
> *of hosts, the God of the armies of Israel, whom thou hast defied.*
> 1 SAMUEL 17:45

EVENING READING

David faced a terrifying enemy with the added pressure of the welfare of his entire nation resting on him. He stood up to Goliath with a courage that can only stem from a true and full knowledge of God's power and love for His people. David knew without a shadow of a doubt that God had a plan for His people and that He would deliver the Philistines into his hand that day. It's much easier to be brave when you know going in that the battle ends in your favor. Through Christ we too can be confident that the war ends in our favor with complete victory over death and sin. Face the world armed with the name of the Lord of hosts.

DAY 138

Joseph's Shepherd

(PSALM 80:1–7)

≫≫≫❀≪≪≪

MORNING PRAYER

Oh Lord my God, You are not only the Shepherd of Israel. You are also the Shepherd of Joseph, Ephraim, Benjamin, Manasseh, and more. You are my Shepherd. You added me to Your flock. You called me by name. I heard Your voice and joined the others in Your sheep pen. Together, we bleat for Your protection. You are enthroned between the cherubim. Your light leads us. Lift up Your hands and save us. When we have wandered astray, restore us. Make Your face shine upon us, that we might be saved. That we might reflect Your glory, our new hearts as white as carded wool. Amen.

Turn us again, O God of hosts, and cause
thy face to shine; and we shall be saved.
PSALM 80:7

EVENING READING

One of the most magnificent sights in nature is when, after a storm, the clouds break to let rays of sunshine through. It's almost as if the very light of heaven has broken through the dark clouds. The language of God's face shining upon His people calls to mind a similar image. Even in the most violent of tempests, God's face is turned toward you, and His everlasting light breaks through the clouds.

Friendship
(1 SAMUEL 20)

❁

MORNING PRAYER

Dear Lord, how I love to read about David and Jonathan. What a king Jonathan might have made. What sacrifice, love, and friendship he offered to David, knowing his best friend would take his place as Israel's next ruler. Oh Lord, when I see someone overtaking me, let me accept them with the same grace. How I grieved at the loss of my first writing friends and missed their support. Yet now You have replaced them with so many others. Thank You, Lord. If we must part ways, let us celebrate the bond You have created between us. I pray that You will go with them and give them success on their journey. Amen.

*When Jesus then lifted up his eyes, and saw a great company come unto him,
he saith unto Philip, Whence shall we buy bread, that these may eat?
And this he said to prove him: for he himself knew what he would do.*
JOHN 6:5–6

EVENING READING

In this passage in John, Jesus asked Philip a question. But He didn't ask it in order to learn the answer. In fact, John tells us that Jesus already knew what He was going to do. When God asks you to walk through a difficult situation, or places questions in front of you that are difficult and painful to answer, take comfort in the fact that He already knows what He is going to do. Stand firmly rooted with faith in His sovereignty.

⋟ DAY 140 ⋞

Bread of Life

(JOHN 6:30–40)

⋟⟩⟩⟩⟩ ❀ ⟨⟨⟨⟨⋞

MORNING PRAYER ·

Bread of Life, fill me, satisfy me. I ate of Your sacrifice and was born anew. Words can't express my gratitude, my deep joy, my soul-deep rest in that salvation. You are my Father, my all in all, and nothing can separate me from You. Now that I have tasted and seen that the Lord is good, I want more, so much more! May I open every crevice of my being for Your Spirit to fill and use me. I hunger for Your righteousness to mark me as Yours. I want a storehouse of Your goodness to give to others. Give me only what I need for today. I thank You that it will be all that I need. Amen.

> *Jesus answered them and said, Verily, verily, I say*
> *unto you, Ye seek me, not because ye saw the miracles,*
> *but because ye did eat of the loaves, and were filled.*
> JOHN 6:26

EVENING READING ·

It is so easy to be lulled into the trap of desiring and seeking God for what He gives rather than for who He is. Like the people in Jesus' time who sought Him because of the tangible food that they ate, we too can often seek Him for the gifts He gives. But there is so much more beauty and fulfillment to be found in seeking God to know Him. Just as Jesus went on to say, don't seek earthly bread from God but rather spiritual bread and an everlasting relationship with Him.

To Whom Shall We Go?

(JOHN 6:67–71)

>>>>> ❀ <<<<<

MORNING PRAYER ·

Lord Jesus, I marvel at the close friendship between You and the disciples. How very human You sounded when You asked, "Are you going to leave Me too?" With Peter, I affirm, "Where else would I go? You alone have the words of life." I have come to believe because of Your gift of grace and faith. It's all from You. Peter saw You were the Messiah, God Himself, the Holy One of Israel. The more time I spend with You, the more I learn. The more I know of You, the more I want to spend time with You. I yearn for eternity with You, when we will speak face-to-face. Amen.

> *Then Simon Peter answered him, Lord, to whom*
> *shall we go? thou hast the words of eternal life.*
> JOHN 6:68

EVENING READING ·

What a beautiful perspective Peter had in today's passage. Having tasted of the words of eternal life that Christ offered, he couldn't imagine ever leaving Jesus for something else. Have you been so touched by Christ as to not be able to fathom life without Him? Or is He merely a supplement to your life to be brought out on the weekends? A true relationship with Him is life changing, so strive to get to know Him more intimately.

DAY 142

David and Saul
(1 Samuel 26)

>>>>> ❀ <<<<<

MORNING PRAYER·· ·

Sovereign Lord, how I thank You that no one is pursuing my life like Saul hunted David. May I have the grace to spare anyone who persecutes me, as David did Saul. I'm tempted to think You've delivered my enemy into my hands so I can act as judge and jury. Open my eyes, that I may see that person as You do. You love him. You want to bring him into the kingdom. You may even have special plans for him. Keep me from doing harm. Lead me in acts of reconciliation and not retaliation. Amen.

> *And David said to Abishai, Destroy him not: for who can stretch forth his hand against the LORD's anointed, and be guiltless? David said furthermore, As the LORD liveth, the LORD shall smite him; or his day shall come to die; or he shall descend into battle, and perish.*
> 1 SAMUEL 26:9–10

EVENING READING ·

David had learned to let God work His perfect plan instead of assuming that God's plan lined up completely with his plan. It's easy for us to decide that we know God's will only because it's what we want. Beware of trying to impose your will on His; disappointment and anger are sure to follow. Rest in God's perfect timing instead of trying to accomplish His work for Him.

Restoration

(JOHN 8:1–11)

❧❧❧❧❧ ❀ ❧❧❧❧❧

MORNING PRAYER ·

Lord Jesus, whatever the textual uncertainty, I love what I learn about You from this story. It's so You. You show Yourself as the author of the wisdom that gave Solomon his reputation. You leveled the playing field. You removed the woman's accusers, their guilt clear, but Your concern was for the woman. They left unforgiven, but You removed condemnation from the accused. Lord, I need that mind-set that releases blame, I who am most guilty of all. Enlarge my heart to welcome the stigmatized and the outcasts. Forgive me. Thank You that You will take me back. Amen.

> *When Jesus had lifted up himself, and saw none*
> *but the woman, he said unto her, Woman, where are*
> *those thine accusers? hath no man condemned thee?*
> JOHN 8:10

EVENING READING ·

The woman in today's passage in John must have been terrified to be dragged in front of a known expert in the Law with a crowd of men desperate to see her stoned. But instead of meeting her accuser in that unofficial courtroom, she came face to face with her Savior. May we be more aware of and more disgusted by our own sin than anyone else's sin. But in our sin, may we always realize that in Christ we have an advocate and Savior, not an accuser.

❧ DAY 144 ❧

1 SAMUEL 30–31 ❀ JOHN 8:12–47 ❀ PSALM 84:1–4

Home Sweet Home

(Psalm 84:1–4)

>>>>> ❀ <<<<<

MORNING PRAYER

Lord Almighty, how lovely is Your dwelling place! You know my multiple addresses. Sometimes it feels like I've had to find a home about as often as the sparrow building her nest every year, and I don't do a good job of maintaining them. Oh, may I not treat Your place with the same disregard. Your house is perfect and beautiful. May I not destroy it by my sin and neglect, starting with my body, Your temple. I cry out for the living God—may I dwell with You forever! I am blessed to live under Your roof. May Your praise be on the tip of my tongue this moment and forever. Amen.

> *My soul longeth, yea, even fainteth for the courts of the LORD:*
> *my heart and my flesh crieth out for the living God.*
> PSALM 84:2

EVENING READING

Do we long for God's presence as though it were the very thing sustaining us? Do we cry out for God as the psalmist does in today's passage? It is an awe-inspiring and humbling thing to be allowed into the presence of a ruler of any nation. And yet, we are invited to come freely into the throne room of the King of kings. This is not something that should be taken for granted. But rather, we should take advantage of this invitation and daily enter into His courts.

Is It Time?

(2 SAMUEL 2:1–4)

>>>>>> ❀ <<<<<<

MORNING PRAYER ·

Lord God, to have the patience of David. When I see an opening for a long-desired opportunity, I run through. Not David. Even after Your promise, even after Saul died, he still asked, "Is it time for me to go up? To present myself as king?" And knowing David, if You had said not yet, he would have waited. When I pray for something, it's as much about the prayer, our communion, my coming to know You and praise You and worship You in the service of my life, as it is about conducting business at the bank of prayer. You want me to ask about every decision and need—because You want to talk with me. Thank You. Amen.

For the Lord God is a sun and shield: the Lord will give grace and glory:
no good thing will he withhold from them that walk uprightly

PSALM 84:11

EVENING READING ·

Whether or not we acknowledge it, we live in a battle of light versus darkness. God is our sun, never allowing the darkness to overtake or overwhelm us. He is also our shield, protecting us from the arrows of the enemy in the heat of battle.

Restore Me Again

(PSALM 85:1–7)

❧❧❧❧❧ ✿ ❧❧❧❧❧

MORNING PRAYER·

God my Savior, how precious is this prayer. Restore us again. Return me to the place of Your favor when I have fallen away. You've done it before. I have once again squandered Your riches in the wasteland of sin. But in Your amazing grace, Your amazing mercy, I can come before Your mercy seat and beg for forgiveness. I fall before You, pleading, "Revive me again." Fill my heart with Your love. Rekindle my soul with fire from above. Show me Your love. Sanctify me, set me apart, making me more and more like You in the here and now. Amen.

> *He answered and said, Whether he be a sinner or no, I know not:*
> *one thing I know, that, whereas I was blind, now I see.*
> JOHN 9:25

EVENING READING

The formerly blind man in today's passage has a wonderful, simple testimony. He knew and testified to one thing—he once was blind but now could see. Christ had changed him in a visible and tangible way. What are some things in your life that clearly point to Christ's work in you?

David's Throne

(2 SAMUEL 7:10–16)

❧❧❧❧❧ ❀ ❧❧❧❧❧

MORNING PRAYER ·

Oh Lord God, to receive Your promise as David did! You only told a handful of people that the Messiah would be one of their direct descendants. How Eve must have rejoiced at the news, after the despair of her sin in the garden. How new, how startling, how marvelous the news came to Abraham, the father of God's chosen people. And then to David, that one of his descendants would rule forever. Last, You told a young, unmarried teenager that her son would be the One. You have a unique message to give to the world in and through me as well. May I shout Your glory aloud. Amen.

> *And David danced before the LORD with all his might;*
> *and David was girded with a linen ephod.*
> 2 SAMUEL 6:14

EVENING READING ·

The total abandon of David in today's passage is refreshing. He was so in love with his God and so thrilled that the ark was returning home that he danced with all his might before God. He wasn't worried about his reputation or how he might look in front of all the people watching. He was simply overwhelmed with the goodness of his God that he couldn't help but show it.

Listening for His Voice

(JOHN 10:11–30)

>꒳꒷꒳ ❀ ꒳꒷꒳

MORNING PRAYER ·

Lord Jesus, You are my Shepherd. As Your ewe, I'm supposed to listen to Your voice. Is a sheep like a cat or a dog? My kitties knew my voice. They waited at the front window at the end of the day and ran to the bedroom as soon as I called their names. They raced to me when they heard me but avoided strangers. Lord, may I hear Your voice like that. May I tune my ear to Your station. May I keep myself in range, where I can hear You easily and quickly. When You whisper my name, let me run to You eagerly, so happy You called. Make me like my pets. Amen.

> *I am the good shepherd, and know my sheep, and am*
> *known of mine. As the Father knoweth me, even so*
> *know I the Father: and I lay down my life for the sheep.*
> JOHN 10:14–15

EVENING READING ·

Do you ever fear that if you were truly known, you couldn't be loved? Your Good Shepherd both knows you and loves you in ways that you can't even fathom. He knew you perfectly before you were even born and continues to know each of your inward thoughts. But in spite of this, He still loves you. This is not a surface love either. It is a love that would drive Him to lay down His life for you. You are intimately known and deeply loved by the Person that matters the very most.

You Are the Man

(2 SAMUEL 12:1–25)

⊰⊱⟩⟩⟩⟩ ❀ ⟨⟨⟨⟨⊰

MORNING PRAYER ·

Lord God, how horrible those months must have been for David, after he'd sinned with Bathsheba and killed her husband. Or was he so in love with her that he numbed himself to what he had done? How I rejoice in Nathan's bravery in confronting him, for all the men and women who are unafraid to denounce sin. I pray that when someone points to the log in my eye, I will repent and accept Your corrective surgery. I have seen the sword fall on my family. How I pray that You will spare my grandchildren. They are innocent of past sins. Let me not be defeated today because of the sins of my forebears. Amen.

> *And I am glad for your sakes that I was not there, to the*
> *intent ye may believe; nevertheless let us go unto him.*
> JOHN 11:15

EVENING READING ·

Sometimes God brings us through difficult circumstances for the purpose of increasing our faith. To those who knew and loved Lazarus, it probably would have felt like Jesus failed at this point. He had healed so many, and yet He wasn't around to heal one of His friends. Little did they know that Jesus had an even bigger miracle in store. His plan was not merely to heal Lazarus but to raise him from the dead. When we feel as though God has missed an opportunity in our lives, we need to remember that His plan is perfect and He may just be preparing for something bigger than we could have imagined.

If the Lord Had Been Here

(JOHN 11:17–43)

>>>>> ❁ <<<<<

MORNING PRAYER ·

Dearest Lord, where have You been? If You had been here, my daughter wouldn't have died. Even as I prayed, You comforted me with the image of welcoming her home in heaven, at peace and rest, full of joy. How else do I understand the depth of Your promise of eternal life, except in the pits of despair after the death of a loved one? How I thank You for Your comfort. I praise You for the promise You gave to me through Martha. You are the resurrection and the life. No one who believes in You will ever truly die. Open my heart to receive more of You during those heavy times of grief. Amen.

> *Jesus therefore again groaning in himself cometh to the grave.*
> *It was a cave, and a stone lay upon it.*
> JOHN 11:38

EVENING READING ·

Jesus groaned as He came to the grave where Lazarus was laid—a grave with a stone rolled over it, similar to the grave that He would be laid in shortly. He was deeply sorrowed over the death that He would soon conquer. Lazarus's resurrection was a skirmish in the ultimate battle of life over death—the battle that Christ would soon be victorious in. Even though we know the end of our story (a glorious eternal life with Christ), it is right and good to mourn over the pain and sorrow of this world as we wait for the fulfillment of God's promises.

Morning and Evening

(PSALM 88:1–9)

❧❧❧❧ ✿ ❧❧❧❧

MORNING PRAYER

Lord God, I come to You because You are the One who saves. I don't know how I got into this mess. I'm exhausted and discouraged, lonely and overwhelmed. Morning and evening I cry out to You. Hear my plea in the morning when the day is young and I hope for a good day. Grant me mercy at night when I'm spent and discouraged, seeking rest. I spread my hands open before You, asking You to fill me with goodness. You are my hope, my all-sufficient hope. If there is something holding back Your blessing, show me, convict me. May my faith increase according to my need, for You are always trustworthy. Amen.

> *But the chief priests consulted that they might put*
> *Lazarus also to death; Because that by reason of him*
> *many of the Jews went away, and believed on Jesus.*
> JOHN 12:10–11

EVENING READING

The chief priests in the Jewish community plotted to kill not only Jesus but Lazarus as well. All throughout history and on into the future, people will oppose Christ and go to great lengths to disprove Him. Those who are walking testimonies of His power and love will be targeted also. But it is far better to live in His truth than to live in the fear of man.

Flight Prayers

(2 Samuel 15:13–31)

⤜⟫⟫⟩ ❀ ⟨⟨⟨⟨⤛

MORNING PRAYER ·

Heavenly Father, even on the run from his own son, David prayed. Oh Lord, give me the grace to approach You in the hardest times. I pray that You will show faithfulness and kindness to the many who have supported me through the years. I seek Your favor both for those who see me face-to-face, in all my petty daily battles, and for those who support me from afar. I ask that Your work will continue unhindered, guiding my steps both away and back again. I need an advocate, someone who will speak up for me and protect me from the harm plotted against me. You are with me, my Rock. Amen.

> *He that loveth his life shall lose it; and he that hateth*
> *his life in this world shall keep it unto life eternal.*
> John 12:25

EVENING READING ·

If you put too much time and effort into making your life exactly how you want it here on earth, you will certainly be disappointed. Holding on to the vision of a "perfect life" will cause you to lose that perfect life. A good life on earth can only be attained when lived out with the perspective of eternity. This perspective will radically change your priorities and the way you live your life.

Jesus Loves Me

(JOHN 13:1–3)

>>>>> ❀ <<<<<

MORNING PRAYER

Dear Jesus, You knew You were going home. Soon You would regain all the glory You had set aside to come to earth. A part of You must have been thrilled, but still I sense Your sorrow. You loved those disciples and those who would come after them. The days ahead would test everything in them, and You poured every last bit of Yourself into them. Son of God and Son of Man, all authority belongs to You. You could have designated tasks to a million angels. Instead, You washed Your disciples' feet. How much do You love me? You give me a pedicure. Amen.

If I then, your Lord and Master, have washed your feet;
ye also ought to wash one another's feet. For I have given
you an example, that ye should do as I have done to you.
JOHN 13:14–15

EVENING READING

Christ preached a very countercultural message. Here was a King who washed the feet of His followers and encouraged them to do the same. Is it any wonder that some people didn't believe that this could be the King and Conqueror that was prophesied of in the Old Testament? And yet, in all His humility, He was and is far more powerful than any earthly king and warrior could ever be. He didn't conquer the oppressive nation of Rome. Instead, He conquered death by being slaughtered as a sacrificial Lamb. This is the kind of King to follow.

Contradictions

(2 Samuel 18:19–33)

⟫⟫⟫⟫ ❀ ⟪⟪⟪⟪

MORNING PRAYER

Heavenly Father, who had turned David's world upside down? A wise man's words disregarded and the king mourning the death of his enemy, his own son—so many of my days are like that, although not usually about such serious matters. For that, I thank You. But almost no days pass without at least one thing jarring the works, stopping things from their usual flow. I want consistency and constancy, familiarity. I don't like change, and my frustration insults those who are trying to change. Forgive me. When my days are in chaos, may I trust in You, the immutable God. Your plan and purpose will never fail. I cling to that, knowing all these other things are secondary to You. Amen.

Thou rulest the raging of the sea:
when the waves thereof arise, thou stillest them.
PSALM 89:9

EVENING READING

God is the only one who can control the wind and the waves of the sea. He is praised for doing so in today's psalm. How poignant it would have been to the disciples when Jesus stilled the storm while they were at sea. They would have recognized that this was truly God walking among them.

Continue the Work

(JOHN 14:12–14)

>>>>> ❀ <<<<<

MORING PRAYER ·

Lord Jesus, did I read that right? "*Whoever* believes in me will do the works I have been doing" (John 14:12 NIV, italics added). Not just the apostles who led the way in validating their claims through supernatural events, but *whoever*. The only condition is that I ask for something that will bring glory to the Father. Forgive me when I turn that promise into a religious catchphrase: "In Jesus' name, amen." Make that the prayer of my inner heart. That I will think, speak, act in Your name. When a mighty work is done, may it bring glory to You and the Father and to no one else. In Your name I do pray, amen.

> *And I will pray the Father, and he shall give you*
> *another Comforter, that he may abide with you for ever.*
>
> JOHN 14:16

EVENING READING ·

God has been moving closer to His people all throughout history. But He couldn't possibly get any closer to His children than when He walked among them on earth, right? Christ's disciples may have thought this, which is why He told them about the Comforter that the Father would send to them. This Comforter doesn't just walk with us; He abides in us. He has no physical restrictions regarding space or time, meaning He can be with all of God's children simultaneously and continuously. He is ever present with you and will be so forever.

2 SAMUEL 22:1–23:7 ❀ JOHN 14:18–15:27 ❀ PSALM 89:19–29

What God Can Do

(2 Samuel 22:26–37)

≈≈≫≫≫ ❀ ≪≪≪≪≈

MORNING PRAYER · •

Oh Lord, how I thank You for David's words in the Bible, for his great gifts of imagery that help express my faith better. Of course Your way is perfect. You're God! But I like exploring how it's perfect. You make my feet like a deer's, where I can climb confidently to the highest of Colorado's fourteeners. I find five-pound weights heavy during exercise; You promise to enable me to pull a heavy bronze bow. You've made the path just wide enough for me so I won't slip, nor will I easily get lost. You are the lamp who shines on my way, revealing the steps I take. The more faithful and pure I am, the more I understand of You. Amen.

For thou art my lamp, O Lord:
and the Lord will lighten my darkness.
2 Samuel 22:29

EVENING READING · •

David spoke from experience when he asserted that God was his lamp to lighten the darkness around him. His life was far from easy. He had friends and family turn against him and force him into a life of running and hiding. But through even the darkest of circumstances, God remained as a faithful light by his side to illuminate his steps and keep him safe from harm. No matter the situation, God is your lamp as well. The darker it gets, the more brilliantly His light shines.

God Is Truth

(PSALM 89:30–37)

⇒⇒⟩⟩⟩ ❀ ⟨⟨⟨⟨⇐

MORNING PRAYER ·

Lord God, am I reading this right? That my future sin cannot change Your past covenant? *"In My holiness I cannot lie. I will never stop loving David, never fail to keep My promise to him."* Oh Lord, how I rejoice in that confidence, knowing that although I am changeable, *You* are not, and You won't desert me even when I seem to turn my back on You. Your holiness, Your immutability, Your faithfulness make me the object of Your ever-present, all-encompassing love. I don't deserve it, never have, never will; but I offer myself as a living sacrifice of praise. Amen.

> *I have made a covenant with my chosen, I have sworn*
> *unto David my servant, Thy seed will I establish for ever,*
> *and build up thy throne to all generations. Selah.*
> PSALM 89:3–4

EVENING READING ·

God made a covenant with His servant David, and He has stood by that covenant through generations and generations. This covenant will stand forever since one of David's descendants sits on the eternal throne. God does not make His promises and covenants lightly because He will never go back on a promise He has made.

The Peace Paradox

(JOHN 16:33)

⇒⟩⟩⟩⟩ ✿ ⟨⟨⟨⟨⇐

MORNING PRAYER ·

Dearest Jesus, this paradox can only make sense in You. You tell me I will have trouble in this world, but I will have peace in You. You have overcome the world. Then how is it that trials and sorrows come? I guess overcoming doesn't mean prevention. It means I can withstand the assault, in You, with Your peace. How much comfort it brings me to know that troubles are to be expected. To be reminded not to ask why but how—*how* do I overcome? In You, always in You, by faith, by Your love and peace. Amen.

These things I have spoken unto you, that in me ye might
have peace. In the world ye shall have tribulation:
but be of good cheer; I have overcome the world.
JOHN 16:33

EVENING READING ·

As Jesus prepared to go to His death, He told His disciples that two things were certain: first, that in the world they would have trials and tribulations, but, second, that in these they would have a joyful peace because Christ had overcome the world. Don't be surprised when trials and difficulties surface in your life. Christ gave us fair warning that these would come. But in Him and in the knowledge of His victory over death, sin, and sorrow, you can have a peace that is unmatched by anything this world can offer. You can indeed face this world with good cheer.

Praying for Those to Follow
(JOHN 17:20–26)

❧›››› ❀ ‹‹‹‹❧

MORNING PRAYER ·

You prayed for me, Lord, at the Last Supper. I bow before You in astonished thankfulness. Such things You asked for me. First I acknowledge the prayer isn't for me, singular; it's for the whole host of people who believe in Your name. You commanded and prayed that we would love one another. Forgive us for falling so far short. You promised Your glory. What a wonder! But none of that happens in a vacuum. You want Your body to stand out in a dark world so that others may come to faith. I pray that will begin here where I live and extend to the farthest reaches of the earth. Amen.

Neither pray I for these alone, but for them also which shall believe on me through their word.
JOHN 17:20

EVENING READING

Isn't it remarkable that in the pages of the Bible is recorded for all time a prayer that Jesus prayed for you? While the inevitability of the cross loomed in front of Him, He prayed for His current followers and all those who would come after. As a follower of Christ, He prayed for you.

All I Ever Wanted

(1 KINGS 3:6–14)

>>>>> ❀ <<<<<

MORNING PRAYER

How exciting, Lord, to see Solomon following in his father's footsteps. His heart must've already been inclined to wisdom to ask for more. He knew he couldn't rule Israel well without guidance. He asked to know the difference between right and wrong. How could he be wise in helping others and so clueless when it came to his own life? But how often am I like that? I can tell others what to do more easily than I can take care of my own problems. As I prepare for the day ahead, let me consider my requests to You. When You ask what I want, let me ask wisely, and not simply for material things. Amen.

Give therefore thy servant an understanding heart to judge thy people, that I may discern between good and bad: for who is able to judge this thy so great a people?
1 KINGS 3:9

EVENING READING

Wouldn't our prayers be so much more productive if we stopped praying for a situation to turn out specifically how we wanted it to and instead prayed for wisdom and discernment? We must humbly realize that God's plan, whatever that may be, is so much better than our plan. So ask Him for wisdom and patience to discern His will.

What Is Truth?

(JOHN 18:28–40)

>>>>> ❀ <<<<<

MORNING PRAYER ·

Dearest Jesus, I bow with You now in this place of life and death, everyone lined up against You and Your closest friends denying You. It's a scary place to be. Even there, You attempted to explain what You were all about, and it feels strange to me that You framed it as "truth." Did Pilate have a clue that You claimed to be the truth? If so, he didn't understand what You meant. I confess I don't understand it completely either. But I trust You as the truth and with my warped perception of reality. Correct my mind to see Your essence more clearly. Amen.

> *A thousand shall fall at thy side, and ten thousand*
> *at thy right hand; but it shall not come nigh thee.*
> PSALM 91:7

EVENING READING ·

When you are one of God's children, held in His powerful hand, you are immortal until the day that He has ordained to bring you home. Nothing can touch you outside of His perfect plan. Even with ten thousand falling at your side, you will stand strong until the day when God has decided to bestow on you the glorious privilege of being admitted into heaven.

Benefits of Loving God

(PSALM 91:11–16)

❧❧❧❧❧ ❀ ❦❦❦❦❦

MORNING PRAYER ·

Ah, Lord God, what beautiful comfort in these words: *You will rescue those who love You.* You initiated that promise. You will protect those who trust in Your name, in all that is revealed about You by the names You have given Yourself. Even before I call, You are with me in times of trouble. When I call, You are sure to answer. You will bring honor to me. Me?! And You hand me the rewards of a long life and of Your salvation. I am unworthy of any of that. I pray that my love and trust for You will increase. The more of You I know and love, the more blessed I am. Amen.

This title then read many of the Jews: for the place where Jesus was crucified was nigh to the city: and it was written in Hebrew, and Greek, and Latin. Then said the chief priests of the Jews to Pilate, Write not, The King of the Jews; but that he said, I am King of the Jews. Pilate answered, What I have written I have written.
JOHN 19:20–22

EVENING READING ·

The irony and stubborn truth displayed in what Pilate wrote for the cross of Christ is really very beautiful. Even during His humiliating death, it was being proclaimed to all who passed by that Jesus was King. The Gospel can never be silenced, not even by an angry mob who killed the very Son of God.

A Place to Meet with God

(1 KINGS 8:1–53)

❧❧❧❧❧ ❀ ❦❦❦❦❦

MORNING PRAYER

Lord God, Solomon's prayer reeks of pride. "Look at me, look at this beautiful and glorious temple I've built!" But then he gets down to business. Will You really live on earth? How, since the highest heavens can't contain You? How much more do I ask the same question today. You have said I'm Your temple. You dwell in me. I am a fragile human shell, the only good in me the righteousness that comes from Your Son. Perhaps I'm not meant to "contain" You. You live in me and You spill out of me to others. You are everything I will ever need, everything the whole world needs. Make me an instrument of that promise. Amen.

And it came to pass, when the priests were come out of
the holy place, that the cloud filled the house of the LORD.
1 KINGS 8:10

EVENING READING

Imagine how awe inspiring it must have been to see the cloud of God's presence fill the holy place. How remarkable it would have been to be one of the people standing there, seeing the very presence of God and knowing that He dwelled with you. And yet, you have a greater gift than that. While the people were unable to enter the holy place, you can go right up to the very throne of God. The curtain that was torn in two at Christ's death will never be sewn together again. You have eternal access to your heavenly Father. His Spirit dwells in and with you.

⇜ DAY 164 ⇝

1 KINGS 8:54–10:13 ❀ JOHN 20:1–18 ❀ PSALM 92:10–15

Warning
(1 Kings 9:1–9)

⇢⇢⟫⟫ ❀ ⟪⟪⇠⇠

MORNING PRAYER ·

Lord God, here's where eternal truth is tested in real time. I've been initiated into service as Your temple. I have the glorious promise: I am Your temple. You dwell in me. I am a living sacrifice. You have set me apart as holy. My purpose is to bring honor to Your name. You are watching over me, for I am dear to Your heart. Now for me to live up to that purpose. But woe to me if I fail in following You. You may bring disaster upon disaster on me. May I obey You with integrity and godliness. Forgive me when I fail. Make me a vessel unto honor in Your service. Amen.

> *They shall still bring forth fruit in old age;*
> *they shall be fat and flourishing.*
> Psalm 92:14

EVENING READING ·

Those who walk with Christ will still be fruitful even in their old age. Far from being forgotten members of society, the older generation has so much to offer about their long and faithful walk with Christ. As an elderly person, don't be afraid to share your testimony of God's faithfulness. As a younger person, seek out those from whom you can gain wisdom and the life perspective of a long life well lived.

Robed in Majesty
(PSALM 93)

❧❧❧❦ ❀ ❦❦❦❦

MORNING PRAYER

Oh God the King, You robe Yourself in majesty. Anyone beholding You will immediately recognize Your greatness, Your right to rule. You are armed with strength. You give Your strength to Your soldiers; they don't make You stronger. You sat on Your throne before time began. You are mightier than anything on earth. You must be! You created everything. What You say cannot be undone, Your laws cannot be changed. You reign throughout all eternity. I am but a soldier in Your kingdom, but I wear the colors of Your majesty and Your glory. Your flag goes before me. Amen.

But these are written, that ye might believe that Jesus is the Christ,
the Son of God; and that believing ye might have life through his name.
JOHN 20:31

EVENING READING

There is not enough room in the Gospel accounts to tell the stories of all the people whose lives were radically changed by Christ. But the accounts of the real Man who touched and changed real people are there so that we too, generations later, can believe in Him. Write down your own accounts of how Christ changes and shapes your life. Remembering His faithfulness will strengthen your faith and give you abundant life through His name.

Do I Love You?

(JOHN 21)

❧>>>>> ❀ <<<<<❧

MORNING PRAYER ·

Lord Jesus, when You ask me, *"Do you love Me?"* I say I do. But how well will my answer stand up to the kind of probing You put Peter through? Do I love You more than the things surrounding me—my friends, my occupation, all those things I hold dear? I like to think so. But when You come back and ask a second time, a third time, I doubt myself. Forgive me for that part of myself that I hold back. Open my eyes to what I cling to over my love for You. Cleanse me, free me, that I may serve Your sheep in whatever way You call me to. Amen.

> *But he forsook the counsel of the old men, which they*
> *had given him, and consulted with the young men that*
> *were grown up with him, and which stood before him.*
> 1 KINGS 12:8

EVENING READING ·

Rehoboam very unwisely followed the counsel of his foolish friends rather than the counsel of the wise men who had far more experience with ruling people. Who are your counselors? Who are you surrounding yourself with whose thoughts and attitudes are rubbing off on you? Choose your friends and counselors wisely since those who are closest to you have a powerful say in your life.

To the Ends of the Earth

(ACTS 1:8)

❧›››› ❀ ‹‹‹‹❧

MORNING PRAYER

Lord of heaven and earth, everyone knows people who don't believe in You. I pray for those lost sheep, starting with people I see every day and extending across the globe. Wherever Your church is, may we spread the Gospel to our own Jerusalem, Judea, and Samaria, in our neighborhoods, communities, districts, and countries. May we speak in the power of the Holy Spirit to those who haven't heard. Use my single voice and the chorus of believers to witness to the nations. Amen.

Blessed is the man whom thou chastenest,
O LORD, and teachest him out of thy law.
PSALM 94:12

EVENING READING

We rarely think that discipline and chastening are blessings. But when God teaches and rebukes you through His Word or through others in your life, you ought to be grateful. He is graciously pulling you back from a dangerous ledge and sparing you from a long fall. Sometimes God's discipline may seem harsher than at other times, but each correction ultimately brings you healing and guides you into a closer walk with God.

What Happened to Matthias?

(ACTS 1:12–26)

❧❧❧❧❧ ❀ ❦❦❦❦❦

MORNING PRAYER· ·

Lord Jesus, Head of the body, I confess I've never quite understood Matthias's role. We only know he was Your follower from this one mention in Acts, but that tells us so much about him. He was a witness to Your ascension and Your resurrection. He followed You before he was one of the Twelve. Then when he finally had his chance, he still disappeared in silence behind Paul's prominence. He reminds me of how I feel, how many times someone else eclipses me. Teach me that joy comes in serving You, wherever and however You call me, not in any fame or attention that is drawn to me. Amen.

> *Nevertheless for David's sake did the LORD his God give him a lamp in Jerusalem, to set up his son after him, and to establish Jerusalem.*
> 1 KINGS 15:4

EVENING READING ·

God does not abandon His plan. He covenanted with David that one of his descendants would always reign. Even with all the evil kings that reigned after David, He did not disregard His promise. And now Jesus, a descendant of David, will reign forever. You know that you serve a God who keeps His promises and doesn't change His mind. Therefore, you can have a sure confidence that no matter what is happening in your life right now, it is definitely part of God's perfect plan.

1 KINGS 16:21–18:19 ❀ ACTS 2:1–21 ❀ PSALM 96:1–8

Sing the Glory of the Lord

(PSALM 96:1)

⟩⟩⟩⟩ ❀ ⟨⟨⟨⟨

MORNING PRAYER · · · · · · · · · · · · · · · · · ·

Lord, may each Christian, wherever we live, declare Your glory and Your marvelous deeds to whomever is around us. May all You are and all You've done spring to the lips of all believers everywhere, especially those who live among those who reject their faith. May we never cease to praise You, even when we travel in places where we are uncertain of the reception of Your glory. May Your people speak of You at all times and in all places. Put a song in our hearts. Show me that one person today who needs to hear Your good news. Amen.

O sing unto the Lord a new song:
sing unto the Lord, all the earth.

PSALM 96:1

EVENING READING ·

The psalmist desires all the earth to sing to the Lord. Generations later at Pentecost, this vision of the psalmist started to become a reality. The Holy Spirit descended, allowing people from many nations to hear the Gospel in their own language. The good news continued to spread from there into all the earth. One day people of every nation will be singing God's praise together in the throne room of their Savior.

What Are You Doing Here?

(1 KINGS 19:9–17)

>->>>> ❀ <<<<

MORNING PRAYER

Lord God Almighty, I should always listen when You speak. When You ask me the same question twice, I had better pay double attention. So what am I doing before You today? Am I like Elijah, feeling like I'm the only one fighting for You and my life is in danger? You talked with him on a regular basis, so what was special about the mountain? Did he need the reminder that a gentle whisper was as powerful as a whirlwind? Perhaps You wanted to quiet his spirit before You stirred the whirlwind of Hazael, Jehu, and Elisha. How thankful I am that just as You met with Elijah on the mountain, You will meet with me today, protect me, save me, and meet my needs. Amen!

And it came to pass at the time of the offering of the evening sacrifice, that Elijah the prophet came near, and said, LORD God of Abraham, Isaac, and of Israel, let it be known this day that thou art God in Israel, and that I am thy servant, and that I have done all these things at thy word. Hear me, O LORD, hear me, that this people may know that thou art the LORD God, and that thou hast turned their heart back again. Then the fire of the LORD fell, and consumed the burnt sacrifice, and the wood, and the stones, and the dust, and licked up the water that was in the trench.
1 KINGS 18:36–38

EVENING READING

Elijah loudly taunted and ridiculed the prophets of Baal, who were enemies of God. But when it came time for him to show Israel who the true God was, his prayer was a beautiful picture of someone who walked humbly with God and had a personal relationship with Him. He asked that God would consume the sacrifice, not so he would look good but so the people would know who their God was. And then God answered the faithful prayer of His servant and shattered any disbelief in the crowd by sending down fire from heaven.

The Seat of Fire

(PSALM 97:1–6)

⇒⇒⟩⟩⟩ ❀ ⟨⟨⟨⟨⇐

MORNING PRAYER·

Oh Lord the King, Your throne sits on a sea of fire. Righteousness and justice are its foundation. Fire goes before You in every place, burning away the dross of evil. None of Your enemies can stand before You. Your fame doesn't just extend to those closest to the throne, but all the way to the farthest reaches of the universe. Heavens and mountains roll away before You, proclaiming Your righteousness, celebrating Your holiness. Let the earth be glad. Let the smallest island in the farthest sea rejoice. Amen.

> *And he leaping up stood, and walked, and entered with them
> into the temple, walking, and leaping, and praising God.*
> ACTS 3:8

EVENING READING

The transformation of the lame man in Acts is a testament to God's ability to completely transform a person. Not only did He fix what was wrong in the man's legs, but He also created muscle strength and coordination that the man would never have had due to his disability—no physical therapy and long rehabilitation necessary. Even with all the incredible medical and scientific advancements we have been blessed to make, we can never match the power of the Creator to restore His broken creation. That is a God who truly deserves to be praised.

Ahab's Repentance
(1 Kings 21)

❧❧❧❧❧ ❀ ❧❧❧❧❧

MORNING PRAYER ·

Lord God, what a surprise to discover that evil King Ahab repented. He learned from David, killing Naboth and taking his vineyard. He went on to encourage worship of Amorite gods and did more to lead Your people further away from You than any other king in Israel's history. But when he repented, You listened. You forgave. Your stamp of forgiveness marked his change of heart as genuine. Oh Lord, how I take comfort from that. If You could forgive Ahab and relent from punishing him, how much more can I trust You will forgive me as well, when I repent and believe in Jesus? Forgive me when I stray. Amen.

> *Ye that love the LORD, hate evil: he preserveth the souls of his saints;*
> *he delivereth them out of the hand of the wicked.*
> PSALM 97:10

EVENING READING ·

It's easy to become overwhelmed by the evil in this world and to loathe its very existence. While we have to live in this imperfect world until Christ brings us home or comes again, take heart that this hatred of evil is a sure sign that you love God. When you have aligned yourself with someone, you end up loving or hating the things that person loves or hates. God hates evil even more than you, and as your heart becomes more like His, you will see things even more vividly from His perspective. Ask Him to continue to mold your heart to be like His.

Praying for Courage

(ACTS 4:23–31)

≈>>>>> ❀ <<<<<≈

MORNING PRAYER·

Oh Lord, that I might have the heart of those early believers. Peter and John returned from the same court that had crucified Jesus. I might be tempted to pray for protection or to escape their notice. But those first-century followers prayed for courage to speak boldly. I don't face those same severe consequences if I testify, and therefore I have all the more reason to be bold. Compel me to share the good news of Your salvation and all Your wonderful deeds for humankind. May You work among us in such a way that people will recognize Your handiwork. Shake our comfort zones, fill us with Your mighty power, that we may give glory to You. Amen.

Before the LORD; for he cometh to judge the earth: with righteousness shall he judge the world, and the people with equity.
PSALM 98:9

EVENING READING

Injustice is rampant on this earth. But God judges with righteousness and equity. He does not judge based on personal bias or prejudice. He does not take into account skin color, age, nationality, or gender. His judgment is pure and holy. He is coming to judge the earth in a way that will finally bring true justice to the wicked and peace and reconciliation to the oppressed.

Pick Up Your Mantle

(2 Kings 2:11–12)

>≥≥≫≫ ❀ ≪≪≪≤≤

MORNING PRAYER

Lord, I love the story about Elisha picking up Elijah's mantle. His excitement upon seeing the chariots of fire, his pain at losing his mentor—his willingness to take over. How much of life is like that? Often a new calling comes hand in hand with suffering. My heart is torn in two when I remember the deaths of those dear to me. Only Your power and love keep my heart together where it's breaking. And in that time of loss, do You have a new work for me to do? I rest in the assurance of the protection of the chariots of fire, even when I don't see them. Whatever You ask me to do, You will also prepare me to complete the task. Amen.

> *Saying, Did not we straitly command you that ye should not teach in this name? and, behold, ye have filled Jerusalem with your doctrine, and intend to bring this man's blood upon us.*
> Acts 5:28

EVENING READING

The apostles were accused of filling an entire city with their doctrine. Their relentless preaching of the Gospel was so pervasive that the officials of the city took note and felt like something had to be done to address the rapid spread of their teachings. Wouldn't it be amazing if we could fill the cities we live in with this same life-giving doctrine? To be accused of the same thing as these faithful and courageous apostles would truly be an honor.

Recognizing I Need Help

(ACTS 6:1–7)

❧❧❧❧❧ ❀ ❧❧❧❧❧

MORNING PRAYER· ·

God who brought order out of chaos, how often are we like the early church, both personally and corporately. Forgive us when we try to do life on our own. Open our eyes to the times we need help. Lead us to people who are respected and full of spirit and wisdom for areas where we lack experience or talent. Let us work as a team. When someone offers to help me, let me also offer to help someone who needs my gifts. As we become one in prayer, love, encouragement, and message, Your truth will spread. Oh Lord, make it so! Amen.

> *Then he said, Go, borrow thee vessels abroad of all thy neighbours,*
> *even empty vessels; borrow not a few. And when thou art come in,*
> *thou shalt shut the door upon thee and upon thy sons, and shalt pour*
> *out into all those vessels, and thou shalt set aside that which is full.*
> 2 KINGS 4:3–4

EVENING READING ·

Could Elisha, through God's power, have solved all the widow's problems in today's passage without having her do anything? Of course he could have. But, instead, we're presented with a valuable model of helping those in need. The woman first worked to get empty vessels from all her neighbors, and then God performed the miracle. As God knew and demonstrated, it is often very constructive to allow the person in need to be part of the solution and not just a bystanding benefactor of it.

Choosing Friends Carefully

(PSALM 101)

❧❧❧❧ ❀ ❧❧❧❧

MORNING PRAYER

Lord God, I start by praising You with songs. I will speak of Your love and justice, and I desire to live blamelessly before You. But do I expect any action on my behalf to earn Your help? It's Your love that makes me worthy. Surround me with people, friends, and helpers who are wise and faithful, above reproach. Let me not cultivate friendships with slanderers or people who are conceited and full of pride. May I not be one of those people. May I be able to stand with Joshua, with David, and say, "As for me and my house, we will serve the Lord." Amen.

> *And he answered, Fear not: for they that be with us are more*
> *than they that be with them. And Elisha prayed, and said, LORD,*
> *I pray thee, open his eyes, that he may see. And the LORD opened the*
> *eyes of the young man; and he saw: and, behold, the mountain*
> *was full of horses and chariots of fire round about Elisha.*
> 2 KINGS 6:16–17

EVENING READING

Oh, that God would open our eyes as He did the eyes of Elisha's servant that we too might see the mighty army arrayed to protect us and to carry out God's will. We are never in this battle alone. How much more courageously would you step into battle if you were aware that you are always surrounded by a victorious, heavenly army?

Stop and Go

(2 Kings 6:24–7:2)

>>>>> ❀ <<<<<

MORNING PRAYER· ·

Lord God, I almost dislike the uncertainty of not knowing when bad times will end as much as the bad times themselves. There are times I rant against You, like the king's servant, in my desire to have the difficulties resolved. Forgive me for my unbelief, especially when the promise comes from Your trusted servant. May I accept Your promise of deliverance without wavering or doubting. When I am in a time of drought, may I trust in You, only You, to see me through and to bring the drought to an end. Amen.

And seeing one of them suffer wrong, he defended him,
and avenged him that was oppressed, and smote the Egyptian.
ACTS 7:24

EVENING READING ·

God does not just save those who are already perfect and have their act together. In fact, the three men who wrote the most books of the Bible are all murderers—Moses (as we read about in today's passage), David (killed Uriah), and Paul (looked on in approval as Stephen was murdered). These three pillars of the faith were far from perfect men. And yet, God used them to carry out His flawless plan. If He could use them, He can certainly use you as well.

Now and Then

(PSALM 102:8–17)

›=›››› ❀ ‹‹‹‹=‹

MORNING PRAYER·· ·

Heavenly Father, I'm not sure if these verses speak about the earthly Jerusalem, the new Jerusalem, or maybe both. How I thank You for Your promise to David that has brought blessing to people everywhere. Hallelujah! David's promised heir, Jesus, will reign on His throne through all eternity, but He won't be King just of a few thousand square feet in the Middle East. He's King of kings and Lord of lords, both on earth and in heaven. You are there, You have always been there, and You will be there when all memory of today has faded. I love every stone in that kingdom, all the living stones You have placed there. Amen.

> *My days are like a shadow that declineth; and I am withered*
> *like grass. But thou, O LORD, shall endure for ever;*
> *and thy remembrance unto all generations.*
> PSALM 102:11–12

EVENING READING ·

The psalmist in today's passage understood his own frailty. He knew that his life was like a flickering shadow and grass that withers rapidly. But he had faith in something greater than himself. While his life was merely a vapor, his God endures forever. While most of us are forgotten soon after we depart this earth, our God will be remembered and praised throughout all eternity. Put your effort into glorifying and magnifying Him during this life rather than magnifying yourself.

The Heavens Opened

(ACTS 7:54–60)

❖

MORNING PRAYER

Dearest Jesus, what a blessed sight. When Stephen was about to experience the severest test, dying for his faith, You gave him the ultimate vision. He saw You standing by Your Father's right hand. And that testimony cost him his life. How often things seem to work like this, that the times of greatest blessing are also the times of greatest trials. I've protested before. I want to enjoy the blessing unhindered by pain. But why do I think I'm any better than Stephen and so many others? Perhaps You give me that great abundance to hold me up during the trying times. Perhaps it takes pain to recognize what is ultimately important. I thank You that You stand by Your Father's side, interceding for me. Amen.

Therefore they that were scattered abroad
went every where preaching the word.
ACTS 8:4

EVENING READING

The people who led the persecution of the early Church must have felt like they were doing a good job of squelching the Gospel of Christ. After all, those who adhered to the teachings of Christ as the Messiah were scattering under the persecution. But God's plan and the inevitable advancement of the Gospel cannot be stopped so easily. In fact, God used the very persecution of His people to more quickly reach others for Christ. Had persecution not forced the Christians away from their homes, it would have taken longer for the good news to spread around the world.

A Glimmer of Hope

(2 KINGS 13:4–5)

❧❧❧❧❧ ❀ ❧❧❧❧❧

MORNING PRAYER ·

Lord God, how much easier it is for my children to learn my poor habits than my good ones. Jeroboam and all his descendants were a bad bunch of rulers. Jeroboam openly and honestly repented, and You cut him some slack. But then his son prayed without repenting. You saved him that one time, but their enemies swarmed back. How I wish I could defeat my besetting sins by one definitive battle, but too often they return to plague me again, and I am forced to call on You again. Show me how to align my life with Your will, to avoid some of the battles. As for the rest—the battle belongs to You. Amen.

And Philip said, If thou believest with all thine heart, thou mayest.
And he answered and said, I believe that Jesus Christ is the Son of God.

ACTS 8:37

EVENING READING ·

God has lovingly planned the steps of His children even down to the smallest details. The eunuch that Philip witnessed to in today's passage was reading in Isaiah 53. He came to embrace Christ that very day. We can only assume that this new believer would have kept reading in Isaiah. A few chapters later in Isaiah 56, he would have come across an exquisite passage specifically talking about the family that a eunuch has as a follower of God. How beautiful that God not only brought Philip to explain the Gospel to him, but that God also showed him through His Word that he was loved and had a place in God's family.

Ananias and Saul

(ACTS 9:1–16)

⇒⇒⟩⟩⟩ ✿ ⟨⟨⟨⟨≪

MORNING PRAYER ·

Lord Jesus, these verses from Acts take me to holy ground. You performed the impossible, transforming Saul from a death-breathing persecutor to one of the greatest proponents of the Way. And to help that happen, Ananias obeyed You, knowing full well the risks he took. When You direct me to go in a certain direction, may I follow You and share Your words with confidence. Even if I don't get the warm welcome Ananias did, let me take joy from being faithful to Your calling. Only You know the eternal consequences of my actions today. Amen.

For he knoweth our frame;
he remembereth that we are dust.
PSALM 103:14

EVENING READING ·

God knows that you are frail. He knows that you are prone to certain weaknesses and sins. He remembers that you were born in sin and must often fight your very sin nature to serve Him. You serve a God who, in His holiness, demands perfection—but who, in His love, has granted you that perfection based on no effort of your own. Don't let guilt or insecurities over your shortcomings have any place in your service to God.

⮒ DAY 182 ⮓

All to Thee I Surrender

(Psalm 103:15–22)

⮒⮓⮓⮓ ❀ ⮐⮐⮐⮐

MORNING PRAYER·· ·

Let all that I am praise You, Lord. Let all my heart, all my soul, all my strength—everything I am and hope to be—praise You. Let me bless You, lift Your name on high. Let gratitude and affection flow from every pore of my being toward You. You are Yahweh, the great I Am, the eternal God. You are Adonai, my Lord Master. You are worthy of all the praise I have to offer, and so much more. May I devote every fiber of my being to praising You. May I join the worldwide chorus in offering praise at Your throne. Amen.

> *But Barnabas took him, and brought him to the apostles,*
> *and declared unto them how he had seen the Lord in the way,*
> *and that he had spoken to him, and how he had preached*
> *boldly at Damascus in the name of Jesus.*
> Acts 9:27

EVENING READING ·

God will build His Church. Sometimes He builds it through the miraculous conversion of enemies of the Gospel—people like Saul. But more often He builds it through the faithful, humble, and relentless service of His children—people like Barnabas and Ananias. Whether your conversion was an elaborate "Damascus road" experience or a simple acceptance of Christ at a young age, it was a miracle that day when God ushered you into the kingdom of His Son. He can and will use every sinner who has been saved by grace.

Rooftop Prayers
(ACTS 10)

❀

MORNING PRAYER

Father God, how appropriate that Peter would be on the rooftop praying when You announced that the good news was meant for Gentiles as well as Jews. How precious to know Peter wasn't alone in his prayers. Cornelius had also been petitioning You. In the middle of the afternoon, no less—the middle of a workday for a Roman centurion. You brought together these two bold, brave men, who might have clashed in any other circumstances, and made them brothers in You. You'll shake up my prayers from time to time. May I listen as well as talk, that I may hear what Your calling is for today. Use me to increase Your kingdom here on earth. Amen.

Then Peter arose and went with them. When he was come,
they brought him into the upper chamber: and all the widows
stood by him weeping, and shewing the coats and garments
which Dorcas made, while she was with them.
ACTS 9:39

EVENING READING

Peter—a miracle-working, mighty, and faithful servant of God—was called to Joppa because another mighty, faithful servant of God had died. This servant, Dorcas, had not restored sight to the blind or raised anyone from the dead, but her work was so significant that a group of people implored Peter to bring her back to life. And God chose to grant their supplication. God can work through miracles, but He can also work through a faithful daughter of His who made garments for those in need.

❧ DAY 184 ❧

Show Them

(2 KINGS 19:14–19)

≽≫⟩⟩⟩ ❀ ⟨⟨⟨⟨≼

MORNING PRAYER· ·

Heavenly Father, You know I have a Sennacherib whispering falsehoods in my ear, just as he did to Hezekiah. Teach me to be as wise as Hezekiah in dealing with it. Oh, deafen me, blind me, to the enemies' claims that they are greater than You. I know the claims are false, from a lifetime of practice and study, but I suspect I could easily fall prey to lies. Whenever I am tempted to doubt, teach me to come to You, asking You to act once again. Strut Your stuff. Remind my enemies they are but pawns in the greatest chess game of eternity, and You are King and Queen and Knight to control and protect. Amen.

> *And Hezekiah received the letter of the hand of the messengers,*
> *and read it: and Hezekiah went up into the house*
> *of the LORD, and spread it before the LORD.*
> 2 KINGS 19:14

EVENING READING ·

Fear is a powerful weapon. The Assyrians understood this as they attempted to destroy the morale of God's people with terrifying taunts. But fear is no match for God. Hezekiah did what we all should do—when confronted with a seemingly indestructible enemy, Hezekiah laid the whole situation before God. He didn't try to figure it out on his own. Rather, he went to the one who was mightier than he or the Assyrians or fear itself.

Memory vs. Record

(2 KINGS 22)

❀

MORNING PRAYER

Wonderful Counselor, I need You these days more than ever, when I can't depend on my memory any longer. Forgive me when I fall into a routine of how I think things are supposed to be done. I think I remember it very clearly. Then I do housecleaning, read an old email, discover an old journal—and it's not so. What a shock to Josiah's helpers when they cleaned the temple. They thought they had been doing things right until they read Your Word again. Give me a teachable spirit and a desire to share what I learn with others, that together we may ever obey You with fuller understanding. Amen.

Now while Peter doubted in himself what this vision which he had seen should mean, behold, the men which were sent from Cornelius had made enquiry for Simon's house, and stood before the gate, And called, and asked whether Simon, which was surnamed Peter, were lodged there.

ACTS 10:17–18

EVENING READING

Cornelius sent men to go visit Peter. This seems like a fairly simple story in the book of Acts. But, it is a glorious step for God's kingdom as it is the official inclusion of the Gentiles into the Gospel of Christ. God made it clear to Peter that there was no longer any national distinction of God's people. People from all nations and languages were made clean and granted the blessing to be adopted as God's children.

A Mutual Love Fest

(PSALM 104:31–35)

>⹁⹁⹁⹁ ❀ ⹁⹁⹁⹁⹁

MORNING PRAYER ·

Lord God, as one doctrinal statement puts it, the chief end of man is to glorify and enjoy You forever. You created me and all people for relationship. You looked on Your creation—people!—and called us very good. Whenever I praise You, You are already rejoicing over me with singing. Like a child, I sit on Your lap, and we play a game of who-loves-whom-the-most. There is no real comparison, of course, but You take great pleasure in hearing my voluntary expressions of adoration, and You cherish those intimate times when You have my full attention. Why would I ever turn away from a time like that? Amen.

And like unto him was there no king before him, that turned to the LORD with all his heart, and with all his soul, and with all his might, according to all the law of Moses; neither after him arose there any like him.
2 KINGS 23:25

EVENING READING ·

Josiah understood who he was and who God was. The title and position of king did not make him think that he was equal to his heavenly King. He understood that all understanding and guidance comes from the Lord. Therefore, he turned to God with all his heart, soul, and might. Have you done the same?

2 KINGS 24–25 ❀ ACTS 12:18–13:13 ❀ PSALM 105:1–7

Your Praise on My Lips
(PSALM 105:1–7)

≥>>>>> ❀ <<<<<≤

MORNING PRAYER ·

Lord God, may Your praise be on my lips for all eternity. Your name is so grand, so glorious, that I have only halting words to speak of it. I rhapsodize about the miracle of creation and revel in Your judgments, testing them to be right and true. I scroll through my scrapbook of memories of Your wonderful acts. The title on each page sums the experience. All I have to do is say "Christmas 1982" and the miraculous way You provided for us that year floods my mind. May I sing, write, and speak of Your wonderful acts in my life and the world in every way I can to every person I can. Amen.

> *O give thanks unto the LORD; call upon his name:*
> *make known his deeds among the people. Sing unto him,*
> *sing psalms unto him: talk ye of all his wondrous works.*
> PSALM 105:1–2

EVENING READING ·

Though your relationship with God is deeply personal, it should not be totally private. You should openly give thanks to God and declare to others what He has done for you. If you truly grasped the depth of His grace to you, you would not be able to contain His praise or keep your love of Him from others. So sing unto Him and talk of His wondrous works.

≳ DAY 188 ≶

Any News?
(ACTS 13:14–43)

≳≫≫≫ ❁ ≪≪≪≲

MORNING PRAYER ·

Heavenly Father, did anyone at that worship service at Antioch of Pisidia have any idea what was happening? The first sermon on Paul's first missionary journey, and wow, what a story he had to tell. Jesus Son of David sounds more like a Wild West legend than a truthful account, and yet the listeners heard and wanted to know more. Lord, open my ears to discern truth from falsehood. May I be driven to speak Your Word boldly, as Paul was. When I communicate, may people hear Your truth. Not only for me, but I pray also for those who go to places where people haven't heard of You or have forgotten. Amen.

> *He hath remembered his covenant for ever, the word which*
> *he commanded to a thousand generations. . . . When they were*
> *but a few men in number; yea, very few, and strangers in it.*
> PSALM 105:8, 12

EVENING READING ·

When God made His covenant with Abraham and promised him that his descendants would be as numerous as the stars, Abraham probably never could have imagined how immensely God would fulfill that promise. God has remembered His covenant and brought to Himself innumerable spiritual descendants of Abraham from all over the earth. Because of your faith in God, you are a direct fulfillment of God's promise.

Asking for More Responsibility

(1 CHRONICLES 4:9–10)

❧❧❧❧❧ ❁ ❧❧❧❧❧

MORNING PRAYER

Lord God, I want to be like Jabez. He didn't wait for relief from pain before he went to work. Instead he went to work. He asked You to take him from where he was to where You wanted him to be. Forgive me for the times I let my circumstances hold me back from following You with all my heart. May I rely on the arms You place around me when I'm ready to give up, fatigued. You have work for me to do, supernatural work that I can only do through Your power and strength. May I return everything You give me as an offering of praise. Amen.

And the disciples were filled with joy,
and with the Holy Ghost.
ACTS 13:52

EVENING READING

In 1 Chronicles 4:10, we read about Jabez, whose prayer for blessing, prosperity, and protection was granted. We can imagine that he would have lived a happy and joyful life. And yet, in Acts we read about followers of Christ who were being persecuted, beaten, and imprisoned. But even in these circumstances, they were filled with joy. When it comes to living a joy-filled life, the circumstances don't matter. Whom you serve does.

Family Business

(1 Chronicles 6:48)

⇝⟫⟫⟫ ❀ ⟪⟪⟪⇜

MORNING PRAYER ·

Lord God, how does this concept of a family business that extends for multiple generations apply today? Aaron and his descendants were priests before You forever. The other Levites were given specific duties. Where is free choice in such an arrangement? My modern sensibilities protest. Then I see my son and how he shares many of my passions, strengths, and weaknesses. That although his life follows a different pattern than mine, we both are drawn to serve You in similar ways. It's both nature and nurture and, most importantly, Your calling and gifting. Whatever that calling is, give me the grace to obey and follow it with my whole heart. Amen.

> *And saying, Sirs, why do ye these things? We also are men of*
> *like passions with you, and preach unto you that ye should turn*
> *from these vanities unto the living God, which made heaven,*
> *and earth, and the sea, and all things that are therein.*
> Acts 14:15

EVENING READING ·

Having been declared gods by the local people, it would have been easy for Paul and Barnabas to see this as their free ticket out of persecution and let the people continue to treat them as gods. But they did not deny their God to take the easy way out. Instead, they declared themselves as mere men. God could (and sometimes does) send impressive angels to declare His Word, but He most often uses flawed and weak humans. Through these broken vessels, He can shine the light of His power more clearly.

Coming to a Consensus
(ACTS 15:1–18)

❧>>❧ ❀ ❧<<❧

MORNING PRAYER·· ·

Heavenly Father, I hate it when I disagree with my brothers and sisters in Christ. How often we have a difference of opinion in our interpretation of Your Word because of our mind-sets. We can't see there's another way to look at it. We bring our culture, religious training, and language to Your Word. No wonder Jews and Gentiles came into conflict. How I need Your mind, that I might ponder soundly, consider things as You would, rather than as a twenty-first century white woman would. Give me a glimpse of Your truth, and enable me to pass it on to others without offending. Amen.

> *And gave them the lands of the heathen: and they*
> *inherited the labour of the people; that they might*
> *observe his statutes, and keep his laws. Praise ye the LORD.*
> PSALM 105:44–45

EVENING READING ·

God miraculously sustained the Israelites through the wilderness and brought them into a rich promised land. He did this so that they might serve and obey Him. But instead, the people more often disobeyed and disappointed Him. God has also brought you into the promised land of His kingdom. Don't make the same mistake as the Israelites who took His blessings and provision for granted. Thank God and serve Him for all He has done for you.

≫ DAY 192 ≪

Breathing You

(PSALM 106:1–3)

≫≫⟩⟩⟩ ❀ ⟨⟨⟨⟨≪

MORNING PRAYER ·

Both now and through all eternity, let us praise You, oh Lord. For You are good and You have done great things, greater than the grandest epics captured by human tongue. I ask You for more "Hallelujah Chorus" moments when I stand to my feet in awe, in praise, for more times when I stumble and bow, swept up in a worship song. May I never tire of the old, old story, because its power continues without pause or alteration, always run by Your love. Make me one who acts justly and who does what is right. I want the privilege of singing in that heavenly chorus. Amen.

And the contention was so sharp between them,
that they departed asunder one from the other:
and so Barnabas took Mark, and sailed unto Cyprus.
ACTS 15:39

EVENING READING ·

Today's passage in Acts 15 feels slightly uncomfortable. Two of the leading apostles who were working together to spread the Gospel had a disagreement so strong that they had to separate. This seems like a major setback in the advancement of the Gospel. But God used even this for His purposes. Instead of working side by side, Paul and Barnabas were able to reach more people by going their separate ways and spreading the Gospel to different countries and people.

Macedonian Call

(ACTS 16:6–10)

❧❧❧❧❧ ❁ ❧❧❧❧❧

MORNING PRAYER ·

Oh Lord Jesus, I sit in Your presence, rejoicing that Paul responded to the cry of the man from Macedonia to go over and help him. When Paul stepped onto the continent of Europe, You thought of me and all the others from that day until now. I am building a monument of thanksgiving at this place, but perhaps You are calling me elsewhere. Give me vision to seek and ears to hear that one person who is eager and ready to receive the good news. Cause our paths to cross and Your name to spring from my lips. Make me visible and verbal with my faith. Amen.

> *Thus they changed their glory into the*
> *similitude of an ox that eateth grass.*
> PSALM 106:20

EVENING READING ·

It seems so absurd that the Israelites would have created an idol of a common animal to replace the God whose very presence they had witnessed in the pillar of fire and cloud. But don't we often do the same thing? We trade the rich bounties that are available to us in God's Word for worthless shows or games. Or we belittle the holy and mighty God into a mere genie whom we only talk to when we want something. Strive to recognize and know the glorious God for who He really is.

⤫ DAY 194 ⤫

A Threesome

(Psalm 106:30–31)

>⟫⟫⟩ ❀ ⟨⟨⟨⟨⟨

MORNING PRAYER ·

Lord God, thank You for the vow You made with Phinehas for a lasting priesthood. Just as there was Abraham, Isaac, and Jacob to father the line of the promise, so here You chose Aaron, Eleazar, and Phinehas to intercede for the people of Israel. Phinehas acted boldly for Your honor, in ways that make me uncomfortable. Does the possibility of drastic action hold me back from total commitment? You've given me a ministry of grace and reconciliation. I ask for two things: that You will provide me with a circle of three godly people to lift one another up, and that I will act without hesitation in whatever fashion You direct when sin strikes our heels. Amen.

> *And when her masters saw that the hope of their gains*
> *was gone, they caught Paul and Silas, and drew*
> *them into the marketplace unto the rulers.*
>
> ACTS 16:19

EVENING READING ·

The concept of Jesus may sound pretty nice, or at least nonthreatening, to most people. . .until He gets in the way of their comfort. We live in a world where comfort and prosperity are god. The Jesus that we preach may be offensive to people, as He forces them to come to terms with their sin and give up things that they have held to be precious. But the riches that are in Christ are far greater than any riches that this earth can offer. We can't dare risk not sharing such an important message because we're afraid of how it will be received.

A Map for Musicians

(1 CHRONICLES 16)

>>>>> ✿ <<<<<

MORNING PRAYER ·

Oh God who is most worthy of praise, I read this official hymn given to the temple musicians and revel in all the emotions and activities of worship. May my times before You, both by myself and with others, reflect the same values. May I proclaim Your name among the nations, making known what You have done. When we sing, may we bring glory to Your name. Give me a heart to seek You, and not just one to glance up and see if You're around. May we tell in song of Your wonderful history with the sons of men. Amen!

> *And when they found them not, they drew Jason and certain brethren unto the rulers of the city, crying, These that have turned the world upside down are come hither also.*
>
> ACTS 17:6

EVENING READING ·

The apostles were accused of turning the world upside down. How incredible would it be if those words were spoken again of God's people? May we so unwaveringly stand for truth in the face of opposition and unabashedly proclaim Christ as the only way to true life that we turn the world on its head.

1 CHRONICLES 18–20 ❀ ACTS 17:15–34 ❀ PSALM 106:44–48

In Partnership

(Psalm 106:44–48)

››››› ❀ ‹‹‹‹‹

MORNING PRAYER· ·

Oh Lord, how glorious to know that You're working behind the scenes. Sometimes You use people to discipline me; other times You use them to show me Your mercy. And You wish to do the same in me, with me, through me. Perhaps there is someone You want to bless through me. Forgive me when I criticize the person You wish to encourage. Use the words I write and speak to build others up. May they comfort others in the same way I've been comforted. Speak to me through them. The same Holy Spirit lives in all of us. May we together give thanks to Your name and praise Your glory. Amen.

> *For in him we live, and move, and have our being; as certain*
> *also of your own poets have said, For we are also his offspring.*
> Acts 17:28

EVENING READING ·

Paul knew and understood the culture in which he was preaching. In today's passage, he even quoted the society's poets. It's important to know whom you are talking to when sharing the Gospel so that you can formulate your message to be the most understandable to your culture. This can be a powerful tool as long as the fundamental message and natural power of the Gospel are not softened or changed.

1 CHRONICLES 21-22 ❀ ACTS 18:1-23 ❀ PSALM 107:1-9

David's Mistakes

(1 CHRONICLES 21)

❧❧❧❧❧ ❀ ❧❧❧❧❧

MORNING PRAYER ·

Heavenly Father, how glad I am that David's life is recorded in the Bible, including his mistakes, even in his later years. If You could love a man who kept making a mess, I dare hope You will love me. In his repentance, I see his wisdom has grown with his age. His sin was his responsibility, his alone, and he refused to allow anyone else to pay for it. He certainly didn't want to take this poor man's farm for free, the way he killed Uriah, and I thank You that however horrible my past mistakes, I don't have to stay that way. You will continue molding me into the image of Christ until the day You call me home. Amen.

And Satan stood up against Israel,
and provoked David to number Israel.
1 CHRONICLES 21:1

EVENING READING ·

Today's passage in 1 Chronicles is one of the few times that Satan is mentioned in the Old Testament. But even when he's not spoken of directly, you can recognize his scent as his evil work is woven throughout the narratives. It is vitally important that we remember that there is a spiritual battle raging in this world at all times. We will be ill-equipped if we don't train for such a battle. Our enemy is real; so be on your guard. But remember that our ally is stronger and can thwart any evil plans the devil can devise.

Teachable Spirit
(ACTS 18:24–28)

❧ ❀ ❦

MORNING PRAYER

Lord God, I pray for discernment and a teachable spirit. Show me the difference between false teaching and differing interpretations. Let me embrace differences with grace but correct where there is falsehood. When You bring an Apollo into my life, let me speak Your words, and let Your Spirit draw me and those I am conversing with together in love and unity. Give me the grace to encourage those You've given me to lead along the way with wisdom and patience. Let me also listen and learn from those who are farther down the road than I am. May we work together to build up Your church. Amen.

And he began to speak boldly in the synagogue: whom when
Aquila and Priscilla had heard, they took him unto them,
and expounded unto him the way of God more perfectly.
ACTS 18:26

EVENING READING

When Aquila and Priscilla heard Apollos speak, they realized that he did not have a completely full or accurate knowledge of the Gospel. In response to this, they did not spend their energy talking behind his back about how ignorant he was. Instead, they took him in and trained him in the fullness of the message of Christ. Wouldn't we spend our time so much more wisely by talking less about a problem and working more to fix it?

Healing

(PSALM 107:20)

>>>>> ❀ <<<<<

MORNING PRAYER·

Divine Healer, more prayer requests are asked for healing than for anything else. Teach me how to pray. Today I bring before You all who are sick. I pray for those whose unwise or sinful ways have led to their illness, that You will heal them in spirit and body. I pray for those with disabilities, whether from birth or from accident, that You would bring them to all fullness, whatever that looks like. Oh Creator of mind and body, heal those with mental illness. Rework the patterns of their minds. For those nearing death, I ask that they will first of all be saved and then that they will have peace and strength, choosing to live each day to the fullest. Amen.

> *Then they cry unto the LORD in their trouble, and he saveth them out of their distresses. He sent his word, and healed them, and delivered them from their destructions. Oh that men would praise the LORD for his goodness, and for his wonderful works to the children of men!*
> PSALM 107:19–21

EVENING READING

The writer of today's psalm had firsthand experience of the love and saving power of God. This personal knowledge drove him to wish that others would praise God and know of His wonderful works as well. Does God's goodness to you inspire you to tell others about Him and cause you to work hard to let others know of His wonderful works?

Choose Your God Here

(ACTS 19:23–41)

❧❧❧❧ ❀ ❧❧❧❧

MORNING PRAYER ·

Lord God, it's disturbing to live in a culture where Christians are rejected because they claim there is only one way to God. But Paul ran into the same problem in Ephesus. Now as then, people want to choose their own deity. How foolish it would be to hold a straw poll to determine whom to worship. Who wants a God who needs an election before taking office, who could be deposed in twelve months? Such a god is no more than I am, hopeless to solve the world's problems. You are God. Period. Thank You for giving me the eyes to see now before the day You force everyone to acknowledge You. May I share the truth of the One true God with love and grace. Amen.

> *And David said to Solomon his son, Be strong and of good courage,*
> *and do it: fear not, nor be dismayed: for the LORD God, even my God,*
> *will be with thee; he will not fail thee, nor forsake thee, until thou*
> *hast finished all the work for the service of the house of the LORD.*
> 1 CHRONICLES 28:20

EVENING READING ·

In today's passage, David spoke beautifully personal words to his son Solomon, encouraging him to be strong and courageous and to rely on God. David knew that his God would continue to be faithful to the next generation. Are you passing on your faith to the next generation? It is a beautiful thing when the surpassing value of a personal relationship with God is passed down to the children's children and so on. It is the best possible inheritance.

Why Them, Not Me?

(2 CHRONICLES 2)

>>>>>> ❀ <<<<<<

MORNING PRAYER

My Lord God, it seems strange that Solomon chose unbelieving foreigners to build the temple. Did Hiram believe in You? He acknowledged You as the creator God. What about the foreigners who were conscripted for labor? Were they people whom You had drawn to Yourself, blessed with the opportunity of a lifetime—to build a temple for You? Did Jewish builders wonder why they were overlooked? Forgive me when I envy the assignments You give to others. You've given me a long list of gifts and opportunities, but I still lust for the one fruit remaining on the branch. Forgive me. Use us together to bring glory to You. Amen.

> *He poureth contempt upon princes, and causeth them to wander*
> *in the wilderness, where there is no way. Yet setteth he the poor*
> *on high from affliction, and maketh him families like a flock.*
> PSALM 107:40–41

EVENING READING

God does not do things as the world does. While we celebrate the rich, beautiful, and powerful, He delights in the poor, lonely, and needy. It would do us good to see the world through His eyes and to value what He values.

Saying Goodbye
(Acts 20:17–38)

>>>>>> ❀ <<<<<

MORNING PRAYER

Heavenly Father, throughout my life, I've had to say farewells, whether I am the one leaving or being left. May I be as gracious in my goodbyes as Paul was. May my record be as consistent as Paul's was—humble, up-front, personal, unprejudiced. Where I have failed in the past, correct me now. May my goal with my peers be to share the good news of Your Son, my Lord and Savior Jesus Christ. May all of us together commit ourselves to finishing the race of faith strong; may all of us together sing of Your salvation. Amen.

Save that the Holy Ghost witnesseth in every city, saying that bonds and afflictions abide me. But none of these things move me, neither count I my life dear unto myself, so that I might finish my course with joy, and the ministry, which I have received of the Lord Jesus, to testify the gospel of the grace of God.
Acts 20:23–24

EVENING READING

Paul knew that bonds and afflictions waited for him in every city where he preached. This knowledge would cause many of us to give up. And yet, Paul talks about finishing his course with joy even in the face of this persecution. The only way that he could have this kind of joyful attitude amid unavoidable suffering was because he knew his God very well. His joy was entirely disconnected from his circumstances and completely rooted in his relationship with God and his hope in an eternity with his Savior.

God's Resting Place

(2 CHRONICLES 6:12–42)

>>>>>> ❀ <<<<<<

MORNING PRAYER

Lord God, Solomon and I wrestled with the same questions. You are God. You can't be contained by Your creation. I'm the smallest Who in Whoville, calling for help. And glory be! You hear me! May Your praises ring the rafters and explode the ceiling—until the news of Your love and salvation spreads from my ears to my neighbors, to my city, and across the earth. May I join with other believers to pray. If my individual cries for help are heard, how much more glorious when they're joined by throngs of others? Amen.

But will God in very deed dwell with men on the earth? behold,
heaven and the heaven of heavens cannot contain thee;
how much less this house which I have built!
2 CHRONICLES 6:18

EVENING READING

Solomon spoke rightly that not even the highest heaven can contain God. Because of this, he wondered that God could ever dwell on earth with men. And yet, He did dwell on earth, as a humble and self-sacrificing Man. And now He dwells in us. That the almighty God condescended to dwell among us and in us is a truth almost too beautiful to fathom.

In Pain

(PSALM 109:21–31)

>>>>> ❀ <<<<<

MORNING PRAYER

Sovereign God, how often the song in my mouth is the prayer in my heart. My prayers turn to You. Where else would I go? You are good. Your love never fails. Your name stands higher than all others. I'm a weak and needy sinner approaching You for help. I've wandered in the darkness of my sin until I'm stretched thin, hardly more than a Gollum in the story of my life. But on that dark journey, You hear my plea for help and deliverance. You bless me and uplift me in the presence of my enemies. I thank You for the storms You've brought me through. Let me extol Your name forever. Amen.

Then Paul took the men, and the next day purifying himself with them entered into the temple, to signify the accomplishment of the days of purification, until that an offering should be offered for every one of them.
ACTS 21:26

EVENING READING

It's important to make wise decisions about when to bend to cultural norms for the sake of the Gospel. In today's passage, Paul purified himself according to Jewish custom. This was not something that he as a Christian needed to do. He did this solely for the sake of the Gospel, believing that it would allow him to reach more people for Christ.

2 CHRONICLES 9:29–12:16 ❀ ACTS 21:33–22:16 ❀ PSALM 110:1–3

What Are You Waiting For?

(ACTS 22:14–16)

⇒≫≫ ❀ ≪≪⇐

MORNING PRAYER·

This hits me square on the chin, Lord. *What am I waiting for?* I come to You, begging for directions. I'm so tired, the task I've been given seems so impossible, my tools so inadequate, that I keep asking for additional help. But what do I think I need? You've already saved me, my future in heaven is secure, and You've given me a task. The time has come for me to stop asking and to start acting on what I know, getting right with You, getting right with others. You will answer when I call as I go about Your business. Amen.

> *And he did evil, because he prepared*
> *not his heart to seek the LORD.*
> 2 CHRONICLES 12:14

EVENING READING

Rehoboam did evil because he did not prepare his heart to seek the Lord. What steps have you taken to prepare your heart to seek God? Do you have a regular devotional time? Do you faithfully attend church? Are you committed to reading and memorizing God's Word? If you have not humbled yourself to seek and serve God, nothing that you do can be righteous in His sight. Set your heart to seek God, and you will find Him. He will reward you for seeking.

2 CHRONICLES 13–15 ❀ **ACTS 22:17–23:11** ❀ **PSALM 110:4–7**

Safe Passage

(ACTS 23:11)

❧❧❧❧ ❀ ❧❧❧❧

MORNING PRAYER·

Dear Jesus, I thank You for Paul's obedience in following Your will, even when he knew it meant imprisonment and possibly death. I just wish the Bible told us more about why he felt compelled to return to Jerusalem. Do You plan for my faith walk to be like that? To pursue a dangerous future without any obvious confirmation that it's of You? May I listen and obey, whether You shout from heaven or simply brush my spirit. How precious Your promise, that You gave Your blessing after he obeyed and was imprisoned. You fulfilled his desire to testify in Rome as well. Charm my inner being so my greatest desires lie in the direction of Your will. Amen.

> *And, behold, God himself is with us for our captain,*
> *and his priests with sounding trumpets to cry alarm*
> *against you. O children of Israel, fight ye not against the*
> *LORD God of your fathers; for ye shall not prosper.*
> 2 CHRONICLES 13:12

EVENING READING

Any battle fought against the living God is a losing battle. The battle to keep your indulgent sins is a battle where you are pitted against God, and you will lose to His holiness. The battle of death over life has already been lost by the devil because he was foolish enough to go up against his Maker. Choose sides with your Savior—you will always be on the winning side.

Honoring Teachers

(2 CHRONICLES 17:7–10)

❧❧❧❧❧ ❀ ❧❧❧❧❧

MORNING PRAYER·· ·

Oh heavenly Father, to have a leader like King Jehoshaphat. It's never too late for a person or nation to repent and follow You. Thank You for his wisdom in sending out his best staff to teach Your Word to the people. How little I know of Ben-Hail, Shemaiah, Elishama, and others, but I thank You for their faithfulness to You and to their earthly king. How heartily they must have studied Your Word to be able to teach it. How You must have transformed their lives. And through them, You transformed the nation. If I can do as the least of them did, I will be a woman of God. That is my prayer, to encourage and teach. Amen.

> *For the eyes of the LORD run to and fro throughout the*
> *whole earth, to shew himself strong in the behalf of them*
> *whose heart is perfect toward him. Herein thou hast done*
> *foolishly: therefore from henceforth thou shalt have wars.*
> 2 CHRONICLES 16:9

EVENING READING ·

It may at times feel like God is not actively involved in the world or that He has given up on a creation that has strayed so far from Him. But this is not true. He is constantly watching the movement of His creation. He shows Himself as a strong defense to those whose hearts are His. God is not an inactive and disconnected observer. He is already aware of your circumstances, so call out to Him in your need.

Praying for My Children

(PSALM 112)

❧❧❧❧ ❀ ❧❧❧❧

MORNING PRAYER ·

Praise You, Lord. Praise Your holy name. I lift up my children, my family, to You. Before I pray for Your blessings, Lord, I beseech You for their character. May they fear You and delight in You. May they be gracious and compassionate in their interactions with people, just and generous in their dealings. I pray that You will keep them close to You, that You will make them mighty and secure, blessed in spirit and in material things, that they will come to You as their Savior and receive Your righteousness forever. Amen.

And the king of Israel said unto Jehoshaphat, There is yet one man, by whom we may enquire of the LORD: but I hate him; for he never prophesied good unto me, but always evil: the same is Micaiah the son of Imla. And Jehoshaphat said, Let not the king say so.
2 CHRONICLES 18:7

EVENING READING ·

Micaiah was faithful in relaying messages from God and was therefore hated by the king of Israel because he never told the king what he wanted to hear. You may sometimes find yourself in the same situation where being faithful to the truth of God and His Word puts you at odds with those around you. May we have the same courage as God's faithful prophets to continue to speak His truth no matter what the reception.

Valley of Blessing

(2 CHRONICLES 20:25)

❧>>>>> ❀ <<<<<❧

MORNING PRAYER

Wonderful Counselor, You are the fount of all comfort, the Creator of my mind, the original and best therapist to me where I'm broken. Help me to unlock the door of my fortress and walk into the fullness You have waiting for me. I've been living on the edge, making unhealthy choices because I see no other way to survive. Forgive me! Remove the scales from my eyes. Shatter the walls of my self-made fortress. Open me to the available abundance instead of the rubbish where I've been living. Life in my valley can be richer than the thin air on the mountaintop. Amen.

> *And said, O LORD God of our fathers, art not thou God in heaven? and rulest not thou over all the kingdoms of the heathen? and in thine hand is there not power and might, so that none is able to withstand thee? Art not thou our God, who didst drive out the inhabitants of this land before thy people Israel, and gavest it to the seed of Abraham thy friend for ever?*
> 2 CHRONICLES 20:6–7

EVENING READING

We ought to pray remembering and relying on God's promises and faithfulness. Jehoshaphat prayed in the light of God's past work and His present promises. Because he knew his God to be a promise keeper, he was able to go into battle praising God (2 Chronicles 20:21). You can march into whatever battle you are facing praising God as well. When the outcome is already decided by the past work of Christ, there is no reason to fear. There is nothing left to do but praise.

Athaliah and Jehosheba

(2 CHRONICLES 22–23)

❧❧❧❧ ❀ ❦❦❦❦

MORNING PRAYER

Lord God, what a scary story—with one ambitious woman throwing the kingdom into upheaval, and another acting with great love and courage to sweep an infant straight out of the royal nursery to safety. As much as I want to be Jehosheba the heroine, at times I display characteristics of the ambitious, murderous Athaliah. Forgive me! Safeguard my mind and heart from jealousy. How easy it is to go from wanting what someone else has to taking it from them. Strike the thoughts from me. Whatever ministry or gifts You have given to me, let me share them with others without pause. Use me to guide those beginners. Amen.

And Paul said, I would to God, that not only thou,
but also all that hear me this day, were both almost,
and altogether such as I am, except these bonds.
ACTS 26:29

EVENING READING

It's easy to dwell on the things in your life that are not going well. But are you aware of how blessed you are solely based on your relationship with Christ? No matter what circumstance you are in, you are beyond fortunate. Paul knew how blessed he was because of his walk with God and wished that others might also know the depths of the riches that he had every day. He had a truly good life that was not affected by chains or suffering.

To God Be the Glory

(PSALM 115:1–10)

❀

MORNING PRAYER

Lord God, to Your name, not mine, be the glory. Make me into a mirror, like the moon, that whatever glory hits me will reflect back to You, that my craters and darkness may fade away and people see only Your shining glory. May they see Your faithfulness and abundant love in the brilliance of Your acts. May I not seek a name for myself but for You. When people think of me, let them remember all the wonderful things You've done on my behalf. When I'm afraid, when I'm blind, let me trust in that glory, love, and faithfulness. You are my help and my shield. You surround me and protect me. Amen.

Now after the death of Jehoiada came the princes of Judah,
and made obeisance to the king. Then the king hearkened unto them.
2 CHRONICLES 24:17

EVENING READING

A good mentor is remarkably valuable. When Jehoiada was alive, Joash did what was right in God's sight. When Jehoiada died, Joash began to be influenced by far less wise people and, tragically, turned from God. Don't be afraid to reach out to mentor someone—it could be the difference between that person choosing to follow God or not. At the same time, seek out a mentor for yourself that will guide you in the way of Christ.

⇒ DAY 212 ⇐

Islands

(ACTS 27:21–41)

⇒⇒⟩⟩⟩ ❀ ⟨⟨⟨⟨⇐

MORNING PRAYER· ·

Oh God to whom I belong, I come before You in the midst of a tremendous storm. A small band sails alone on treacherous seas. You know my heart, that I look forward to going home but believe You have work yet for me to do. Oh, thank You for the reassurance that Your calling is sure! It will happen, maybe not how I pictured it. Like Paul, a prisoner, I'm not alone in the squall. I pray for the lives of everyone around me. I pray that no one with me will be given over to destruction. Use me to encourage those around me to endure and survive life's shipwrecks together. Amen.

> *Wherefore, sirs, be of good cheer: for I believe God,*
> *that it shall be even as it was told me.*
> ACTS 27:25

EVENING READING ·

Paul knew the plan that God had for him and recognized that he was immortal until that plan was fulfilled. His faith in God's purposes was rock solid. Not even things as lethal as a shipwreck or poisonous snake could alter the course that God had set for him.

Not My Father

(2 Chronicles 28:1–29:19)

⇒⇒⟩⟩⟩ ❀ ⟨⟨⟨⟨⟨

MORNING PRAYER ·

Loving Father, I can't wrap my head around a father who would sacrifice the son of his own body to a god of fire. What a stench it must have made to Your nostrils. How I thank You for Hezekiah's testimony. He broke the pattern of generational sin. Oh, to live like him, where he made his first order of business to repair the broken places. How I rejoice in not having to be defined by my parents, and I pray the same for my children. How thankful I am for the things they have done well. Make me a Hezekiah in my time and before my children, and not an Ahaz. Amen.

> *But we desire to hear of thee what thou thinkest: for as concerning this sect, we know that every where it is spoken against.*
> ACTS 28:22

EVENING READING ·

The "sect" of Christianity was spoken against everywhere. The adherents to this sect preached of life that was released from the bonds of the Law. They preached of salvation based on no merit of one's own. They spoke of eternal life with God in heaven secured by the sacrifice of His Son. Isn't it remarkable that there could be so much resistance to such a beautiful message?

A Reputation Like Rome's

(ROMANS 1:7–10)

>->>>> ❀ <<<<<

MORNING PRAYER

My reputation, Lord. What is it? What do the people I know, from my neighbors to people who have never met me in person, think of me? Forgive me when my flame spreads muddy ash instead of burning brightly for You. Make me like the believers in Rome. Thank You that You have called me as part of Your holy people. I pray that whenever other people think of me, they will think of You. That I will play some part, however small, in spreading the good news of Your salvation across the earth. And lead me to fellowship with others who are Your called, wherever they are from. Amen.

Precious in the sight of the LORD
is the death of his saints.
PSALM 116:15

EVENING READING

For those of us who have lost loved ones who are in Christ (or for those who are facing an imminent death), keep in mind that the death of God's saints is not the end. The death of His children is precious in His sight. We do not pass from this world into the next forgotten and on our own. Rather, we are led through by our faithful guide who overcame death on our behalf. A beautiful celebration awaits us on the other side. Celebrate the lives and deaths of God's children, for our Father does.

All You Peoples

(PSALM 117)

>>>>> ❀ <<<<<

MORNING PRAYER

God of the universe, the heavenly host, and all mankind—I add my voice to the throng. Whenever we gather, two or three together, let us add our prayers, cries, and praise to the church universal. May we join our petitions with the persecuted church, with those living without freedom of religion. You reign, and my prayers rise up to You along with those of every tribe and tongue. How I look forward to the day when we will all understand one another's speech. You are great and Your faithfulness never fails. You are the only One greater than we ourselves. Amen.

> *Be strong and courageous, be not afraid nor dismayed for the king*
> *of Assyria, nor for all the multitude that is with him: for there be*
> *more with us than with him: with him is an arm of flesh; but with us*
> *is the LORD our God to help us, and to fight our battles. And the*
> *people rested themselves upon the words of Hezekiah king of Judah.*
> 2 CHRONICLES 32:7–8

EVENING READING

What a beautiful and inspiring speech we read from King Hezekiah in today's passage. The terrifying and brutal force of Assyria was threatening God's people. But instead of giving in to fear, Hezekiah relied on his God. No matter how big or fearful a force is up against you, you will always have more on your side because you have a heavenly army led by the everlasting God fighting for you. Being on God's side automatically puts you in the majority.

Your Love Never Quits

(Psalm 118:1–18)

≈≈≫≫≫ ✿ ≪≪≪≪≈

MORNING PRAYER ·

Loving God, I'm running to You, crawling if that's all the strength I have. Because now, this morning, there is a fresh supply of Your compassion. Your faithfulness will never expire or be out of date. You'll never hang an Out of Stock sign on Your door and turn me away. I'm sticking with You. From the wide-open spaces of eternity, You come to me in my here and now. My life seems to hang by a thread, and the enemy's scissors are closing in. My Rock, my Shelter, come to my aid. Cover me in the shadow of Your wings until I am strong enough to stand. Amen.

> *For when the Gentiles, which have not the law, do by nature the things contained in the law, these, having not the law, are a law unto themselves: which shew the work of the law written in their hearts, their conscience also bearing witness, and their thoughts the mean while accusing or else excusing one another.*
> Romans 2:14–15

EVENING READING ·

We have an innate understanding of the moral law written on our hearts that proves the existence of a higher order. No matter how hard people may fight against the idea of a Creator, their very innermost conscience speaks and witnesses of Him. An instinctual knowledge of Him is inevitable. This means that however hard some people may work to harden their hearts and minds to Christ, they are without excuse on the day when they stand before their Maker.

The Haves and Have-Nots

(ROMANS 3:1–26)

>>>>>> ❁ <<<<<<

MORNING PRAYER ·

Oh Lord God, I was once lost but now am found. I once was a sinner, a mouse trying to jump over the moon of Your holiness, the distance too far for me to travel in a million lifetimes. And yet, incredibly, I am righteous, justified, transformed by Your Son's atoning blood. No matter how often I repeat the good news, I still tremble at the law I spurned and rest in Your amazing grace. Whatever separates me from other believers, this brings us back together. Thrust apart by sin, brought together by grace. Make it so in the places we brush against each other. Amen.

Even the righteousness of God which is by faith of Jesus Christ
unto all and upon all them that believe: for there is no difference:
for all have sinned, and come short of the glory of God.
ROMANS 3:22–23

EVENING READING ·

When it comes to our presalvation standing before God, we are all on an even playing field. We have all sinned and are in desperate need of His righteous covering. In God's eyes, there is no difference regarding race, gender, socioeconomic status, physical ability, or beauty. None of us can attain to His standards on our own. If God does not cater His message based on physical, financial, or social standards, then neither should we.

Today Is the Day

(PSALM 118:24)

❧❧❧ ❀ ❧❧❧

MORNING PRAYER

Today is the time to praise You. It's the only day I have. I can't make up for what I didn't do yesterday or store up praise for tomorrow. This is the day You have made, and therefore it is good and fitting, Your gift to me to turn back as an offering to You, every minute a new beginning. You not only made today and gave it to me; You also are acting in my now, on my behalf. Oh, let me join my voice with other believers to say, "This is the day which the LORD hath made; we will rejoice and be glad in it" (Psalm 118:24). Amen.

> *This is the day which the LORD hath made;*
> *we will rejoice and be glad in it.*
> PSALM 118:24

EVENING READING

"This is the day which the Lord hath made; we will rejoice and be glad in it." This is a mind-set and a decision to be made each and every morning—*God has made today; therefore I will be glad.* If at the moment your life is such that it is hard to find things to rejoice in, at least you can be glad that God has given you another new day with new opportunities and new blessings from Him. He has planned out this day for you. Rejoice in the new day that God gives you.

Hope Is My Middle Name

(ROMANS 5:1–5)

>>>>>> ❀ <<<<<<

MORNING PRAYER

God of all comfort, thank You for all the ways hope works in my life. I hope while I'm suffering, because I know You won't leave me stranded but will always rescue me and set me on a rock. You keep me safe. You are present with me in my trials. Hope fills me with Your love. Without troubles, how could I know of Your deliverance? If I don't recognize Your tender care in the depths, how will I recognize it in the heights? I boast of that hope and all the wonderful things You have for me. Amen.

*Therefore being justified by faith, we have peace with God through
our Lord Jesus Christ: by whom also we have access by faith into
this grace wherein we stand, and rejoice in hope of the glory of God.*
ROMANS 5:1–2

EVENING READING

Where does your peace come from? Not from relationships, physical healing, or more money. It comes from being justified before God. You know you stand clean and spotless before a holy God and that because of this you are guaranteed a life of eternity in His glory. This is true peace, to know that you have been saved by grace and that nothing can touch you outside of His will for you.

EZRA 4–5 ❀ ROMANS 6:1–7:6 ❀ PSALM 119:9–16

Sanctify Me
(ROMANS 6)

>>>>>> ❀ <<<<<<

MORNING PRAYER ·

Lord and Master, with each passing moment, remind me that I have a choice because I am no longer under the law and the power of sin, but under grace. Make me an instrument of righteousness. Bring that choice to my mind when I'm the most tired, the most likely to let sin rule. Let me test the fruit of my choices, that I may judge them accurately. Have I chosen what appeals to my eyes, my fleshly desires? Or have I lifted my eyes like Isaiah to see You in Your majesty and holiness? Cleanse me of sin and impurity. Renew my spirit. Amen.

> *Thy word have I hid in mine heart,*
> *that I might not sin against thee.*
> PSALM 119:11

EVENING READING ·

Memorize God's Word. Having God's Word in your heart and mind is remarkably powerful. It has the ability to keep you from sinning and to guide you in the will of God. When temptations arise, quote scripture to yourself and brandish the sword that God has given you in His Word. The devil will flee from a fight where the unerring Word of God is boldly used as a defense. Let God's Word reign in your heart to dethrone the sin that Christ sacrificed so much to conquer (Romans 6:12).

God of Heaven
(EZRA 6)

꙳꙳꙳ ❀ ꙳꙳꙳

MORNING PRAYER ·

God of heaven, when people look back on today, will they see Your hand at work as clearly as I see it in Bible times? Make it so. Like Darius, I worship You, the God of heaven. I praise You that in these latter days You have caused Your name to dwell both in the grandeur of the heavens and in the flesh of Your Son, full of grace and glory. I pray today for our leaders, for their well-being, for Your wisdom to fall on them as they lead us. Like Darius, may they recognize You. Amen.

> *Moreover I make a decree what ye shall do to the elders of these*
> *Jews for the building of this house of God: that of the king's goods,*
> *even of the tribute beyond the river, forthwith expenses be*
> *given unto these men, that they be not hindered.*
> EZRA 6:8

EVENING READING ·

The stories recorded in Ezra and Nehemiah are a marvelous demonstration of how God is in control no matter how out of control a situation may appear to our eyes. The people's mission to rebuild the house of God was constantly facing the threat of termination. In today's passage, King Darius (a ruler from an enemy nation that had captured God's people) not only allowed them to continue work, but he even assisted them with their project. God has never lost control. He is always sovereign.

Not Asking for Help

(EZRA 8:21–23)

⇝⟫⟫⟩⟩ ❀ ⟨⟨⟨⟨⟨⟨

MORNING PRAYER ·

Gracious God, how I thank You for the many times You send aid from the hands of Your children and even from unbelievers. I stand in awe of Ezra's faith. He refused to ask for help because he had bragged that Your hand was on everyone who looked to You. Forgive me if my doubt brings shame on Your name. I humble myself before You, for I am nothing, and ask You for a safe journey from now to the end of my days. Great God of heaven above, how I thank You that You hear and answer my prayer. Amen.

There is therefore now no condemnation to them which are in
Christ Jesus, who walk not after the flesh, but after the Spirit.
ROMANS 8:1

EVENING READING ·

There is no condemnation for you who are in Christ. Do you really grasp that? Covered by Christ's blood-washed robes, you cannot be condemned. You no longer need to live under the yoke of slavery to sin and the Law. Your freedom in Christ releases you from a life of desperately trying to reach an unattainable standard. This doesn't mean that you shouldn't strive to live a righteous life. But now that righteous life is inspired not by a need to be right before God but by a gratefulness for what God has already done for you.

Daily Walk

(PSALM 119:41–64)

❈

MORNING PRAYER

Heavenly Father, I am physically pained, mentally fatigued, and discouraged. Remember Your Word to me, for my hope is in Your unfailing love. Every day You offer a new batch of compassion, and I trust Your history of faithfulness. From the days when I first came to know You, oh God, I've believed Your promise that forgiveness requires only simple, honest confession and repentance. But willfulness and rebellion make my faults stick in my throat. Though I ache to admit them, they hold me. Free me, Savior, to open my soul to You. May my heart run to You to seek Your pardon. Cleanse me from all sin, and glorify Yourself in my life. Amen.

> *Nay, in all these things we are more than*
> *conquerors through him that loved us.*
> ROMANS 8:37

EVENING READING

The end of Romans 8 is one of the most exquisitely victorious passages in the Bible. Bookmark it in your Bible so that anytime you feel as though you are caught in a losing battle, you can be reminded that in Christ you are more than a conqueror. Absolutely nothing has the power to separate you from the love of Christ. God alone is powerful enough to separate you from His love by deciding to take it away. But He has shown you through the sacrifice of His own Son that He will stop at nothing to be able to keep loving you. You are secure in His love and will be for eternity.

Hardened Hearts

(ROMANS 9:18)

>⟫⟫ ❀ ⟪⟪⟪

MORNING PRAYER ·

Sovereign Lord, as Your daughter, I tumble with laughter and tears into Your lap. How grateful I am that You had mercy on me, on my family, and on so many who are near and dear to me. I am saddened when I see people who refuse You repeatedly. Is that when You harden their hearts? Is that what happens to those nations of the earth, those who are most resistant to the good news, Your own special people, the Jews, chosen by You? Oh, how I beseech You that the scales will fall from their eyes! You don't want any to perish. Break apart those bars of iron on darkened hearts. Amen.

Then the king said unto me, For what dost thou make request?
So I prayed to the God of heaven.

NEHEMIAH 2:4

EVENING READING ·

Nehemiah is standing in the courts of the king, and the king asks him what he requests. What would be your knee-jerk reaction in this intimidating situation? Nehemiah's reaction was to pray. Even in the middle of the king's court, his dialogue with God continued. Nehemiah was constantly in the court of his heavenly King. Prayer is too often a second or third resort for us. Strive to be more like Nehemiah where the natural thing to do is to pray.

NEHEMIAH 3:17–5:13 ❀ ROMANS 9:19–33 ❀ PSALM 119:73–80

The Results of Meditation

(PSALM 119:73–80)

❧❧❧❧❧ ❀ ❦❦❦❦❦

MORNING PRAYER

Oh Lord, how wonderful to read of the power of Your Word. It's not simply meant to tickle my ears. May it change me. Because I hope in Your Word, may others rejoice. Because Your laws are righteous, convict me of my sin. I find comfort in Your promises. Your compassion gives me light as I delight in Your law. The better I understand Your statutes, the more prepared I am to teach others. May I meditate on Your precepts and follow Your decrees with all my heart and soul, that I might not shame Your name. Amen.

Nay but, O man, who art thou that repliest against God? Shall the thing formed say to him that formed it, Why hast thou made me thus?
ROMANS 9:20

EVENING READING

Romans 9:20 gives us an apt answer to a plethora of our doubting questions—who are we to reply to God? God's ways, thoughts, wisdom, and knowledge are so far above ours as to be incomprehensible to us. A dose of humility and trust in the love of God would do us good when facing life's hard questions.

Strengthen My Hands

(NEHEMIAH 6:9)

>>>>> ❀ <<<<<

MORNING PRAYER •

My Lord God, when enemies taunt me, saying I can't finish the work, strengthen my hands. When foes accuse me for the wrong reasons or of unfair tactics, pour purpose into my actions. If people speak against me in the name of God, turn it back on them. When the days seem long and the task seems harsh, steady my hands. When I am faint, when I doubt the work I'm engaged in, renew my vision, that I may renew my commitment. When I feel alone in the work, bring helpmates to labor beside me. And when the task is done, may I return all glory and praise to You. Amen.

> *For they all made us afraid, saying, Their hands shall*
> *be weakened from the work, that it be not done.*
> *Now therefore, O God, strengthen my hands.*
> NEHEMIAH 6:9

EVENING READING •

Nehemiah 6:9 records a quick prayer that Nehemiah spoke to God in the face of fearful circumstances—"O God, strengthen my hands." We can probably assume that his life was punctuated perpetually with this type of prayer. He was in constant conversation with the one who was so much greater and more able than himself. May your thoughts be similarly inseparable from an inner conversation with your Father.

NEHEMIAH 8:1–9:5 ❀ **ROMANS 10:14–11:24** ❀ **PSALM 119:89–104**

How Shall They Hear?

(ROMANS 10:14–15)

❧❧❧❧❧ ❀ ❦❦❦❦❦

MORNING PRAYER ·

Lord Jesus, the irrefutable logic stirs me from the bottom of my heart. People who haven't heard of You can't call on You, and they can't hear without a preacher. How I thank You again that I grew up in a land where Your Word is abundantly spoken. I beg You, make me both a preacher and a sender. Make the wheels on my chair and my fingers on computer keys beautiful as I write and speak of Your wondrous salvation. May I also play my role in sending preachers to those who haven't heard. May the day come ever nearer when every tribe and tongue and nation has heard. Amen.

Unless thy law had been my delights,
I should then have perished in mine affliction.
PSALM 119:92

EVENING READING ·

David had learned to delight in the Word of God. It had become his sustenance. In today's reading, he cited his knowledge of and delight in God's law as the reason he didn't perish in his affliction. Knowing God's Word will keep you from falling, sustain your soul during grief, and bolster you with courage when you are afraid. It's through His Word that you can get to know God. Don't miss out on such a glorious opportunity.

NEHEMIAH 9:6–10:27 ❀ ROMANS 11:25–12:8 ❀ PSALM 119:105–120

Trifling Hardship?

(NEHEMIAH 9:6–37)

⇒⇒⟩⟩⟩ ❀ ⟨⟨⟨⟨⟨⇐

MORNING PRAYER ·

Lord God, what a bold prayer! Thank You for the Levites' example to bring even my trifling problems to You. You are the highest God of the highest heaven, from the depths of the sea to the far ends of the universe, so how is it that You see me? I'm just a pebble upon which my troubles are dust, and yet You know the weight of them on me. Oh, I fall in worship and thanksgiving. You are a forgiving God, gracious and compassionate, slow to anger and abounding in love. Your Spirit instructs me in all matters, great and small. I praise You and thank You. Amen.

Thy word is a lamp unto my feet, and a light unto my path.

PSALM 119:105

EVENING READING ·

David asserted that God's Word was a lamp to his feet and a light to his path. If you are lacking direction in your life, go to God's Word. He has already provided you with the very light that you so crave to illuminate your future. Delve into this life-giving Word and seek to know all that you can from it. God will in turn use His Word to light your way. Use the lamp that He has provided.

Coal Bearer

(ROMANS 12:20–21)

❧❧❧❧❧ ❀ ❦❦❦❦❦

MORNING PRAYER·

Lord Jesus, as a pale imitation of Your sacrifice, You tell me to feed my enemies, to care for them, until the coals You've placed in my hands burn away the hostility between us as well as between them and You. Make me a coal bearer today. Use those burning coals to purify me and to draw my enemies closer to You, no matter how painful. How often I feel overcome by the circumstances of living in a fallen and imperfect world. Make me a force for good. Let me be an inspiration and not a drain on those around me. Amen.

> *Be of the same mind one toward another. Mind not high things,*
> *but condescend to men of low estate. Be not wise in your own conceits.*
> ROMANS 12:16

EVENING READING

Why is it that knowledge of spiritual matters often makes us feel arrogant? This is unacceptable. We are not to be wise in our own eyes. If we feel arrogant that we know God better than someone else, then it's probably safe to say that we don't actually know Him at all. The God who humbled Himself to dwell and die on earth is not a God who takes delight in any form of arrogance or prejudice.

Keep Me from Sin

(PSALM 119:129–136)

❧❧❧❧❀❦❦❦❦

MORNING PRAYER ·

Living Word, You are the Light of the World, and Your wonderful words give light. May I never wander beyond the reach of Your light. I pant for Your words, hungry for the righteousness and truth they provide. They show me the way I should walk and keep my feet from slipping. Direct my footsteps according to Your Word, that I might not sin. And when I do sin, have mercy on me. Your lovely name speaks of Your abundant love and forgiveness. Let not the sins of those around me turn me away from You. I pray not only for myself, but also for all who need this prayer. Forgive us, Lord. Amen.

Thy testimonies are wonderful:
therefore doth my soul keep them.
PSALM 119:129

EVENING READING ·

It is astounding and convicting to read through Psalm 119 and see the immense love that David had for God's Word. As someone who was so intimately acquainted with God's laws and promises, it is no wonder that David was a man after God's own heart. His heart is displayed to us in His Word. We come to know and love Him more fully the more time we spend in it.

ESTHER 1:1–2:18 ❀ ROMANS 14:13–15:13 ❀ PSALM 119:137–152

Different Is Okay

(ROMANS 14:13–15:13)

≈≫⟩⟩⟩ ❀ ⟨⟨⟨⟨≪≈

MORNING PRAYER ·

Our Lord and Savior, may I join together with other Christians, even if our practices differ. Together we ask You to fill us with joy and peace, that we may overflow with hope in the Holy Spirit. Our unity comes from You, not from the exact things we eat or the way we dress. Teach me, humble me, to not judge others whose theology and values differ from mine. Let me not create a stumbling block for someone else by my behavior, but rather live in such a way that leads to building each other up toward good works. Amen.

> *Now the God of hope fill you with all joy and peace in believing,*
> *that ye may abound in hope, through the power of the Holy Ghost.*
> ROMANS 15:13

EVENING READING ·

Biblical hope is not a vain wish for something that might happen but rather a steadfast faith in something that is sure to happen. God is the God of hope because He is the very author of our hope. Without His work and His promises, there would be nothing sure in which to have faith. Along with Paul in Romans 15:13, ask that God would fill you with joy and peace so that you would overflow with hope through the Holy Spirit.

Perfect Peace
(PSALM 119:165)

≽≫≫≫≫ ❁ ≪≪≪≪≼

MORNING PRAYER

Dear Lord, how I hunger for peace. I crave an inner peace that keeps me on an even keel. Make my outside calm, with my faith planted in the ground of Your faithfulness, so that I won't stumble. Prince of Peace, rule me inside and out as I struggle with daily life and health issues. Let my passion for Your Word fill my body, soul, and spirit. Loosen the grip of temptations on my life; show me how to live in peace in spite of my weaknesses. For in You, when I am weak, then I am strong. Amen.

> *For if thou altogether holdest thy peace at this time, then shall there enlargement and deliverance arise to the Jews from another place; but thou and thy father's house shall be destroyed: and who knoweth whether thou art come to the kingdom for such a time as this?*
>
> ESTHER 4:14

EVENING READING

God is not directly referenced in the book of Esther. Still, the evidence of His work is woven throughout the entire narrative. Even if you don't acknowledge or notice God's work directly, be confident that He is constantly working out His will for you. Just like Esther, He may place you in a situation that does not seem to have any correlation with His will. And yet, you'll find that He has put you there for a very specific reason. . ."for such a time as this."

Means Fighting
(ESTHER 8)

⇒⇒⟩⟩⟩ ❀ ⟨⟨⟨⟨⟨

MORNING PRAYER

Lord God, Your hand is so evident in Esther's narrative. You gave Mordecai opportunities within the palace, made Esther queen, and gave her favor when she sought the king's help. But when it came down to Your solution, they still had to fight. I shouldn't be surprised when that happens. I pray, asking a way out of the dangerous situation. When the battle comes upon me, I wonder if You failed to answer my prayer. Open my eyes to the weapon You've placed in my hands. Train my hands to fight. Remind me that You don't always spare me the battle, but You will always give me victory. Amen.

> *Let thine hand help me;*
> *for I have chosen thy precepts.*
> PSALM 119:173

EVENING READING

David professed that he had chosen God's precepts. Desiring to know and follow God's Word is a choice and a commitment. Sometimes we get so caught up in avoiding legalism that we allow a healthy diligence and obedience to slide. Make a commitment to read, memorize, and meditate on God's Word. You will only ever be blessed by this kind of commitment.

Mountain-High Help
(PSALM 121)

❧❀❧

MORNING PRAYER

Maker of heaven and earth, what comfort and courage I take from Your words. Stand guard over me when I walk in Your way. You won't let me fall down. Your attention is constantly upon me; You have no need of rest. You even provide shade from the burning sun and hide me from my enemies. You watch over me, both when I go out to work and when I come home, in the intimate details of my family life. I look to the grandeur of the mountains because they remind me of how much greater You are. Amen.

> *For your obedience is come abroad unto all men. I am glad*
> *therefore on your behalf: but yet I would have you wise*
> *unto that which is good, and simple concerning evil.*
> ROMANS 16:19

EVENING READING

Be wise in what is good and simple concerning evil. In today's culture, it often seems that we are more well versed in and familiar with what is evil than what is good. Yet Paul entreats the Romans to be simple concerning evil. Don't pursue knowledge of things that tear down, that promote violence or abuse, or that are simply worthless. Instead, do pursue knowledge of what is good and lovely and valuable. Be an expert in these things.

Grief

(JOB 1:20)

>>>>> ❀ <<<<<

MORNING PRAYER ·

Oh Father, when tragedy strikes, may I show the same wisdom and faith as Job. He grieved first, throwing himself into mourning rituals. May I never feel ashamed of my feelings, but like Job, may I bring them to You. May I, like him, thank You for the gift of those so near and dear to me, especially my daughter who is now dead. And just as You gave her to me for a short time, You called her home. It is all through You and for You. May Your name be praised in my grief even as I praised You at her birth. Through it all, may I trust in You. Amen.

> *And said, Naked came I out of my mother's womb,*
> *and naked shall I return thither: the LORD gave, and the*
> *LORD hath taken away; blessed be the name of the LORD.*
> JOB 1:21

EVENING READING ·

Job understood that God is wiser than he could ever be and that if God could give immense blessing, He also had every right to take it away. He understood that he came into the world with nothing and that he could take nothing with him into the next life. He therefore had a loose hold on his earthly possessions and relationships. He chose to bless the name of the Lord even in the midst of unspeakable suffering.

God Helps the Needy

(JOB 5:15–16)

MORNING PRAYER

Heavenly Father, how thankful I am for Job's example. His faith remained strong when You stripped him of his riches and health. He remained committed to You when he was poor. He knew that You still cared for him as You care for the poor and needy. I pray for the needy around me, for children who are abandoned, neglected, abused. God, rescue them! I pray for those in nursing homes, whose minds wander and who feel the pangs of loneliness. Protect them; ease their spirits. For those who are refugees in war-torn lands, oh, shut the mouth of injustice so that they might have hope. I pray for Your strong arm of comfort for the grieving. Show me what role You want me to play in their lives. Amen.

> *But God hath chosen the foolish things of the world to confound the wise; and God hath chosen the weak things of the world to confound the things which are mighty.*
> 1 CORINTHIANS 1:27

EVENING READING

God uses the weak, broken, and foolish things of the world for His purposes. We see this concept all throughout scripture. Just as a piece of pottery can only let light through if it has cracks, so too God's light shines more clearly through those who do not have it all together. When God chooses to use us for His kingdom, it is our brokenness and weakness that allow God's power to become all the more visible to those around us.

My Body, the Temple

(1 CORINTHIANS 3:10–16)

>>>>>> ❀ <<<<<<

MORNING PRAYER· ·

Lord Jesus, You are the cornerstone of the church, and I am Your temple. As unlikely as it was that You would dwell in a temple made of wood and stone, how much less that You would live in a child born of sin? But You redeemed me, purified me, and now You dwell in me. Let me be careful about what I use to build on that foundation: gold and silver or hay and wood. You live in me. Transform my thoughts, that I may better understand. Mold me into Your likeness. With all Christians, may we reflect the fullness of You. Amen.

> *I know it is so of a truth: but how should man*
> *be just with God? If he will contend with him,*
> *he cannot answer him one of a thousand.*
> JOB 9:2–3

EVENING READING ·

Job asked a very astute question in chapter 9: How can a man be just with God when he has nothing to bring to the table? The answer, of course, is Christ. Job obviously did not have the blessing of knowing what Christ would do on the cross, and so his standing before God seemed rather hopeless based solely on his own merit. We have the immense privilege of living in the new covenant, having been justified by our faith in Christ based solely on God's grace. Christ answered for God's wrath so that we would never have to.

Hope in the Depths

(JOB 11:18)

>>>>> ❀ <<<<<

MORNING PRAYER ·

Heavenly Father, You have given me the ultimate security of salvation and Your indwelling Spirit, the environment of Your never-failing love. Thank You for planting that hope in my heart! When I overcome obstacles or I'm optimistic, it's because of the hope You have given me. When I'm restless during the night, troubled by the events of the day, shine Your light into the darkness of my soul and remind me that You are my safety net, my secure tower. I can rest in peace. Without You, I am nothing. With You, I have everything I will ever need. Thank You. Praise You! Forgive my doubts. Amen.

For I know nothing by myself; yet am I not
hereby justified: but he that judgeth me is the Lord.
1 CORINTHIANS 4:4

EVENING READING ·

Paul knew of nothing against himself. Can you say the same of yourself? Do you strive to live a life where you can have a clear, guiltless conscience before God? You shouldn't strive for holiness as a way to be right before God, because you can never attain that on your own. Rather, your obedience should be a response to the grace that God has already shown you by making you clean before Him. You are already blameless in His eyes, so live that way.

Waiting with Bated Breath

(PSALM 130)

❀

MORNING PRAYER

Heavenly Father, I'm waiting with bated breath, pregnant with anticipation, fainting from thirst and hunger, as desperate as a junkie in need of a fix, as tired as a worker waiting for their relief to show up. As wakeful as I am, wishing I could sleep, I wait for You. I can't let go—I won't let go—for with You there is unfailing love, full redemption, and peace. My hope comes from You. I'm not looking for salvation from any other corner. You are the morning star, the harbinger of my hope. You never have, never will, and never can disappoint. You always deliver on Your promises. Your guarantee is more important than anything else I'm hoping for. Amen.

I wrote unto you in an epistle not to company with fornicators:
Yet not altogether with the fornicators of this world,
or with the covetous, or extortioners, or with idolaters;
for then must ye needs go out of the world.
1 CORINTHIANS 5:9–10

EVENING READING

In today's passage, Paul explained to the Corinthians that he never intended for them not to associate with sinners. He asserts that as Christians we ought to be in the world, getting to know the sexually immoral, greedy, and idolatrous. To not associate with these nonbelievers would be to miss the point of our pilgrimage here on earth. God's light shines the brightest when brought into the darker corners of the world.

A Weaned Infant

(PSALM 131:1–2)

⇒⋙ ❁ ⋘⇐

MORNING PRAYER ·

Loving Father, I want to be like the person in this psalm, knowing contentment like that of a weaned child, the continual reassurance that I am loved and special. Help me to grow into that independence. I want to change from a demanding infant to a child who confidently runs to You but leaves and plays, satisfied to know You are near. May I live and work under the shadow of Your wings, secure and confident. Like a child, keep me from worrying about matters too wonderful for me. I seek to know You, to become more like You, my Father. Amen.

> *For I know that my redeemer liveth, and that he shall stand*
> *at the latter day upon the earth: and though after my skin*
> *worms destroy this body, yet in my flesh shall I see God.*
> JOB 19:25–26

EVENING READING

Job had a remarkably clear vision of God's coming to earth and the subsequent resurrection of his own body. How he knew that his Redeemer would one day stand on earth and that one day he would see God in his own body, we don't know. But God had provided him a priceless comfort in his suffering to know that this was not the end of his body and that his Redeemer would one day make all things right.

Being Single
(1 CORINTHIANS 7:1–16)

❧❧❧❧❧ ❀ ❦❦❦❦❦

MORING PRAYER· ·

Heavenly Father, I thank You that I have enjoyed both the joys of marriage and the blessings of the single life. I pray for those believers who are single like me. That if it is Your will, You will bring a spouse that's a perfect fit for us. If not, then let us be at peace and rejoice in our calling. Let us pursue You with all our heart and give doubly of ourselves. For those who are single parents, grant them a double measure of grace as they do a job You designed for two people to carry. I pray for increased understanding and support for single adults among our churches. Amen.

But he knoweth the way that I take:
when he hath tried me, I shall come forth as gold.
JOB 23:10

EVENING READING ·

Job had a right understanding of suffering. He understood that through his trials God was polishing him as you would a dirty piece of priceless gold. Often it is the battering of trials that brings out the power of God that dwells in each of His children. We can all testify to knowing someone who has gone through immense trials but is all the stronger and more grounded in God because of them. The end result, a glittering piece of gold, is worth the process of polishing.

Understanding God

(JOB 26:13–14)

⇉⟩⟩⟩ ❀ ⟨⟨⟨⇇

MORNING PRAYER· ·

Lord God, we see Your hand at work in nature—in each day's sunrise, in the physical properties of earth and sky, in growing plants and animals that live and breathe, with man at the apex. And yet all that is only the flaming edges of Your glory. Our sin can't obscure You totally, only present a partial eclipse of all You are. When You burst through that darkness, when You strike in Your mighty power, who can withstand You? Open my eyes to see Your handiwork in the beating of a hummingbird's wings. Forgive me when I fail to acknowledge Your rightful place. Amen.

> *Behold, how good and how pleasant it*
> *is for brethren to dwell together in unity!*
> PSALM 133:1

EVENING READING ·

It is a good and pleasant thing for God's people to dwell together in unity. Relationships are hard. People will disagree and cause contentions. But the value of having fellowship with other believers is precious enough that we should be striving to live in peace and unity with our brothers and sisters as much as possible. God has given us one another to bolster, uphold, soothe, convict, and encourage each other. Don't miss out on the value of spending time with His people.

Reasons to Praise

(PSALM 135)

❧❧❧❧❧ ❀ ❀❀❀❀❀

MORNING PRAYER ·

We praise You, oh Lord, in the sanctuary. We praise You at our home altars. Let all who minister before You praise You. Let all who share a love for the name of Jesus with me join me in praise. For You are great, greater than anything we have ever seen, and I long to hear the testimony of others about You. I've felt You in the mountains. Let me hear from those who've met You in the rainforests and in the deserts. Let us together remember the great things You've done for Your people and take hope for today. Your name endures forever and Your compassion for eternity. Amen.

> *And if any man think that he knoweth any thing,*
> *he knoweth nothing yet as he ought to know.*
> *But if any man love God, the same is known of him.*
> 1 CORINTHIANS 8:2–3

EVENING READING ·

In the whole scheme of things, we know so very little. It's true that the more we learn, the more we realize how little we know. So make it a priority to seek out the most valuable kind of knowledge. Seek to know your God. Though our knowledge of God will always be limited in this life because of our finite minds, we are known perfectly by Him. He knows us better than we know ourselves.

In the Courtroom

(JOB 31:35)

>>>>> ❀ <<<<<

MORNING PRAYER ·

El Shaddai, I have long worshipped You as the almighty God of the universe, but I usually approach You as my Abba Father. If I came before You in court, I would be like Job, puzzled and uncertain. At least he recognized that he was on trial, that he had an accuser, although he didn't know the full story. How I thank You that You included the courtroom scene in Your Word. If Satan comes to accuse me, Your Son stands at Your right hand, speaking on my behalf. You justified me; You'll toss out any complaint placed at my door. Oh Lord, may I live in that freedom—even when I'm under attack. Amen.

O give thanks unto the LORD; for he is good:
for his mercy endureth for ever.
PSALM 136:1

EVENING READING ·

The refrain "for his mercy endureth for ever" occurs twenty-six times in Psalm 136. Each verse is punctuated by that phrase. Shouldn't our lives be punctuated by that refrain as well? After every chapter and verse of our lives, we can truthfully say, "His mercy endures forever." His mercy is woven all throughout the small, insignificant days as well as the life-changing events of our lives. It endures forever and will buoy us into the next life.

Temptation

(1 CORINTHIANS 10:12–13)

≈≫≫≫ ❀ ≪≪≪≈

MORNING PRAYER

Heavenly Father, You know how easy it is for me to strut like a peacock, unaware that I'm about to fall into sin. Forgive me. May I keep in mind my own history and the examples of those who have gone before me. The older I get, the more I realize that none of the trials and temptations that come my way are unique. Thank You for the testimonies of those who have overcome similar circumstances, for their support. But mostly I need to depend on You. Even when it feels like I have more than my fair share of problems, You have promised to make a way out or to give me strength to endure. I cling to that hope. Amen.

> *To the weak became I as weak, that I might gain the weak: I am made*
> *all things to all men, that I might by all means save some. And this I*
> *do for the gospel's sake, that I might be partaker thereof with you.*
> 1 CORINTHIANS 9:22–23

EVENING READING

Paul strove to reach as many people as he possibly could for the sake of the Gospel. His own sense of self or personal reputation was of no concern compared to the need he felt to tell people of Christ. He became as a servant, as a Jew, as one under the Law, as one outside of the Law, and as weak in order to reach those in each category. The Gospel requires sacrifice and a giving up of oneself. But Paul would assert that this sacrifice was well worth it so that he could share in the riches of the Gospel with those he had reached.

Glorify God in Everything

(1 CORINTHIANS 10:31)

≈≫≫≫ ✿ ≪≪≪≈

MORNING PRAYER ·

Lord God, through the years, churches have created different lists of how Christians should behave. I don't always agree. I'm an American, and I'm prone to claim my rights. Forgive me when I harm my fellow Christians as I claim my freedom. If I am choosing an activity, let me keep Paul's questions in mind: Am I gratifying the flesh, or is it beneficial to myself and others? How will my choice seek the good of others? Oh Lord, I fall so far short in this area. May I live in such a way as to glorify You and to build others up. Amen.

> *Where wast thou when I laid the foundations of the earth?*
> *declare, if thou hast understanding.*
> JOB 38:4

EVENING READING ·

When God speaks back to Job, it is an awe-inspiring, terrifying, and humbling thing to read. Imagine being there and seeing and hearing the power of God. How could we ever begin to think that we know better than God? Were we there when He created the earth? Do we hold the universe together from day to day? It has taken us millenia to even begin to discover the depths of the mysteries of this world that He created by simply speaking it into existence. And yet, we sometimes dare to assume that our will is better than His.

God Answers Job

(JOB 42:1–6)

>>>>> ❀ <<<<<

MORNING PRAYER

Oh Lord God! When I truly encounter You, how I fall in awe and tremble before You. How I thank You for Job's story. He spoke truth, but he had limited knowledge. How I need these reminders that You are God and I am not. As Job says, sometimes I speak of things too wonderful for me. Who am I, a poor woman, to question the hand of my Creator? I am nothing. Every now and then You bring me to a place where I see a glimpse of You, more than I have seen before, and I am humbled before You. As I run to my Abba Father, remind me that You are the sovereign God of the universe and to trust in You. Amen.

I know that thou canst do every thing, and that no thought can be withholden from thee. Who is he that hideth counsel without knowledge? therefore have I uttered that I understood not; things too wonderful for me, which I knew not.
JOB 42:2–3

EVENING READING

Job's response to God is the only possible response to an encounter with God—complete and utter humility of oneself coupled with the utmost praise of God. Job's life would never have been the same after this. Imagine how radically your life would change after having been directly spoken to by God. And yet, He has given us access to Himself every single day. Listen for His voice as you read His Word and pray. May it humble you and cause you to praise and magnify Him.

I Am Known

(PSALM 139:1–6)

⇝⟩⟩⟩⟩ ❀ ⟨⟨⟨⟨⇜

MORNING PRAYER ·

Creator God, You knit me together. But Your involvement doesn't stop at conception. You keep a detailed diary of my comings and goings. You would be the perfect expert witness in a trial, explaining where I was, what I was doing, and why, at any point in time. I can't hide before You. I can't escape. You know the words I'm going to speak before they come out. If I back away, You're there. I can't run away—You're in front of me. You are so big, so powerful, so awesome that I can't understand. And yet You still want to be in a relationship with me. The tiny little insignificant speck that I am. I praise You and thank You! Amen.

> *Vanity of vanities, saith the Preacher, vanity of vanities;*
> *all is vanity. What profit hath a man of all his*
> *labour which he taketh under the sun?*
> ECCLESIASTES 1:2–3

EVENING READING ·

Ecclesiastes is a remarkably apt description of life apart from God—life "under the sun." Apart from the purposes of God, all that we do on this earth is vanity and a passing shadow. God has put eternity in man's heart (Ecclesiastes 3:11) so that we inevitably realize that there has to be something more to life. Only a life that is lived with an "over the sun" perspective will provide true fulfillment and joy.

Think Before Speaking

(ECCLESIASTES 5:1–7)

❧>>>>> ❀ <<<<<❧

MORNING PRAYER ·

When I come to worship, Lord, let me bring listening ears. I am prone to ramble, to say what I think You want to hear. Test me and know my thoughts. You, the God I serve, want an eager learner rather than someone who mindlessly follows rules without seeking the purpose behind them. Keep me from rash promises and, even worse, from making vows. I thank You for Your forgiveness in the past, but keep me from repeating that sin again. Stop me from jumping into things without counting the cost. Forgive me, Lord, when I do. For You know the best course of action always, and when I don't understand, I know Your ways are higher than my ways. Amen.

> *Thine eyes did see my substance, yet being unperfect; and in*
> *thy book all my members were written, which in continuance*
> *were fashioned, when as yet there was none of them.*
> PSALM 139:16

EVENING READING ·

God formed you in the womb and knew you before anyone else was even aware of your existence. Before the first beat of your heart, He planned out a life for you in which you would have the unmatchable privilege of knowing Him. For Him to have spent this much thought on your life means that you are exceptionally valuable to Him. The opinions that people on earth may have of you are nothing compared to the opinion and love that God has for you.

Transparency

(PSALM 139:23–24)

❧❧❧❀❧❧❧

MORNING PRAYER

My Lord and Master, I don't want anything to come between us. You know me better than I know myself. Search me, know my heart, reveal me to myself. Roll my anxious thoughts around in the palm of Your hand. Crush the boulders that crush my spirit into sand; blow them away by the breath of Your Spirit. Reveal to me any offensive way. Convict me of sin. Reveal any patterns of behavior that will lead me into harm. Open my eyes to warning signs that I'm headed in the wrong direction. May I follow the straight and narrow path outlined for me; lead me in the way everlasting. Amen.

Whatsoever thy hand findeth to do, do it with thy might;
for there is no work, nor device, nor knowledge,
nor wisdom, in the grave, whither thou goest.
ECCLESIASTES 9:10

EVENING READING

Now is the time to work hard, to invest in people's lives, and to seek after wisdom and knowledge. In heaven we won't have the opportunity to speak of God to the lost. In heaven we won't have the opportunity to bind up the broken and heal the sick. Obviously, the perfection of heaven is incomparably preferable to the fallen state of this world, but you should make the most of your time here. It will be all the chance you get to be a light for God in the darkness.

Orderliness

(1 CORINTHIANS 14:40)

＞＞＞＞ ❀ ＜＜＜＜

MORNING PRAYER

Lord Jesus, the head of the church, how sad You must be to see the partitions we carve into it. The divisive, selfish behavior at Corinth deeply disturbed Paul. Today we worship and serve in the culture of fractured churches, denomination fighting denomination. I pray my church will come together in a unity of spirit and broadness of mind. May we reach decisions by prayer and in order, centered on hearing from You and worshipping You as one, not bent on individual preferences. To the extent it's possible, let community churches set minor differences aside to spread the good news to those who haven't heard. Amen.

Let us hear the conclusion of the whole matter: Fear God,
and keep his commandments: for this is the whole duty of man.
For God shall bring every work into judgment, with every
secret thing, whether it be good, or whether it be evil.
ECCLESIASTES 12:13–14

EVENING READING

The conclusion of Solomon's study into life is this: "Fear God, and keep his commandments." God is the one who will ultimately bring judgment on all that you have done in life. His opinion should be of the utmost concern to you. Your life should be lived to glorify and enjoy Him. Because in the end, the conclusion of your whole life will consist of what you have done for others and for the kingdom.

Celebrating Spring

(SONG OF SOLOMON 2:11–13)

❧❧❧❧ ❀ ❧❧❧❧

MORNING PRAYER ·

Lord God, how I treasure these beautiful verses about spring—and their association with love. Even in Bible times people's thoughts turned to love as the season changed. No wonder so many couples marry in June. The arrival of spring enlivens my senses. Flowers bloom on trees and bushes, in gardens, and along the ground. Doves coo and songbirds sing as they repeat their mating rituals. The aroma of fruit and flowers and rain fills the air. An explosion of color dispenses with the white of winter. And in all this, we celebrate the promise of eternal life through the resurrection. Thank You, Lord. Amen.

If in this life only we have hope in Christ,
we are of all men most miserable.
1 CORINTHIANS 15:19

EVENING READING

Christianity hinges on the reality of Christ's death and resurrection. Without the person of Jesus, your faith is worthless. It would be the easiest religion to disprove if only someone would have found the bones of Jesus. And yet, no one did because Christ rose from the dead, appeared to many people on earth, and currently sits on His throne in heaven. We have hope in Christ not only in this life but in the next as well. Instead of the most miserable of all people, we are the most blessed and should be the most grateful.

Where Is Death's Sting?

(1 CORINTHIANS 15:55)

=>>>>> ❁ <<<<=

MORNING PRAYER ·

Oh everlasting God, how glorious. This mortal body won't trap me forever. One day I will be fully restored in body, mind, and spirit. At last, I will be everything You created me to be, inside and out. I will join with all creation to glorify You and enjoy You forever. I don't have to worry about those who have gone before me. They're in heaven waiting for me—the ones I've met, those I never met, and those who will come after me. My eternal life offers so much more than my few years on earth. Let me make the most of my years here, and may I use them to prepare for everlasting life. Thank You! Praise You! Amen.

> *Set a watch, O LORD, before my mouth;*
> *keep the door of my lips.*
> PSALM 141:3

EVENING READING ·

Psalm 141:3 is a prayer that we should pray every day—*Lord, set a watch on my mouth and keep the door of my lips.* How much less trouble would we get into if our thoughts and words were always filtered through the grace of God? What if everything we said built others up and glorified Him? What if our thoughts were always pure and lovely? Ask God to protect your words and even your very thoughts.

Walking in the Light with the World

(ISAIAH 2:1–5)

❧⟩⟩⟩⟩ ❀ ⟨⟨⟨⟨❧

MORNING PRAYER

Mighty God, I read these verses and weep in wonder. Now nations gather in the mountains for the Winter Olympics. I watch the spectacle and imagine the day when people from all the nations of the earth will gather at Your holy mountain to seek You. Speed the day when everyone will want to know and obey Your ways. Hasten that day of peace. Only Your kingdom will bring freedom from war machines. With that bold of a dream, may I boldly walk the streets of my earthly city, a beacon of light to the world around me. Amen.

> *Wash you, make you clean; put away the evil of your doings from before mine eyes; cease to do evil; learn to do well; seek judgment, relieve the oppressed, judge the fatherless, plead for the widow.*
> ISAIAH 1:16–17

EVENING READING

Verse 16 is a beautiful turning point in chapter 1 of Isaiah. The start of the chapter is desolate as God recounts all the evil that His people have done and how they have not served Him as they should. Verses 16 and 17 are a call to repentance—wash, put away evil, do well, relieve the oppressed. And then verse 18 is a refreshing picture of redemption—our scarlet sins will be washed as clean as snow. This is how the Lord deals with His people. He does not leave us in our sin.

Comfort

(2 CORINTHIANS 1:1–11)

⇒⇒⟩⟩⟩ ❀ ⟨⟨⟨⟨⇐

MORNING PRAYER ·

Wonderful Counselor, I can never thank You enough for Your comfort, given to me so that I may in turn comfort those around me. Open my eyes to those who are in pain. May I never speak of my troubles without testifying to Your loving care. Give me the grace to relieve the sorrow and be transparent so that I may encourage those who are going through their own difficult times, those who are hurting. May Your constant comfort strengthen our feet and spread among Your people. Together, may we be the arms and feet of Your love to the world. Amen.

> *And now, O inhabitants of Jerusalem, and men of Judah, judge, I pray you, betwixt me and my vineyard. What could have been done more to my vineyard, that I have not done in it? wherefore, when I looked that it should bring forth grapes, brought it forth wild grapes?*
> ISAIAH 5:3–4

EVENING READING ·

God told a tale of a vineyard in Isaiah 5 as an analogy of His people. It is a heartbreaking look into God's relationship with a sinful and ungrateful nation. He lovingly planted and tended to the vineyard only for it to rebel against Him. He then asked of the people, "What else could I have done for My vineyard?" God has poured out blessings on us, yet how often do we rebel against Him and bring forth the wild grapes of our rebellion instead of the fruit of our gratefulness?

ISAIAH 6–8 ❀ 2 CORINTHIANS 1:12–2:4 ❀ PSALM 143:7–12

Burning Coals

(ISAIAH 6:6–7)

❀

MORNING PRAYER

Lord God, when Your Word speaks of fire, I flinch. Help me to understand how fire plays a role in the life of a believer. Whether Your discipline comes in a fierce firestorm or from the touch of a single live coal, burn away the impurities and make me holy. I thank You for loving me enough to make me all I was created to be in the heat of Your fire. Its touch on my lips may burn for a moment but will not consume me. You refine me to send me with Your message. Set my lips on fire wherever I go. Amen.

Also I heard the voice of the Lord, saying, Whom shall I send,
and who will go for us? Then said I, Here am I; send me.
ISAIAH 6:8

EVENING READING

Isaiah saw God in all His terrifying and majestic glory. When God asked whom He should send, Isaiah immediately and emphatically replied, "Here am I; send me." This is the only possible reaction of someone who has seen God enthroned on high. To know that God sits on His throne in victory should inspire us to respond to His call to go and spread His Gospel as enthusiastically and unhesitatingly as Isaiah did.

DAY 257

A Son Is Born

(ISAIAH 9:1–7)

❯❯❯❯❯ ❀ ❮❮❮❮❮

MORNING PRAYER

Lord God, Your names roll off my tongue as Handel's music resonates in my mind. Wonderful Counselor, Mighty God, Everlasting Father, Prince of Peace. But this passage also reminds me of the transformation Your coming made in my life, the salvation exchange: You replace dishonor with honor, shut out darkness with light, and fill me with life, joy, and freedom from oppression. You have put me under a rule of justice and righteousness. The more I mature in faith, the brighter Your light shines. I'm on my way to the eternal city where You are the light. Amen.

> LORD, what is man, that thou takest knowledge of him! or the
> son of man, that thou makest account of him! Man is like
> to vanity: his days are as a shadow that passeth away.
> PSALM 144:3–4

EVENING READING

Who are you that God should take notice of you? How is it that a life that is a mere shadow in the scheme of history could be intimately cared for by God? But He does care for you more than you even know. It is a remarkable and incomprehensible concept. If you could grasp how deeply God knows and loves you, would it change your life? We feel important if we know someone famous on earth whose life is of the same value as ours—how much more worthy should we feel that we know and are known by the almighty God? We should indeed be happy that God is our Lord.

ISAIAH 11–13 ❀ 2 CORINTHIANS 3 ❀ PSALM 145

Find Words
(PSALM 145)

⇾⇾⟩⟩⟩ ❀ ⟨⟨⟨⟨⇽

MORNING PRAYER ·

My mouth speaks in praise of You, oh Lord. Your wonders fill the accounts of my days. Forgive me when I allow foul talk or speech to cross my lips. When I speak of You, I never run out of news to report, good news to cheer and build people up. You are God my King. No matter how accurate my instruments, how precise my words, I fall short of measuring Your greatness, Your wonder, and Your splendor. Use me in my weakness. May I pass on the stories of Your goodness to others. May Your praise remain constantly in my mouth. Amen.

> *Seeing then that we have such hope,*
> *we use great plainness of speech.*
> 2 CORINTHIANS 3:12

EVENING READING ·

In Christ we have an unmatchable hope and a glorious assurance of eternal life. Because of this, we should be bold to speak of it. How can we keep such a gift to ourselves? Do you not feel sufficient enough to share the Gospel? The good news is that you aren't sufficient in yourself, which is why you must rely on the impassable sufficiency of God (2 Corinthians 3:5). It's through His power that you can have the boldness to share His Word.

All Good Gifts

(PSALM 146)

❧❧❧❧❧ ❀ ❦❦❦❦❦

MORNING PRAYER ·

My Lord and God, I am blessed. Whatever happiness, peace, and hope I have comes from You, the great I Am that Abraham and Moses served. How can I be anything but blessed when I can follow in their footsteps? I thank You that my days will unfold exactly as You order them to be. You are the Creator God, and You are forever faithful to Your people. This is why I ask You to uphold the cause of the oppressed and those who suffer, wherever they are. You love the righteous. You love me, and I giggle at the thought. The God who created everything sees me. You know me and love me still. Hallelujah and amen.

> *Which made heaven, and earth, the sea, and all that therein is: which keepeth truth for ever: which executeth judgment for the oppressed: which giveth food to the hungry. The LORD looseth the prisoners.*
> PSALM 146:6–7

EVENING READING ·

God's power, as demonstrated in His ability to create and sustain the entire universe, is incomparable to anything we know. But unlike so many humans who use power for personal gain or superiority, God uses His power to help the oppressed, release the prisoner, feed the hungry, and care for the orphan and widow. His power and justice are never separated from His love, kindness, and mercy.

Reconciliation

(2 CORINTHIANS 5)

⇒⇒⟩⟩⟩ ❀ ⟨⟨⟨⟨⇐

MORNING PRAYER ·

Heavenly Father, You have reconciled the world to Yourself in Your Son, Christ, and entrusted that message—more than a message, a ministry—to Your church. May we work for intentional reconciliation. May I speak and live this truth in every way to every person that I meet today. Send ministers of reconciliation, whether missionaries, residents, tourists, businessmen, or others, among people who don't know You. May a passion for reconciliation burn within Christians who encounter those who have rejected You. May Your new life be evident to all, and may they be prepared to give all honor to You. Amen.

> *For the love of Christ constraineth us; because we thus judge,*
> *that if one died for all, then were all dead: And that he died for all,*
> *that they which live should not henceforth live unto themselves,*
> *but unto him which died for them, and rose again.*
> 2 CORINTHIANS 5:14–15

EVENING READING ·

Paul told the Corinthians that the love of Christ constrained (or compelled) him. What does that look like for Christ's love to compel you? Every action would be inspired by the love of Christ. Every word would seek to disperse His love to others. Every prayer would be said in the light of our standing before God, which was secured by His sacrificial love. You truly would no longer live for yourself but rather for Him who gave up His life so that you might live.

Letter of Recommendation

(2 CORINTHIANS 6:3–10)

❧❧❧❧❧ ❁ ❧❧❧❧❧

MORNING PRAYER

Lord God, when I read Paul's summary of his ministry, I scratch my head. I don't understand the economy of Your kingdom. How is it a commendation to be regarded with dishonor, rejected as imposters? Paul contended that he was willing to be dismissed by the world to bring about the glorious news of Your kingdom. Then I think of people like Martin Luther King Jr. who were willing to be despised for the sake of peace. If great men have suffered for worldly peace, how much more should I risk my reputation and my finances on Your behalf? Not foolishly, but let me not hold back a penny or an ounce of myself worrying about others' opinions of me. Amen.

> *For he hath strengthened the bars of thy gates;*
> *he hath blessed thy children within thee.*
> PSALM 147:13

EVENING READING

The psalmist in today's reading praised God for having strengthened his gates. In order to allow them to open and close, the gates would inevitably be the weakest part of a fortified city. Therefore, it was essential that the gates be strong. Have you identified what the weakest points are in your defense against the enemy? Where is it in your life that sin creeps in the easiest? Ask God to strengthen your gates and to help you be proactive in protecting those particular areas.

Two Sides

(ISAIAH 24:14–17)

⤳⟩⟩⟩⟩ ❀ ⟨⟨⟨⟨⤸

MORNING PRAYER· ·

Lord God, shouts of joy come from the west. The east gives glory to You. The islands rise out of the sea to exalt Your name. Worldwide. You are glorified as the Righteous One. Praise rises to You from sunset to sunset, in waves as the earth whirls through its day. But sometimes those praises are reduced to a whisper in the din of sinful voices, when the darkness of men's hearts inundates my senses. Thank You that Your light breaks that darkness and I hear Your voice because I am Your sheep. May more and more people across the globe join in the song until at last no other sound is heard. Amen.

> *For godly sorrow worketh repentance to salvation not to*
> *be repented of: but the sorrow of the world worketh death.*
> 2 CORINTHIANS 7:10

EVENING READING ·

Grief and sorrow over sin is good so far as it leads to repentance. Understanding the weightiness of sin and how abhorrent it is to God is essential as you strive to banish it from your life. But sorrow over sin that leads to undue guilt is not healthy. As a redeemed child of God, holding on to the guilt of sin is essentially not to accept Christ's work on the cross for you. When you sin, grieve over it, repent, and then accept God's grace and forgiveness.

The Last Psalm

(PSALM 150)

>>>>> ❀ <<<<<

MORNING PRAYER

Almighty God, this is such a perfect psalm to end the Bible's hymnbook. May we praise You in Your sanctuary. May our praises echo from the heavens. Let us speak of Your power in action, of Your greatness beyond compare. May our voices, our instruments, our very bodies join together as one, praising You. Let everything on earth, from the rippling waterfall to trees whistling in the wind and rain pounding on the earth, bring glory to Your name. Let everything that has breath—a bee's buzz, a whale's song, an infant's cry—praise You. Amen.

*Let every thing that hath breath
praise the LORD. Praise ye the LORD.*
PSALM 150:6

EVENING READING

Psalm 150 is a glorious picture of how all of God's creation should be and how it will be one day. One day everything that has breath will praise the Lord. In the meantime, our praise of Him should fill our lives and spill over into the lives of others. He is entirely worthy of all our praise. He is worthy simply because of who He is—the great God above all gods. But He is also worthy because of the wonderful things He has done for us. Praise Him now and continue to praise Him until all the earth and the entire universe join in.

Cheerful Giving
(2 CORINTHIANS 9:6–8)

MORNING PRAYER

Lord Jesus, I thank You for people who exemplify cheerful givers, like George Müeller, Albert Schweitzer, and my daughter. Thank You for the joy of giving. Show me where and to whom and what to give. Let me give endlessly of nonmonetary gifts like prayer. But especially help me to give my money cheerfully. Forgive me when I'm stingy. Give me fiscal sense to give wisely. Yet let me not depend on "my" job or "my" bank account to tide me over. You will always make sure I have everything I need for every good work, including generous giving. Amen.

And therefore will the LORD wait, that he may be gracious unto you,
and therefore will he be exalted, that he may have mercy upon you:
for the LORD is a God of judgment: blessed are all they that wait for him.
ISAIAH 30:18

EVENING READING

Just as a loving parent will wait for a wayward child to behave, so too will God wait patiently to be gracious to you. He will not get fed up with you. You won't be able to try His patience beyond what He can handle. He desires that you walk with Him and keep His commandments. He will never give up on those who are His.

Making My Mind Obey

(2 Corinthians 10:5)

❧❧❧❧❧ ❀ ❦❦❦❦❦

MORNING PRAYER ·

All-wise God, thank You for addressing my doubts in the past. But my intellectual questions are only half of the problem. I fight to bring my thoughts into obedience when emotions and memories from my past attack, trying to take over how I think. The battle continues all day long. Satan wants to plant thoughts that are contrary to Your truth in my mind. Lift me high above the din of the arguments. Give me a voice to shout down falsehoods with sacrifices of praise. May I drown the false accusations and incorrect thoughts by hiding Your Word in my heart. Amen.

(For the weapons of our warfare are not carnal, but mighty through
God to the pulling down of strong holds;) Casting down imaginations,
and every high thing that exalteth itself against the knowledge of God,
and bringing into captivity every thought to the obedience of Christ.
2 CORINTHIANS 10:4–5

EVENING READING ·

So often our greatest struggles are against intangible things like our thought life or wayward desires. Fortunately, God has provided us weapons with divine power, capable of fighting the most insidious of enemies. Ask that God might help you take every thought captive in obedience to Christ—imagine how different (and more productive) your thought life would be! God is powerful enough even to conquer your most private thoughts of insecurity, pride, lust, or fear.

The Way of Holiness
(ISAIAH 35)

≈≫⟩⟩⟩ ❀ ⟨⟨⟨⟨≈

MORNING PRAYER ·

Lord God, You've set me and all Your people on the way of holiness. You strengthen my unfit, arthritic limbs and put on my walking shoes. It's time for me to get into shape. I want to be strong, not fearful, obeying Your command. I can't wait to see the wonders You will perform, both in the spiritual and in the natural realms. I look forward to seeing people with physical disabilities restored to full physical health. I want to travel the new earth after the wastelands of our planet pass away. Thank You for the redeemed who stroll by my side. Your gladness and joy rest on us as we walk hand in hand toward our eternal home. Amen.

> *If I must needs glory, I will glory of the things which concern*
> *mine infirmities. . . . And through a window in a basket*
> *was I let down by the wall, and escaped his hands.*
> 2 CORINTHIANS 11:30, 33

EVENING READING ·

Paul was not in the least concerned about keeping up personal appearances. In fact, if he were to boast, he would boast in the very things that most of us would desire to keep hidden. Embarrassing accounts of how he, the mighty apostle of God, had to be saved from situations in the most humble of ways were merely fodder for his message about God's power. Don't be afraid to tell the stories that make you "look bad" but showcase the goodness and power of God.

DAY 267

ISAIAH 37–38 ❀ 2 CORINTHIANS 12:1–10 ❀ PROVERBS 1:27–33

Glory in Weakness

(2 Corinthians 12:9–10)

>>>>> ❀ <<<<<

MORNING PRAYER

Omnipotent God, many times I've felt weak in the frailty of my humanity. This is one of those times. Instead of rejecting my weakness, teach me to rejoice because whatever I accomplish will come from You, not myself. There is no better position for me to be in. In this hour, when I own my faint and feeble nature, I also gain strength. For that reason, I will boast about my weaknesses so that any good that comes will point others to You. May I disappear completely, my life a trophy in the showcase of Your grace. Amen.

> *Whom hast thou reproached and blasphemed? and against whom*
> *hast thou exalted thy voice, and lifted up thine eyes on high?*
> *even against the Holy One of Israel.*
> Isaiah 37:23

EVENING READING

Those who reproach and revile God's people are really reproaching God Himself. Situations in which you are berated for being a Christian can make you feel very vulnerable and alone. But remember in those circumstances that God is standing right there beside you, bearing the revilement with you. Though you may feel like the target, it is really the Holy One of Israel that those people are pitting themselves against. It may be easy to scorn another human, but taunting the Maker of heaven and earth is never a good idea.

≽ DAY 268 ≼

Open for Business

(ISAIAH 40:28–29)

≥≫⟩⟩⟩ ❀ ⟨⟨⟨≪≤

MORNING PRAYER

Eternal, always-faithful God, what a promise You made for the times I feel forgotten or overlooked. You're not a "here today, gone tomorrow" kind of God. You don't say, "See you later," or hang a sign saying OUT TO LUNCH. You don't come and go. You're always open for business 24-7, 365 days a year, and You're always at peak performance. Your care doesn't change based on the time of day, the month or year. You don't need updates. You know all there is to know about everything. What an awesome God I serve! And You share all that energy and power and strength with me. Amen.

> *Behold, the Lord GOD will come with strong hand, and his arm shall rule for him: behold, his reward is with him, and his work before him. He shall feed his flock like a shepherd: he shall gather the lambs with his arm, and carry them in his bosom, and shall gently lead those that are with young.*
> ISAIAH 40:10–11

EVENING READING

There is a beautiful juxtaposition in Isaiah 40:10–11 that speaks clearly of God's character. Verse 10 depicts a strong warrior king who comes to rule the earth with a strong arm. Verse 11 completely changes imagery and speaks of a caring shepherd who carries the lambs in His arms and gently leads His sheep. We serve a God who is so powerful that He conquered death and evil but so good and loving that He gently leads and cares for us. In His mighty arms can be found true protection and blissful rest.

ISAIAH 41–42 ❀ GALATIANS 1 ❀ PROVERBS 2:16–22

Place of No Return

(PROVERBS 2:16–22)

❧❧❧❧❧ ❀ ❧❧❧❧❧

MORNING PRAYER ·

Heavenly Father, I tremble at these words: "Surely [his] house leads down to death" (Proverbs 2:18 NIV). How I thank You for keeping me from sexual impurity. But You know the temptations of my mind. I thank You for the glorious beauty of the marital relationship, for the picture of a man and woman unified in marriage, for its sheer joy. Guard my mind and heart for You, that You will be at the center of any friendship I have with a man. I pray also for others who are married, church leaders, families, and friends: Keep their bond strong. Keep them from falling into adultery, which can lead to death and destruction in marriages and families. Amen.

Thou whom I have taken from the ends of the earth, and called thee from the chief men thereof, and said unto thee, Thou art my servant; I have chosen thee, and not cast thee away. Fear thou not; for I am with thee: be not dismayed; for I am thy God: I will strengthen thee; yea, I will help thee; yea, I will uphold thee with the right hand of my righteousness. . . . For I the LORD thy God will hold thy right hand, saying unto thee, Fear not; I will help thee.
ISAIAH 41:9–10, 13

EVENING READING ·

God has chosen you. He set you aside as one of His children before the foundation of the world. There is nothing to fear when you grasp that your whole life was planned far in advance by a loving Father. And in those times when fear is too strong to hold at bay, He holds you by the hand to reassure and strengthen you. Listen as He says to you, "Fear not; I will help you."

New Road Ahead

(Isaiah 43:16–21)

❧❧❧❧❧ ❀ ❧❧❧❧❧

MORNING PRAYER· ·

Heavenly Father, I confess my tendency to dwell on the past, on the mistakes I made and the way I hurt myself and those I love. Transform the patterns of my mind. May I put those mistakes behind me, as far as the east is from the west. Open my eyes to the new road You are paving ahead. In the wilderness of life, it springs forth like a well-marked path through the forest. It will lead me from harm to Your good, perfect, pleasing will. May I follow Your lead by the light of Your Word. Amen.

Since thou wast precious in my sight,
thou hast been honourable, and I have loved thee:
therefore will I give men for thee, and people for thy life.
Isaiah 43:4

EVENING READING ·

Do you truly believe that you are precious in God's eyes? Do you believe that He loves you as fully as He says? Do you believe that He would go to the ends of the earth in order to bring you back? With the fallacy of love that we've all experienced in this world, it's sometimes easier not to believe that we can be perfectly and fully loved. And yet, your heavenly Father, who considers you precious, will prove His love for you as He ceaselessly seeks you to draw you to Himself.

Forever Family

(ISAIAH 45:22–24)

⇝⇝⟫⟫ ❀ ⟪⟪⇜⇜

MORNING PRAYER ·

Everlasting Father, You never take away Your promises. Your blessings on me today are due in part to a faithful ancestor of mine a thousand years ago. I thank You for that person's faithfulness, whoever they were. I find comfort in knowing You'll show similar favor to my descendants. You'll watch over them and correct them when they go astray. I pray that they'll live faithfully before You. How thankful I am for Your faithfulness. You haven't forgotten that squire in medieval England, that peasant listening to Saint Patrick, or perhaps even a Viking. You will remember all of us and one day return for us. Amen.

> *The LORD by wisdom hath founded the earth; by understanding hath he established the heavens. By his knowledge the depths are broken up, and the clouds drop down the dew.*
> PROVERBS 3:19–20

EVENING READING ·

The book of Proverbs has lots to say about wisdom—its value, how we should search for it, and how a wise person behaves. Why is wisdom so important? Because it is an attribute of God. In wisdom, God created the earth and established the universe. Attaining wisdom will make us more like God. To be more like God is truly of more value than any gold or jewels.

≥ DAY 272 ≤

Refine Me

(ISAIAH 48:10–11)

≥≫≫≫ ✿ ≪≪≪≤

MORNING PRAYER ·

Thank You, Lord, for testing and refining me instead of washing Your hands of me. Why did You choose such a fragile vessel? In faith I believe Your choice makes me worthy and capable. Forgive me for shaming You before others. You won't let anything take Your rightful place as Lord of my life. I praise You for Your discipline that comes from Your heart of love. When Your work is finished, I can join others in lifting up Your name above every name. Burn away my sin and impurities, that I may better reflect Your glory. Amen.

> *Stand now with thine enchantments, and with the multitude*
> *of thy sorceries, wherein thou hast laboured from thy youth;*
> *if so be thou shalt be able to profit, if so be thou mayest prevail.*
> ISAIAH 47:12

EVENING READING ·

The idols that we so foolishly cling to are no match for God. We work so hard to develop and protect our idols. We hold on to them as something precious. But there is no chance that any of those things could prevail against God. All our idols and foolish sins will be cast down before the throne of Christ, and we will have no answer as to why we exchanged the unmatchable glory of God for a filthy and worthless idol.

Engraving

(ISAIAH 49:18)

❧❧❧❧❧ ❀ ❦❦❦❦❦

MORNING PRAYER ·

Lord God, I got to hold my great-granddaughter for the first time yesterday. When her long fingers, short compared to mine, grip my hands, I feel a fierce love for this new person asleep in my arms. I can't imagine forgetting her or failing to do everything possible to help her. So how is it that I doubt, wondering if You have forgotten me? As incredible, as impossible, as it seems, You have engraved me on the palm on Your hands. I am etched on Your heart, Your favorite accessory. May I live and move in that confidence. Amen.

> *I, even I, am he that comforteth you: who art thou, that thou shouldest be afraid of a man that shall die, and of the son of man which shall be made as grass; And forgettest the Lord thy maker, that hath stretched forth the heavens, and laid the foundations of the earth; and hast feared continually every day because of the fury of the oppressor, as if he were ready to destroy? and where is the fury of the oppressor?*
> ISAIAH 51:12–13

EVENING READING ·

Why do we fear the power and opinions of man? We get so caught up with people pleasing and appearances that we forget the one whom we should actually fear—the one who has the power to destroy or sustain, to curse or bless. Humans are inherently mortal. God is everlasting. Whose side would you rather be on?

Childlessness

(GALATIANS 4:27)

>>>>>> ❁ <<<<<<

MORNING PRAYER

God of all comfort, there are few things more painful than the empty arms of a woman longing for a child. My arms ache for my daughter who died. I met a woman whose infant only lived for minutes, but we both felt as one. I think of those women who have not yet carried a child to term. For those who are unmarried and celibate, childless. That longing for motherhood can only come from You. But You don't leave us there. You bring us joy for sorrow, fullness for emptiness, an enlarged territory instead of narrow spaces—whether that comes by children or in our relationship with You or through a myriad of other ways. Amen.

Keep thy heart with all diligence;
for out of it are the issues of life.
PROVERBS 4:23

EVENING READING

Be diligent to guard your heart. Don't fill it with worthless lusts and empty entertainment. Be more concerned about your own heart than anyone else's. Hate your sins more than the sins of your friends or family. How easily we fall into busying ourselves with accusing others while our own hearts are harboring sin. Be diligent over your own heart—the life that will overflow from a well-kept heart will in turn bring others to Christ.

House of Prayer for the Nations

(ISAIAH 56:6–8)

⇒⟩⟩⟩⟩ ❀ ⟨⟨⟨⟨⇐

MORNING PRAYER

Father God, I thank You for gathering outsiders to Your holy mountain, that You welcome me to come and worship alongside Your holy people. May the news reach those who haven't received an invitation yet. Make the hearts of those who have rejected You tender. Bombard them with invitations time and time again, until the gathering is complete. I look forward to the day when all may know the God of the nations, the God of justice, salvation, and right. When You call us, may we gladly respond, accepting Your forgiveness and binding ourselves to You in Your great love. Amen.

Stand fast therefore in the liberty wherewith Christ hath made us free, and be not entangled again with the yoke of bondage.

GALATIANS 5:1

EVENING READING

Stand firm in the freedom that you have in Christ. In what areas of your life do you tend to slip into legalism or moralism? You cannot possibly earn your salvation. Christ's work alone is what grants you righteousness and salvation. If your equation for salvation is Christ plus anything else (good works, keeping the Ten Commandments, etc.), then you have lost your stand in Christ's freedom and have slipped into a false gospel. Our standing before God is based on a past action of Christ on the cross. Our obedience to God is an outworking of our gratefulness to Him for our salvation.

Sowing and Reaping

(GALATIANS 6:7–10)

⪢⪢⪢⪢ ❀ ⪡⪡⪡⪡⪡

MORNING PRAYER

Lord of the harvest, I thank You for rewarding the faithfulness of those who come to the nursing home where I live, teaching, loving, ministering. You have increased their flock with new people eager to learn and participate. I come back to You, pleading for your workers with willing hearts and hands to join their efforts. I pray that they will continue to sow without growing weary. May I follow their example, and Your command, to do good to all people, especially to believers who live in the nursing home with me. You are faithful, even here. Amen.

Is it not to deal thy bread to the hungry, and that thou bring the poor that are cast out to thy house? when thou seest the naked, that thou cover him; and that thou hide not thyself from thine own flesh? Then shall thy light break forth as the morning, and thine health shall spring forth speedily: and thy righteousness shall go before thee; the glory of the LORD shall be thy reward. Then shalt thou call, and the LORD shall answer; thou shalt cry, and he shall say, Here I am.
ISAIAH 58:7–9

EVENING READING

God promises to bless, heal, and answer us and to grant us righteousness when we feed the hungry, bring the homeless into our homes, and clothe the naked. God's love and care for the needy is impossible to miss while reading through the Bible. His heart is fully turned toward those who have no voice of their own. If this is where His heart is, isn't it where your heart should be as well?

The Year of the Lord's Favor

(ISAIAH 61)

MORNING PRAYER

Sovereign Lord, the greater my trouble—the more contempt hurled at me—the more fervent my prayer. In fact, teach me to shout for joy, because for every godly trouble on earth, there's increase and treasure in heaven. It can never be stolen or tarnished. Let all that is in me thank You when times grow dark, because that's where I see Your love and glory most clearly. The year of the Lord's favor—how I thank You that I live on this side of the cross in history. Clothe me in a garment of praise instead of a spirit of despair. Grow my life, branch by branch, until I am a tall oak in the garden of Your splendor. Amen.

> *According as he hath chosen us in him before the foundation of the*
> *world, that we should be holy and without blame before him in love:*
> *Having predestinated us unto the adoption of children by Jesus*
> *Christ to himself, according to the good pleasure of his will.*
> EPHESIANS 1:4–5

EVENING READING

God chose you as His child before the foundations of the world were set. He has ordained that you be holy and without blame before Him. He planned far ahead of your physical birth that you would be adopted as one of His children and fully invited into His family. He did all this simply because it pleased Him to do so. There is no ulterior motive or manipulation. A love this full and this pure is virtually impossible for us to comprehend but something for us to be grateful for every single day.

Changing Habits

(EPHESIANS 2)

❧❧❧ ❀ ❧❧❧

MORNING PRAYER

My Lord and Savior, I have a shameful past like everyone else. There was a time I gave into the cravings of the flesh, with its sinful desires. *But*—that glorious word—You wiped that away. The deed is done. Oh, make Your new life in me evident to all. Free me from that shame. Forgive me when I react in anger born out of past hostilities. Break down the walls I put in place to protect a frightened and helpless child. May I ever reach out from the position of Your peace and Your love and not from my pain. Amen.

> *That in the ages to come he might shew the exceeding riches*
> *of his grace in his kindness toward us through Christ Jesus.*
> EPHESIANS 2:7

EVENING READING

At the start of Ephesians 2 is a list of the things that God has done for you—loved you, made you alive, saved you, raised you up, and seated you with Christ. Why would He do all these things for you? Does He want something in return? The astounding and humbling answer comes in verse 7—He did all these things so that He might show you His grace and His kindness toward you. His desire is to shower you with love and grace. How undeserving we are to belong to a God who is so selflessly gracious to us.

One Hope

(EPHESIANS 4:4)

>>>>> ❀ <<<<<

MORNING PRAYER

Lord God, thank You for the hope I share with all Christians. One body, one Spirit, at birth. You gave me hope when You called me, a hope that I will know the Son of God in all His majesty and fullness and that I'll be unified with other Christians and with You. Let us exercise our gifts to build up one another. Use my gift of encouragement to share that hope, and may I receive what others have to share with me. Teach us not to neglect the times we are to gather together to give and receive. We are so much stronger together than standing alone. Amen.

> *And to know the love of Christ, which passeth knowledge,*
> *that ye might be filled with all the fulness of God.*
> EPHESIANS 3:19

EVENING READING

Paul prayed that the Ephesians would know the love of Christ that surpasses knowledge. He wanted them to know the unknowable. Christ's love for us is so vast that our finite minds cannot grasp it. But to know even the smallest drop of this unknowable love would be life changing. Ask God to begin to help you comprehend His incomprehensible love.

⇒ DAY 280 ⇐

Speak the Truth in Love
(EPHESIANS 4:22–27)

⇒⇒⟩⟩⟩ ❀ ⟨⟨⟨⟨⇐

MORNING PRAYER ·

Lord Jesus, clean my vessel, my being inside and out, today. Wash away the stench of deceitful desires. Fill my mind with a new attitude so that I might pour out new wine, righteous and holy. When something comes up today that frustrates or angers me, let me release it right then. Replace that resentment with insight and compassion for the one who has hurt me. Let me speak truth in love, seeking to build others up and not to tear them down. Make love the constant that quickly smothers sparks of anger. May I learn about trusting others by trusting You. Amen.

> *Before I formed thee in the belly I knew thee; and before*
> *thou camest forth out of the womb I sanctified thee,*
> *and I ordained thee a prophet unto the nations.*
>
> JEREMIAH 1:5

EVENING READING ·

God knew the entire plan He had for Jeremiah's life before he was even born. He knew him better than anyone would know him before he was even conceived. He was completely sovereign over his life. He is completely sovereign over yours as well. The same care with which He formed Jeremiah in the womb He used to form you. Take courage. God is fully aware of the circumstances in your life—He knew about them before they had even happened. You don't have to fill Him in or catch Him up—He is the perfect one to go to with your fears and petitions.

Breaking Up the Ground

(JEREMIAH 4:3–4)

⋙❀⋘

MORNING PRAYER

Lord God, how am I supposed to apply these verses? Am I to break up the sins in my heart into tiny pieces? If people could do that on their own, Jesus wouldn't have had to die. Maybe it's more like Hebrews 12, where I'm told to remove everything that distracts me and leads me to sin. Or maybe You want to soften the hardness of my heart so that I may choose to believe and live. You're there, rooting for me, but You don't decide for me. May I use the rake of Your Word to crisscross the soil of my heart, digging up hidden thorns and rocks, so that I can produce a more fruitful crop. Amen.

And have no fellowship with the unfruitful
works of darkness, but rather reprove them.
EPHESIANS 5:11

EVENING READING

Don't even let yourself toy with the works of darkness. They are entirely unfruitful, worthless, and destructive. Instead of ignoring or trying to hide the sin in your life, expose it. Sin is strongest in the darkness; being exposed to the light will cause it to shrivel and weaken. Talk to other trustworthy Christians who can help you throw off the load of sin so that you can spend your time and effort pursuing works of righteousness.

Children and Parents
(EPHESIANS 6:1–3)

⇻⇻⇻⇻⇻ ✿ ⇺⇺⇺⇺⇺

MORNING PRAYER ·

Heavenly Father, before all societies and government came into being, You instituted the family—husband, wife, children. It's meant to be one of Your best gifts to us, but too often things go wrong. I no longer have a husband or small children, but I pray for those who do, starting with my own son. May their offspring obey their parents as children and honor them as adults. I pray for fathers, that they won't infuriate their children but teach them gently, training them in Your ways. Although Paul only mentions fathers, I pray the same things for mothers. May homes be filled with Your love, and not anger or abuse. Amen.

For we wrestle not against flesh and blood, but against principalities,
against powers, against the rulers of the darkness of this world,
against spiritual wickedness in high places.
EPHESIANS 6:12

EVENING READING ·

How often do you consider the spiritual warfare that is raging at this very moment in the world? While it would be unfruitful to fixate on these thoughts, it is important to keep in mind the gravity of the battle at hand. Use prayer as a weapon against the powers and rulers of the darkness in this world. Work to spread God's light to conquer the darkness.

Paul's Prayer for the Philippians
(PHILIPPIANS 1:4–11)

≈≈⟩⟩⟩ ❀ ⟨⟨⟨≈

MORNING PRAYER

Lord Jesus, what comfort I take in Paul's confidence. You began the good work in me, and You will finish it when I see You. I would certainly fail on my own. And between now and then, I ask that my love will abound both in wisdom and in depth of insight. May I gain not only head knowledge but also understanding. May I put Your principles into practice. I pray the same for others who believe in You. Lead us into purity, blamelessness, and holiness. May all that knowledge permeate our lives, increasing the crop of righteousness to the glory and praise of God. Amen.

Being confident of this very thing, that he which hath begun a good work in you will perform it until the day of Jesus Christ.
PHILIPPIANS 1:6

EVENING READING

God is a promise keeper. He has proven Himself as such throughout history. Because of this, you can trust Him fully to fulfill His promise that He will perfect the good work He has started in you. This means that no sin, guilt, or apathy can keep Him from working in your life. Thoughts of your own worthlessness have no room or authority in your heart and mind. God will make perfect His work that He started in you—you can count on it.

JEREMIAH 7:27–9:16 ✿ PHILIPPIANS 1:27–2:18 ✿ PROVERBS 8:12–21

Spiritual MRSA

(JEREMIAH 8:20–22)

≈≫≫≫ ✿ ≪≪≪≈

MORNING PRAYER

Lord, how foolish the Israelites were, to seek peace at any price instead of going to You to cure their incurable wound. How foolish I am at times, when I reject Your good and perfect will and instead look for healing elsewhere. I keep holding out a palm branch, seeking allies, but my choices have turned the ground beneath my feet into quicksand. Forgive me. Turn my heart to You. Open my eyes to Your commands. Instead of seeking help elsewhere, may I turn to my balm in Gilead. Let me meditate on Your precepts. Show me how to put them into practice. May I commit them to memory, that they will spring to mind when I am tempted to go in the wrong direction. I want to be a faithful resident in Your kingdom. Amen.

Do all things without murmurings and disputings: That ye may be blameless and harmless, the sons of God, without rebuke, in the midst of a crooked and perverse nation, among whom ye shine as lights in the world.
PHILIPPIANS 2:14–15

EVENING READING

You have daily opportunities to shine God's light into this crooked and perverse world. Something as simple as doing everything without grumbling or complaining makes it apparent to the watching world that there is something different about you. Conversely, to fit right into the world with its grumblings and disputes does absolutely nothing for the cause of Christ. Seek ways to be a light. Let the world know through the way you live that you are a child of God.

JEREMIAH 9:17–11:17 ❀ PHILIPPIANS 2:19–30 ❀ PROVERBS 8:22–36

Reasons to Boast

(JEREMIAH 9:23–24)

❧ ❀ ❧

MORNING PRAYER

Lord God Almighty, it's okay to boast, but I have to carefully consider what's worth shouting about. If I think I'm smart, wise, strong, or rich—even if it's true—those attributes don't come from me. They are from You, Your good gifts. I struggle with how to share my good news without feeling like I'm bragging. But may I gladly share what You've taught me about Yourself. I have learned a small part of who You are. Your kindness, justice, and righteousness dictate all You do. That's how I live and thrive. They are Your delight; make them my joy and my boast. Amen.

Thus saith the Lord, Let not the wise man glory in his wisdom, neither let the mighty man glory in his might, let not the rich man glory in his riches: but let him that glorieth glory in this, that he understandeth and knoweth me, that I am the Lord which exercise lovingkindness, judgment, and righteousness, in the earth: for in these things I delight, saith the Lord.
JEREMIAH 9:23–24

EVENING READING

In what do you find your worth? In your strength? Athletic ability? Looks? Social status? Good works? Knowledge? Though all these things can be gifts from God, the only thing in which you should truly glory is knowing the Lord. When thinking about the blessings in your life, does knowing God typically make it on the list? It is a privilege beyond anything else we can experience on this earth. Work to be defined more by how well you know your Savior than by anything else.

Wisdom's Pillars

(PROVERBS 9:1–6)

>>>>>> ❀ <<<<<<

MORNING PRAYER

Lord God, I'm standing in the house with wisdom's pillars and I'm not sure what I'm looking at. She encourages me to seek insight rather than to live according to what makes sense in my own eyes. You don't want me to ask for wisdom from my acquaintances. Your Word is the banquet You have spread open for me. Each bite increases my insight; each taste presents new truth. You have so very much to teach me. I can never eat too much, and there is a continual supply. This is where I should come to feast. Amen.

And be found in him, not having mine own righteousness,
which is of the law, but that which is through the faith
of Christ, the righteousness which is of God by faith.
PHILIPPIANS 3:9

EVENING READING

The "famous" followers of Christ are not perfect people. Rather, they are people who are especially aware of their imperfections and who, because of their flaws, learn to rely more on Christ. They know that even when they stumble, they are covered by Christ's righteousness.

⇒ DAY 287 ⇐

JEREMIAH 14–15 ❁ PHILIPPIANS 4 ❁ PROVERBS 9:7–18

Peace in Chaos

(PHILIPPIANS 4:7)

⇒⋙ ❁ ⋘⇐

MORNING PRAYER·· ·

Prince of Peace, You know how interruptions disturb my serenity. I like things in the order I prefer. How often that fails to happen. Guard my heart and mind with Your peace. May I rest and wait in quiet, whether the hour is early or late, whether I am longing for the arrival of sleep or bemoaning the lack of promised human help. May I remain happy and content, calm and not flustered when prolonged delay becomes a flurry of activity. Have I made time my god? Forgive me. Let me not allow time to be my taskmaster, but my slave to put to work for You. Amen.

Be careful for nothing; but in every thing by prayer and supplication with thanksgiving let your requests be made known unto God.

PHILIPPIANS 4:6

EVENING READING ·

Philippians 4:6 is not just a pleasant suggestion or a quaint platitude. It is a command—do not be anxious. Bring your prayers and supplications to God. Paul could give this command because he was absolutely certain that worrying was of no benefit. He was also absolutely sure that no anxiety-producing situation was too big or difficult for God to handle. To be anxious is to question that God is doing the right thing in your life. There is, therefore, zero reason to be anxious because He is undoubtedly in control and doing the right thing. So, instead of worrying, carry your burdens to Him and drop them at His feet.

A Deceitful Heart

(JEREMIAH 17:7–10)

>>>》》 ❀ 《《《<

MORNING PRAYER· ·

Lord God, these words simultaneously offer hope and fear. If I trust in You, I am blessed. But when You search my heart, will You find deceit? Do I say I trust You but instead rely on what I can see and touch? Am I underhanded with You, claiming to follow You while going my own way? Forgive me. Thank You for replacing my incurable heart with the new one given to me at salvation, that I may serve You with all that I am. Only when I place 100 percent of my confidence in You will You plant me like a tree by streams of water. Only Your pure water will produce constant, unhindered growth. Amen.

> *For this cause we also, since the day we heard it, do not cease to pray for you, and to desire that ye might be filled with the knowledge of his will in all wisdom and spiritual understanding; That ye might walk worthy of the Lord unto all pleasing, being fruitful in every good work, and increasing in the knowledge of God.*
> COLOSSIANS 1:9–10

EVENING READING ·

Paul did not cease to pray for the Colossians that they would be filled with knowledge and wisdom and that they would "walk worthy of the Lord" in good works. Is there anything that you care about enough to never cease to pray for it? Maybe start with this prayer in Colossians 1.

JEREMIAH 18:1–20:6 ❀ COLOSSIANS 1:24–2:15 ❀ PROVERBS 10:6–14

Stirring Up Conflict

(PROVERBS 10:12)

MORNING PRAYER

Lord God, I'd rather skip this verse. I hate conflict, my part in it, how my stomach churns and I wince at the approach of my opponent. How easily I go from resolving differences to sinning against my fellow man and You. If hatred stirs up conflict, then it starts in my mind and heart. I feel like I've been wronged, and often I have valid reasons. But You expect better of me. You invite me to cover other people's offenses with love instead of responding with hate. You provided the perfect example. Make me like You. Where there is hatred, let me sow love. Amen.

> *Blotting out the handwriting of ordinances that was against us,*
> *which was contrary to us, and took it out of the way, nailing*
> *it to his cross; and having spoiled principalities and powers,*
> *he made a shew of them openly, triumphing over them in it.*
> COLOSSIANS 2:14–15

EVENING READING

Christ made a public spectacle of the devil on the cross. The devil must have thought that he had finally triumphed over God as he saw Christ hanging on the cross. Little did he know that in that moment was his greatest loss. The curtain that had separated God from His people was torn in two, the dead were raised, and the very earth quaked under the weight of the victory of Christ. On that cross, any hold that the devil had over us was destroyed as the decree that documented our debt was nailed to the cross and erased by Christ's blood. In Christ's death and resurrection was His and our victory.

JEREMIAH 20:7–22:19 ❀ COLOSSIANS 2:16–3:4 ❀ PROVERBS 10:15–26

Depression

(JEREMIAH 20:14–18)

>>>>> ❀ <<<<<

MORNING PRAYER

My loving Father, I thank You that Jeremiah's deep emotions are included in Your Word, as painful as they are. How apt I am to think that when I'm depressed, I must be doing something wrong. That You can't use me until I get over it. Here's the example of a prophet, the one You used to confront Judah during the final years of her downward spiral. How much truth would be lost to the world without his book of prophecy? And yet he felt worthless. Like You did for Jeremiah, do also for me: keep me going even when I don't feel it in my heart. You are always able, even when I wish I were someone, anyone, else. Amen.

> *He judged the cause of the poor and needy; then it was*
> *well with him: was not this to know me? saith the LORD.*
> JEREMIAH 22:16

EVENING READING

What is it to know God? God said that King Josiah knew Him because he pled the cause of the poor and needy. We could probably think of far more glamorous ways to know God. And yet, this is what God Himself says it means to know Him. Could His heart for those in need be any more clear? And could His call for you to minister to the poor and needy be any more obvious?

A New Wardrobe

(COLOSSIANS 3:12–13)

⇒⇒⟩⟩⟩ ❀ ⟨⟨⟨⟨⟵

MORNING PRAYER

Lord God, the next time I go shopping for new clothes, let me remember this list from Paul. May I be more concerned about expanding my spiritual wardrobe to accommodate my new self than purchasing new outfits for my body. May I choose compassion, kindness, humility, gentleness, and patience as staples. None of those come naturally to me, Lord, but they are mine because You are in me. Add Your love and forgiveness as the necessary accessories that will bind the church together in unity. Choose my clothing and dress me in kingdom fashions. Amen.

> *And let the peace of God rule in your hearts, to the which*
> *also ye are called in one body; and be ye thankful.*
> COLOSSIANS 3:15

EVENING READING

"Let the peace of God rule in your hearts." You are not called to "make" the peace of God rule in your heart or even to "ask for" it. Rather, you only need to let it rule. God's peace already dwells in your heart. Stop trying to anxiously figure out your life, and instead, let His peace rule your every thought and action. Don't allow any room for doubt or fear to usurp the throne in your heart.

Sent Away for My Own Good

(JEREMIAH 24:4–7)

≽≫≫≫ ❀ ≪≪≪≼

MORNING PRAYER

Lord, did men like Daniel, Ezekiel, and Mordecai realize they had been sent away from Israel for their good? You protected them from the desolation of Judah's final days and kept them from annihilation. You sent them to a place where they would prosper and to a king who was sympathetic to their faith. There, and back in Israel, You wanted to build them up and give them hearts to know You. Maybe that's why You turned me aside from the plans I believed You had for me and led me elsewhere, to my place of exile. Here You have prospered me and given me friends and a ministry I never expected. Thank You. Amen.

> *And I will give them an heart to know me, that I am the LORD:*
> *and they shall be my people, and I will be their God:*
> *for they shall return unto me with their whole heart.*
> JEREMIAH 24:7

EVENING READING

God gives you a heart to know Him. On your own you would be helpless in seeking out God. But He desires that you know Him, and He does not hide from you. He has given you all that you need to know Him. The Lord controls the hearts of everyone on this earth and can turn them wherever He chooses. If your heart is His, it always will be.

JEREMIAH 26–27 ✿ 1 THESSALONIANS 1:1–2:8 ✿ PROVERBS 11:12–21

Faith, Hope, and Love at Work
(1 Thessalonians 1:2–3)

MORNING PRAYER·

God my Father, what do people think of when my name comes to mind? Oh, to have a testimony such as the church at Thessalonica had. May others remember my work produced by faith. May any good I do, any words I write, speak of You and all You have done and not of me and all I have done. May my labor be prompted, not by duty or selfishness, but by Your love flowing through me. When I am called to endure—which in a sense is every day until I get to heaven—may hope inspire me. In work, in labor, in endurance, keep my eye on the prize of living in You. Amen.

> *A talebearer revealeth secrets: but he that is*
> *of a faithful spirit concealeth the matter.*
> PROVERBS 11:13

EVENING READING

How many grudges, arguments, and lost relationships could have been avoided by concealing a matter? Gossip is often used to allay our own insecurities. If we can just get someone else to look bad, we assume that we'll look so much better. There are much more productive ways of dealing with insecurities. Dwell on how much you, as an image bearer, are loved by your Creator. And dwell even more on how much everyone around you is also highly valuable simply for bearing the image of their Father. Be a secret keeper and not a talebearer.

Finding God

(JEREMIAH 29:11–13)

❧❧❧❧ ❀ ❧❧❧❧

MORNING PRAYER ·

Lord God, You want to be found. If I seek Your face with all my heart, I will find You. It's like following a maze and catching glimpses of You each step of the way. Each one shows me more. Even when I'm in heaven, where You are the light and I am worshipping before Your throne, I'll rejoice in spending eternity coming to know You in all Your fullness. Because I have seen You only in part, I only comprehend a small portion of Your plan. You say You have given me new hope and a future. I accept Your promise by faith. I thank You for what I have already seen of You. Amen.

And the Lord make you to increase and abound in love one toward another, and toward all men, even as we do toward you: To the end he may stablish your hearts unblameable in holiness before God, even our Father, at the coming of our Lord Jesus Christ with all his saints.
1 THESSALONIANS 3:12–13

EVENING READING ·

Paul prayed that the Thessalonians' love would increase for each other and for all people. Why? So that God would establish their hearts as blameless and holy at the coming of Christ. Love for one another is so central to the message of the Gospel. This is not a surface love that allows others to do whatever they want as long as it makes them happy, even if it's ultimately detrimental. Rather, it's a love that encourages and spurs each other on to live a blameless and holy life. How often do you think about the people you love standing in judgment before a holy God? Would that perspective change the way you love them here on earth?

Saving Lives

(PROVERBS 11:30)

>>>>> ❀ <<<<<

MORNING PRAYER

Heavenly Father, what a foolish, self-serving person I can be. I rejoice that I am a living tree growing by the stream, for the fruit that grows on my branches. And I do rejoice in the fruit You give me—abundant fruit with a heavenly flavor that can only come from You. But that fruit isn't meant for me alone. You give it to me to share. If I'm planted by Your stream, if I'm wise in how I prune and fertilize, through me You'll save lives. I'll minister to here-and-now needs. I'll also point the lost to You, their Savior. Give me the wisdom to know how You want me to reach out. Amen.

> *The Lord hath appeared of old unto me, saying,*
> *Yea, I have loved thee with an everlasting love:*
> *therefore with lovingkindness have I drawn thee.*
> JEREMIAH 31:3

EVENING READING

Even when God reprimands and punishes His children, He still loves them. In fact, it's because He loves His children that He rebukes them. But no matter what trials He may bring you through, His love is everlasting and therefore will not cease or fail you. With loving-kindness He will draw you in, and one day you will see the clearest evidence of His love threading all the way through your life, both in the trials and in the joys.

A Timeless Covenant

(JEREMIAH 31:31–36)

>>>>> ❀ <<<<<

MORNING PRAYER ·

Everlasting Father and Prince of Peace, oh, what a joy to read the promise and know I received a new covenant in Your Son. You have remade me, a dwelling place for Your Spirit. I don't have to ask someone else to explain it, because You make it clear. I'm also in covenant with Your people, the community of believers, yet Your plan for me doesn't rest on what happens to my spouse, child, or neighbor. You have placed Your will in my mind that I may remember it and written it on my heart that I may obey. While my body will one day crumble into dust, Your covenant with me will remain strong and unbreakable. Amen.

Faithful is he that calleth you, who also will do it.
1 THESSALONIANS 5:24

EVENING READING ·

We all know the feeling of being let down, of watching promises be broken, of seeing expectations shattered. In this life we can expect to be disappointed and hurt. This is why it is so important that we have a God who will never fail us. He is perfectly and unwaveringly faithful. What He has promised to do He will do. No exceptions. It's in the chaos and uncertainty of this world that we begin to more fully appreciate the steadfastness of God.

It's a God Thing

(JEREMIAH 33:6–9)

❧⟫⟫⟫ ❀ ⟪⟪⟪❦

MORNING PRAYER ·

Lord God, no wonder You told Jeremiah that You were doing wonderful things in answer to his prayer. Like me, his petitions focused on his needs. You answered his prayer with tremendous promises. You would bring the Jews back to the land, to prosper them, if only they would obey You. You offered to restore, heal, and rebuild with peace, security, and forgiveness. But all those things had a single purpose: to glorify You. The transformation brought You not only praise and honor, but also renown and joy. It caused people from across the globe to seek You. You share the joy of restoring the praise of human voices with me. Lord, whatever good happens to me, let me turn it back to You. Amen.

> *Call unto me, and I will answer thee, and show thee*
> *great and mighty things, which thou knowest not.*
> JEREMIAH 33:3

EVENING READING ·

God promises that if you call on Him, He will answer you. This in itself is a remarkable promise that the God of the universe will always answer you when you call on Him. But He doesn't just promise to give a quick answer and then move on before you take up too much of His time. On the contrary, He will invest in you, guide and teach you, and show you great and mighty things. The amount of time and energy that God chooses to put into such insignificant creatures as ourselves is truly breathtaking.

⇌ DAY 298 ⇌

Peace at All Times

(2 THESSALONIANS 3:16)

❖

MORNING PRAYER ·

Lord of lords and Prince of Peace, I pray You will spread Your peace at all times and in every way. I want a perfect personal peace, but I pray even more for my community of faith. You are with all of us. Your grace lies on us. You are unchangeable. So how is it we find so much to disagree about? Let me seek that peace for myself and for others. Let us make harmony our goal daily, especially in times of potential strife and even when the battle rages. May You give wholeness to us in every way, free from war and disturbance. Amen.

But ye, brethren, be not weary in well doing.
2 THESSALONIANS 3:13

EVENING READING ·

Do not grow weary in doing good. Doing good should not just be something on the side. It should be a lifestyle, something that defines who you are. The power of a kind word, a listening ear, or time taken out of your day for someone else should not be underestimated. Be hospitable. Reach out to the lonely and needy. Listen to the grieving. Serve as Christ served while He walked among us.

JEREMIAH 36:11–38:13 ❀ 1 TIMOTHY 1:1–17 ❀ PROVERBS 13:1–4

Pursuing Good or Bad

(PROVERBS 13:2–3)

⟫⟫⟫⟫ ❀ ⟪⟪⟪⟪

MORNING PRAYER

Lord God, I'm gaining a greater appreciation for Solomon's commonsense couplets. He packs in so much! And he doesn't always make the obvious connection. In today's passage, he doesn't say the opposite of good things is the lack of them. Instead, he expresses the results of unrighteousness: the unfaithful have an appetite for violence. How ugly. My heart's desires, left unchecked, will lead me to selfish, demanding, angry thoughts that tend toward violence in what I say and do. Rather, teach me to be wise, to seek righteousness, to protect my lips, that I may preserve life and not destroy it. Replace any angry thoughts within me with Your love and peace. Amen.

He that keepeth his mouth keepeth his life:
but he that openeth wide his lips shall have destruction.

PROVERBS 13:3

EVENING READING

It's no mistake that in several places in the Bible emphasis is put on the dangers of what you say. Would you have fewer regrets in life had you faithfully kept your mouth as Solomon advises in Proverbs? Life is the outcome for those who are wise and uplifting with their words. But destruction waits for those who use their words carelessly.

JEREMIAH 38:14–40:6 ❀ 1 TIMOTHY 1:18–3:13 ❀ PROVERBS 13:5–13

Then There's Pride

(PROVERBS 13:10)

>>>>> ❀ <<<<<

MORNING PRAYER ·

Wonderful Counselor, You know how I've struggled my whole life with wanting to be proven right. I've never thought of that as pride, but it certainly leads to strife. Forgive me. I thank You for the maturity to accept others' theological and ideological beliefs. Teach me that same wisdom in my daily life, especially in the circumstances I live in. May I listen more than I speak, that I may learn from the wisdom of others. Make me more eager to gather wisdom than to spread it, for my wisdom is no wisdom at all unless it comes from You. If I boast, let it be that I know You, the One true God. Amen.

There is that maketh himself rich, yet hath nothing:
there is that maketh himself poor, yet hath great riches.
PROVERBS 13:7

EVENING READING ·

Where does your wealth lie? Are you making yourself rich on things that amount to nothing? Or are you in possession of greater riches than this world could ever offer? The treasure that will last is your relationship with God and your investment in other people for the kingdom. These riches are those that are stored up in heaven. Everything else cannot come with you. Invest in the riches that will last into eternity.

In Training

(1 TIMOTHY 4:6–10)

❧❧❧ ❀ ❦❦❦

MORNING PRAYER

Lord Jesus, what a difference in priorities between what Paul advocates and what we hear today. Physical regimens? Useful but not as important as godliness. Seeking God offers profit in every area of my life, including the physical, both in this world and the next. It's a good investment—give me the eyes to see what a blessing it is. Keep me from being sidetracked by myths and old wives' tales. Fill my mind with Your truth. If my life isn't godly, if it doesn't measure up to what I say, then no one will listen to my words. Because of my hope in You, I labor and strive toward godliness. Amen.

For bodily exercise profiteth little: but godliness is
profitable unto all things, having promise of the
life that now is, and of that which is to come.
1 TIMOTHY 4:8

EVENING READING

Physical exercise is healthy and good but is only profitable in this lifetime. Spiritual exercise is profitable not only in this lifetime but in the one to come. Put the same effort into spiritual fitness as an Olympian would into physical fitness. Set aside time each morning for "training." Meditate on God's Word throughout the day. Recite God's Word to yourself as you fall asleep.

How to Love My Children
(PROVERBS 13:22)

>>>>>> ❀ <<<<<

MORNING PRAYER ·

Heavenly Father, the One who also cares for us like a mother, how I thank You for Your parenting guidance. My children are grown, but there never comes a time when I stop being a mother, in the unique role that grandparents play. What better incentive to pursue righteousness than to know it will bless my grandchildren? Let me be thoughtful about what kind of riches I am storing away for them to receive and to remember me by. Let me set a good example of faith, love, and life. If they follow in my footsteps, may they follow You. Amen.

But she that liveth in pleasure is dead while she liveth.

1 TIMOTHY 5:6

EVENING READING ·

Are you giving in to a sin that is killing you even while you live? God has promised you abundant life; don't throw that away for something that will only deaden your soul. Though we like to think that sin is a private matter, it almost inevitably affects more than just ourselves. Don't poison yourself and slowly suffocate the spirits of those around you for something worthless. Ask the giver of life to take away your desire for sin and in its place give you an all-consuming desire for Him.

Escaping with My Life

(JEREMIAH 45:5)

❧❧❧❧❧ ❀ ❦❦❦❦❦

MORNING PRAYER ·

Heavenly Father, it sounds like Baruch dreamed of great things. I know I do. I want a comfortable life, with my physical needs met. I long to see the work I do for the kingdom reach a large number of people, and so I fail to see the individuals in the crowd. Humble me; teach me to be satisfied with the small things. Let me not expect to escape disaster when it falls on the city where I live, the place where I work, on my nation. I thank You that in the worst circumstances, You promise to deliver me. I will survive. How foolish I am to want more when I see people falling on every side. Amen.

But godliness with contentment is great gain. For we brought
nothing into this world, and it is certain we can carry nothing out.
And having food and raiment let us be therewith content.
1 TIMOTHY 6:6–8

EVENING READING ·

Paul's perspective on contentment is an excellent one. Why would we desire for more than we have when we are fully aware that just as we brought nothing into this world, we can certainly take nothing out of it? Our simple sustenance and clothing is all that we really need. The rest of what we have is a blessing and a gift from God. Be grateful for what God has given you, but hold on to your worldly possessions with a loose hand, for the seed of discontent quickly grows into bitterness.

Second-Generation Christians

(2 TIMOTHY 1:3–8)

>>>>> ❀ <<<<<

MORNING PRAYER ·

Lord Jesus, I'm so thankful that the faith I received from my mother now burns brightly in my son. How Lois and Eunice must have rejoiced in Timothy. As beautiful as the legacy of faith in a family is, that flame is different for someone who is the first in their family to be saved. Forgive me when I allow other things, like timidity and fear, to smother the flame and the gifts You want to light with it. When I allow insecurity to hold me back, fill me with power, love, and self-discipline. Let me jump at the chance to share the Gospel. Amen.

> *But is now made manifest by the appearing of our*
> *Saviour Jesus Christ, who hath abolished death, and hath*
> *brought life and immortality to light through the gospel.*

> 2 TIMOTHY 1:10

EVENING READING ·

Christ abolished death, having completely decimated it when He rose from the dead. Covered in His blood shed for you, death cannot touch you either. This means that you are immortal until the day that God has long ago appointed for you to go home to Him. And even then, death is nothing to fear, merely a necessary doorway into life everlasting—a passage through which Christ will walk with you as He has already walked before.

Starting Over

(JEREMIAH 50:4–5)

❧❀☙

MORNING PRAYER

Oh Lord my Guide, I come to You, seeking You, sadness in my heart for the neglected days, thankful for fresh health and alertness. Thank You for renewing Your covenant with me, not because You had forgotten it, but because I had forgotten You. I kneel before You, acknowledging Your gracious provision, confessing my sin, asking You to cleanse and renew me. May I not go astray, but instead seek Your guidance at every twist in the road ahead. Forgive me when I do stray and bring me back. Thank You for Your eternal embrace. Amen.

> *If we believe not, yet he abideth faithful:*
> *he cannot deny himself.*
> 2 TIMOTHY 2:13

EVENING READING

Thank God that our lack of faith and obedience doesn't affect Him. Even when we are unfaithful and stumble badly, God remains entirely faithful and secure. Our sins do not mar Him since they are now and evermore carried in the scars of Jesus. For our sins Christ was sacrificed. By His wounds we are forgiven. Because God cannot deny Himself, this sacrifice was necessary. But because God is merciful beyond anything we deserve, He gave His Son in our place.

Small Stuff
(PROVERBS 14:29)

MORNING PRAYER

Oh Lord, I need this one today. Make me as slow to anger as You are, that I may mine the ores of Your understanding and compassion. How can I claim to know You and Your Word if I lose my patience easily? It makes me think of the saying "Don't fret the small stuff, and it's all small stuff." Compared to the grandeur of Your plan, and with the understanding that nothing happens to me without Your knowledge, I can accept what is, showing patience, waiting for You to fulfill Your will. Keep me from folly, and let me trust in You. Amen.

> *Their Redeemer is strong; the LORD of hosts is his name:*
> *he shall throughly plead their cause, that he may give*
> *rest to the land, and disquiet the inhabitants of Babylon.*
> JEREMIAH 50:34

EVENING READING

Your Redeemer is strong; the LORD of hosts is his name. There is no shortcoming on your part that He can't fill. There is no fear that He can't conquer. There is no wound that He can't heal. There is no grief that He can't assuage. There is no mourning that He can't turn into dancing. This is your God. He pleads your cause. Rest in Him.

The Two-Sided Tongue

(PROVERBS 15:1–7)

＞＞＞＞＞ ❀ ＜＜＜＜＜

MORNING PRAYER ·

God who spoke the world into being, You have given great power to the tongue. Forgive me when I abuse that power. Cleanse and renew me when I stir up anger and crush spirits with harsh words. Correct my foolish speaking. In its place give me a gentle spirit to respond to anger. May I relay Your wisdom and not my own folly. Let my speech soothe the spirits of those in despair, offering the shade of the tree of life. May I speak of what is upright and true and know when to be silent. Amen.

> *Notwithstanding the Lord stood with me, and strengthened me;*
> *that by me the preaching might be fully known, and that all the*
> *Gentiles might hear: and I was delivered out of the mouth of the lion.*
> 2 TIMOTHY 4:17

EVENING READING ·

Paul recounted one of many times that the Lord stood by him. Christ stands by His people even though no one stood by Him in His hour of need. The abandonment and loneliness He felt on the cross is a grief and a pain that we can never imagine—nor will we ever have to since He bore it for us. We will never be forsaken, because He was. We will never be alone, because He was. We will never bear the just wrath of God, because He did. You can be confident that Christ will always stand by you because He does so based on no merit of your own.

It's Not Worth It

(PROVERBS 15:16–18)

❧❧❧❧❧ ❀ ❧❧❧❧❧

MORNING PRAYER ·

Lord God, once again You're reminding me that conflict isn't the best answer, and it's often the last choice to consider. You know my struggles. Perhaps that's why You give me so many opportunities to change and grow, that I will be calm in the face of conflict. Use me to calm troubled people instead of stirring up strife. Oh, make it so. I also pray for those nearest and dearest to me, that I will eat that plate of food I don't like rather than create a fuss. Keep me from allowing momentary problems to fester and grow into a hate-filled boil. Lance me with Your Spirit. Amen.

In hope of eternal life, which God, that cannot lie,
promised before the world began.
TITUS 1:2

EVENING READING ·

God cannot lie. This means that the promises and truths He speaks in His Word are fully reliable and trustworthy. He has promised eternal life to those who are His children. Therefore, as a child of God, you have a true and sure hope in eternal life with Him. This life and all its grief and sorrow is not even a drop in the ocean compared to the life of perfect joy and blessing that you have waiting for you.

Wives and Mothers

(TITUS 2:4–5)

❧❧❧❧❧ ❀ ❦❦❦❦❦

MORNING PRAYER

God who created families, I pray for young mothers and wives. May their love for their husbands and children burn fiercely and in purity. Make them sensible in their management and modest in their dress, thoughts, and behavior. May they work hard at home and on the job. Teach them to be kind to friends, neighbors, and strangers. I lift up those wives whose husbands aren't believers, that they will know how to both honor their husbands and obey You, especially when their husbands' wills contradict Yours. I pray for their spouses' salvation and that unity will rule in their hearts. Amen.

It is of the Lord's mercies that we are not consumed, because his compassions fail not. They are new every morning: great is thy faithfulness. The Lord is my portion, saith my soul; therefore will I hope in him.

LAMENTATIONS 3:22–24

EVENING READING

This beautifully uplifting passage in Lamentations 3 is often taken out of context. It's easy to think that this sentiment was spoken by someone whose life was going well, who woke up every morning excited for a new day. But these precious verses are all the more beautiful because they were written from the pit of despair. This faith in God's daily compassion was held to in a dark place. These words were spoken by someone who clung to God's mercies as the only hope of life. No matter the darkness, God's light will find its way to you.

You Answered My Call

(LAMENTATIONS 3:55–58)

❧❧❧❧❧ ❀ ❦❦❦❦❦

MORNING PRAYER ·

Lord God, when I tumble to the bottom of a pit, like the Jews who were taken into captivity, I'm weary in mind, body, and spirit. I am too crushed to utter any prayer beyond my cry for help. Oh, the wonder of the Holy Spirit, who takes that wordless prayer and intercedes for me. Like the father of the prodigal son who actively looked for his son's return, You actively await my pleas. You run to me and assuage my fears. You take up my case, redeem me, and change me. You prepare me for a better quality life—the life I was designed for, eternal life. Praise the Lord. Amen and amen.

The heart of the righteous studieth to answer:
but the mouth of the wicked poureth out evil things.
PROVERBS 15:28

EVENING READING ·

"Think before you speak" may seem like a tired adage, but it's a valuable one nonetheless. A righteous person studies his answer before making a reply. A wicked person pours forth evil and worthless things with no thought or care. Whose speech do your words resemble more—the wicked, careless person or the righteous, mindful person?

No Longer a Slave

(PHILEMON 14–17)

≫≫〉〉 ❀ 〈〈≪≪

MORNING PRAYER

Lord and Master, to whom I owe my service, Onesimus's story makes me think about the continuing racial strife because of the legacy of slavery. I don't understand, can't understand, what it's like to be black in America today, because my skin is white. I can imagine how hard it was for Onesimus to return to the situation he'd fled, uncertain of his reception. Like Onesimus and Philemon, many of us who were once on the outside are now brothers and sisters in Christ. Let our oneness in You be a new beginning, Your Son's blood the thing that binds us together. We are forever family. Let us stand up for one another. May churches take the lead in healing the racial divide. Amen.

A man's heart deviseth his way:
but the LORD directeth his steps.

PROVERBS 16:9

EVENING READING

No matter what plans you devise in your own heart regarding how your life should go, God is the one who ultimately guides your steps. He may (and often does) take you down a totally different path than you had planned. The story of Onesimus in the book of Philemon is just one example of this. Onesimus left Philemon as a runaway slave and was commended by Paul to return to Philemon as a fellow brother in Christ. It is doubtful that this was at all the plan that Onesimus had for his life when he ran away. But the story God crafted for him was more glorious than anything he could have devised.

❧ DAY 312 ❧

Working Things Out

(PROVERBS 16:20)

>>>>> ❀ <<<<<

MORNING PRAYER

Eternal, wise God, I boast that everything will work out when Your Word permeates my life, when I live according to Your revealed will. If I use the Bible as a handbook for my business and personal affairs, I will enjoy a good, if not wealthy, life. The better I understand Your Word, the greater the chances my efforts will succeed. The more I study, the greater my skill set. When I turn to Your Word, I don't have to anticipate the future. You've already paved the way before me. Past experience has demonstrated the truth of Your Word. Its pages fill my mind and mouth with wisdom. Thank You! Amen.

How shall we escape, if we neglect so great salvation;
which at the first began to be spoken by the Lord, and was
confirmed unto us by them that heard him; God also bearing
them witness, both with signs and wonders, and with divers
miracles, and gifts of the Holy Ghost, according to his own will?
HEBREWS 2:3–4

EVENING READING

We cannot deny the Gospel. We cannot overlook the work of God that is so evident in the lives of the people whom He touches. We cannot reject the work of the Holy Spirit as He turns hearts of stone into hearts that fervently seek the Lord. We cannot escape the condemnation that comes to those who disavow their Creator who put His fingerprints so clearly over all creation. Only through accepting and embracing the work of Christ can you be truly free. Spread this essential news to all around you.

Crown of Glory

(PROVERBS 16:31)

＞＞＞＞ ❀ ＜＜＜＜

MORNING PRAYER ·

God Almighty, my gray and hoary head grows more glorious by the day, as gray gives way to white. If those snowy locks testify to a God-loyal life, make every one of them bright and as stain-free as the righteousness You have given to me. Since I live in a culture that doesn't treasure our elders, I thank You for this reminder of how You see me. May I treat my fellow senior saints with honor and dignity. May I see Your beauty in their clouded eyes and gnarled hands. May I accept my long life, and the limitations age brings, as a mark of distinction, bestowed upon me by You. Amen.

Forasmuch then as the children are partakers of flesh and blood, he also himself likewise took part of the same; that through death he might destroy him that had the power of death, that is, the devil; and deliver them who through fear of death were all their lifetime subject to bondage.

HEBREWS 2:14–15

EVENING READING ·

Death has no power in your life. The conqueror of death now rules in your heart, leaving no room for fear. The effects of death are temporary and fleeting and quickly give way to a more glorious reality. Christ has turned the devil's greatest weapon into His most beautiful gift, for through death is the doorway to a much better life.

Housecleaning

(HEBREWS 3:13)

>>>>> ❀ <<<<<

MORNING PRAYER·

Gracious, holy Lord, I come to these chapters in Hebrews with fear and trembling. I confess I don't understand what hardening of the heart means for the Christian and what the consequences are. Such things are too wonderful for me. I pray that instead of hardening, believers in danger will be built up. When I see a brother or sister who is struggling, may I offer my support and prayers. May I not overlook my pesky sins. Forgive me for what I overlook. Sweep the house of my heart clean; dig up any moldy sin that wants to take root. Fill my mind with Your Word and Spirit, that I might not be deceived. Amen.

Whoso mocketh the poor reproacheth his Maker:
and he that is glad at calamities shall not be unpunished.
PROVERBS 17:5

EVENING READING

It is undeniably evident all throughout scripture that God defends and loves the poor and needy. As a God who is defined by love and justice, it's no wonder that He pays special attention to those who through injustice receive little love. Those who mistreat or mock the poor are really just mocking their Maker, which is an enormously bad idea. Those who speak up for and defend the poor become more like their Maker in that very act.

Keeping My Mouth Shut

(PROVERBS 17:9)

≽≫≫❀≪≪≼

MORNING PRAYER

Loving God, You speak to me in truth and love. You deal with me directly. You don't whisper bad things about me in the ears of others. Oh, that I would be like You! Oh, that You will burn away the disease of my forked tongue, which speaks love with one side and gossips with the other. Sew it back together by Your Holy Spirit; heal it with the ointment of Your *agape* love that will cover a multitude of sins. Forgive me when I repeat that which is best kept secret, and give me the wisdom to know the difference. Amen.

> *Let us therefore come boldly unto the throne of grace, that we*
> *may obtain mercy, and find grace to help in time of need.*
>
> HEBREWS 4:16

EVENING READING

We are to come boldly to the throne of grace. Why? So that we might receive grace and mercy. If we need grace and mercy, then it means we are far from perfect. In our imperfection, what right do we have to enter into the throne room of a holy God? And yet, God calls us to come—and to come boldly no less. Clearly, this is not an us-centered boldness based on what we have done and how clean our man-made robes are. Rather, it is a God-centered boldness based on what He has done and how clean the blood-washed, heavenly robes are that we have been given.

EZEKIEL 13–14 ❀ HEBREWS 5:11–6:20 ❀ PROVERBS 17:13–22

My Lifeline

(HEBREWS 6:18–19)

❧❧❧❀❧❧❧

MORNING PRAYER

My Lifeline and my promised Hope, I have run to You for my life. I hold on to the sure hope of that sanctuary as my lifeline. I cling to it with everything I have, trusting in nothing and no one else. It guides me past appearances and takes me to Your presence. I hold on with both hands, not letting go to reach for passing fads. Up ahead of me I see Jesus, who has gone before me. May I follow the trail He has blazed. Prepare me to breathe in Your rarefied spiritual air. Amen.

> *Which hope we have as an anchor of the soul, both sure*
> *and stedfast, and which entereth into that within the veil.*
> HEBREWS 6:19

EVENING READING

If a ship is moored by a trustworthy anchor, it can only go a certain distance from that anchor. It may be tossed around by the wind and pummeled with waves, but the anchor will not let it break free and get pushed out into the ocean. So too the hope that we have in God will never allow us to drift out to sea. We may be tossed and battered by life's waves, but only within the confines of the anchor's reach. God has anchored our soul to Himself through Christ's work on the cross. No matter how big the waves get, we have a hope in something sure.

⊱ DAY 317 ⊰

Perfect Fit
(HEBREWS 7:25–27)

⇒⇒⟩⟩⟩ ❀ ⟨⟨⟨⟨⇐

MORNING PRAYER

Lord and Savior, I live in a one-size-fits-all world that meets most of my needs but doesn't cater to me. The solutions offered for my problems come with no guarantee of success. Praise to You that Your sacrifice on the cross was a perfect cover for every sin. There are no sins that are excluded (except for the unforgiveable sin, and I'll ask You about that another time). There is no small print. No limitations on how many or which people may come. There is abundant grace, and exactly enough, for everyone born among men. I praise You that You are absolutely, eternally perfect. Amen.

But this man, because he continueth ever, hath an unchangeable priesthood. Wherefore he is able also to save them to the uttermost that come unto God by him, seeing he ever liveth to make intercession for them.
HEBREWS 7:24–25

EVENING READING

Christ intercedes for you. Have you ever really pondered that? As you would lift up in prayer a family member or friend that you care deeply about, so too Christ your truest friend intercedes for you to the Father. You could not ask for a better advocate. He has been where you have been and has seen and felt the weight of this world. That the Son of God would know how your suffering feels is astonishing. He is deeply connected to your human needs and desires. Having been your sacrificial Lamb, He is now and forever will be your High Priest.

Cedars

(EZEKIEL 17:22–23)

≈≫≫❀≪≪≈

MORNING PRAYER

Living Lord, You are a splendid cedar, a life-giving vine, the tree that provides shade everywhere on earth. Your chosen people were branches on that tree, and now You have grafted me in, giving me a new identity I don't deserve. Thank You for the tree that allows me to nest, to rest and multiply, a concert hall where we raise songs of praise. I want to eat Your fruit and drink Your water, both for myself and to offer it to others. Prune me, that I will bear fruit. Use me to spread the seeds of Your life to others, that they may also come to You. Amen.

Behold, this was the iniquity of thy sister Sodom, pride, fulness of bread, and abundance of idleness was in her and in her daughters, neither did she strengthen the hand of the poor and needy. And they were haughty, and committed abomination before me: therefore I took them away as I saw good.
EZEKIEL 16:49–50

EVENING READING

We often comfortably compare ourselves with Sodom, knowing that we are far more holy than the people living there who were truly evil and debased. And yet, what are the sins cited against Sodom? Pride, careless prosperity, idleness, and an inattention to the poor and needy. . . All of a sudden this seems a little uncomfortable. Is your life free of these sins? Just like the people of Sodom, we are wretched sinners whom God has every right to do away with. But He chose to redeem us and make us one of His family instead. Praise be to Him!

She Will Surely Live

(EZEKIEL 18:5–9)

MORNING PRAYER

Living God of truth, is this a promise or a description? Pondering it again, I'm struck that You've given me a definition of what real life is. You don't prescribe a trade for extra years but instead paint a portrait of a good, full life. You want me to treat others well, to work at relationships. A good life involves abstaining from instant gratification through things like food or irresponsible spending. You offer me the true life today, if I want it. May Your righteousness in me cause me to seek after what is just and right. Amen.

Yet ye say, The way of the Lord is not equal. Hear now, O house of Israel; Is not my way equal? are not your ways unequal?

EZEKIEL 18:25

EVENING READING

We have all heard the accusation that God is not fair. In fact, maybe you've thought that at times in your life. But how do we have any right to say that God's ways are not fair? To begin with, we can't even come close to comprehending the plans that God has for us. Also, we have done nothing for God compared to the matchless gifts and grace that He has given us. With all our fickleness, lack of gratefulness, and idolatry, we are the ones who are not fair.

Friends

(PROVERBS 18:24)

❧>>>>> ❀ <<<<<❦

MORNING PRAYER ·

Heavenly Father, sometimes I would rather live without the nuisance of pesky people, the kind of undesirable friends that Solomon wrote about. But You have made me for community. You placed me in my family unit, through the wonderful years as the middle of a three-generation sandwich and now as the elder of the clan. You've also given me all believers as my brothers and sisters. But perhaps the ones I appreciate the most are those who choose me as a friend. I can't thank You enough for all we have meant to each other. I pray for those who don't have much support. Bring someone alongside them, and shelter them within a loving community. Amen.

But this man, after he had offered one sacrifice for
sins for ever, sat down on the right hand of God.
HEBREWS 10:12

EVENING READING ·

Christ sat down at the right hand of God. The action of sitting down signified that His work was completed. It was finished. Unlike the other priests who would have to continually offer sacrifices, Christ's sacrifice was so powerful it put an end to the need for any further sacrifices. His work is finished, which means that your sins are already paid for. There is nothing that you have done that will fall outside the boundaries of His atoning sacrifice.

Holding On

(HEBREWS 10:36)

>>))>> ❀ <<<<<<

MORNING PRAYER ·

Author and Finisher of my faith, I have confidence knowing that You'll bring my faith race to completion in Christ. But that doesn't mean my steps today come easily or that I never question the cost or doubt the outcome. Replace my questions with acceptance. Overcome my doubt with patience so that I might persevere until the finish line. Give me the endurance to walk when I can't run, to crawl when I can't walk. Prod me to my feet and move me forward when I've fallen. Make me dogged in following Your will. How sweet the day will be when I receive Your promise. Amen.

It is a fearful thing to fall into the hands of the living God.

HEBREWS 10:31

EVENING READING ·

God's love fully encompasses who He is. But to only consider that He is a loving God is to truncate your knowledge of Him, to diminish His glory, and ultimately to lack a full understanding of His love. God is also a God who can be moved to wrath. He is a God to be feared in all His unattainable holiness. He can either create or destroy with a simple word. Knowing the power and fearfulness of God only makes the truth that He loves and cares for you more glorious.

Proof
(HEBREWS 11:1)

❧>⟩⟩⟩⟩ ❀ ⟨⟨⟨⟨⟨❧

MORNING PRAYER·

Unseen God, thank You for the gift of faith, for it is a gift. I don't know why I see You clearly when people I admire deny Your existence for lack of empirical evidence. I thank You for sight and pray for them. In the classroom, faith enables me to comprehend as fact what I can't see or touch. In the courtroom, it's the proof that determines the verdict. Faith is both the confirmation of what I've received from You and the title deed to my inheritance. It gives substance to my spiritual diet. Thank You for the gift of faith that enables me to live in light of Your reality. Amen.

> *For they that say such things declare plainly that they seek a*
> *country. . . . But now they desire a better country, that is,*
> *an heavenly: wherefore God is not ashamed to be called*
> *their God: for he hath prepared for them a city.*
> HEBREWS 11:14, 16

EVENING READING

Would those who interact with you on a daily basis recognize that you seek a homeland that is not of this world? Does your anticipation of your true home seep into your words and actions so much that it inspires others to seek this kingdom as well? What are you doing to seek out this heavenly land of which you are a citizen? Just as refugees on this earth often surround themselves with the comforts and reminders of their country of origin, so too remind yourself often of where you are going.

Man Proposes but God Disposes

(PROVERBS 19:21)

>>>>> ❀ <<<<<

MORNING PRAYER ·

Sovereign Lord, I love to make plans. I lay out the hours of my days. In my work, I count the cost before I commit to a project. Daily, I discipline myself to accomplish predetermined goals. Then there are the times You step in. You hand me a new assignment. Illness creeps in, and I must turn to You for wisdom and strength in completing my assignment. You turn my small things into big things and my big things into small ones. I seek to make wise use of time, but You operate the stopwatch, reminding me to trust You with my seconds and minutes. Amen.

(Of whom the world was not worthy.)
HEBREWS 11:38

EVENING READING ·

In Hebrews 11 is a small parenthetical phrase that just may be the most powerful words ever put into parentheses—"Of whom the world was not worthy." This comfort-driven world is not worthy of people who will gladly be killed, beaten, and exiled so that they might follow their Savior. This selfish world is not worthy of people who value their lives so lightly that they would give them up for the sake of another. This compromising world is not worthy of people who refuse to budge an inch on the truth of the Gospel even when this steadfastness will cost them in this life. This world is not worthy of them. . .but they are worthy of their homes in heaven where every day they will dine with the Savior they so faithfully followed.

The Christian Race

(HEBREWS 12:1–2)

❧❧❧❧❧ ❀ ❦❦❦❦❦

MORNING PRAYER ·

Wonderful Counselor and Coach, strip me of everything that hinders my race. Author and Finisher of the race, lead me in Jesus' steps and be the wind at my back until I reach the finish line. Thank You for burning away the hindrances and impurities that keep me from running straight for the prize. I trust the transformation process to You as I hide under the shelter of Your wings. You are the instigator of the race and its Reward. You're also the pattern for how to run. If I don't know what steps to take in training, I only need to turn to Your example. Amen.

> *But if ye be without chastisement, whereof all*
> *are partakers, then are ye bastards, and not sons.*

HEBREWS 12:8

EVENING READING ·

Chastisement and discipline from God are not things that we generally look forward to. And yet, to not be disciplined is far worse. God will inevitably reprimand His children—it is how He lovingly makes us more like Himself. If you have not been corrected by Him, the sobering truth is that you may not truly be a child of His. Though it may seem a bit frightening, ask for God to make you more like Himself no matter what it takes—for it is far better to be one of His children than an outsider to His family.

Bitterness

(HEBREWS 12:14–15)

❧)))) ❀ ((((❧

MORNING PRAYER ·

Lord God, woe is me! When I look at myself in the mirror of this scripture, I see how ugly I am, what awful things I've done. So often I'm tempted to bitterness, resentful of all the things I would change about my life if I could. So often I'm known as a complainer instead of someone who builds others up. Praise You, I'm changing, but I cringe to think of all the people my negative attitude may have pushed away from You. Forgive me! As Saint Francis said, "Make me an instrument of Your peace. Where there has been hatred, let me sow love." Amen.

Most men will proclaim every one his own goodness:
but a faithful man who can find?
PROVERBS 20:6

EVENING READING ·

Be careful to avoid being the kind of person who proclaims your own goodness but in whom none of this proclaimed goodness can be found. Rather, be the kind of person who doesn't speak much of yourself but, through your actions and character, proves yourself a faithful person. Be more concerned about building others up. Humbly let your praise come from God or others.

Sacrifice of Praise

(HEBREWS 13)

>>>>> ❀ <<<<<

MORNING PRAYER

Lord God, every minute of the rest of my life, teach me the delightful sacrifice of praise—even on days like today, when I feel out of sorts and fear things will never improve. May Your peace, love, and hope take the place of all those concerns. I praise You because nothing happens to me without Your permission. Everything that I experience works together for Your glory, if not my idea of comfort. With that in mind, may I sing of Your praises in the assembly. Together with Your children, may we shout hallelujahs to our Lord and Savior, Jesus Christ. May the canyons of my despair echo my whispered affirmations of Your love, until they grow stronger and more powerful with each passing day. Amen.

Wherefore Jesus also, that he might sanctify the people with his own blood, suffered without the gate. Let us go forth therefore unto him without the camp, bearing his reproach.
HEBREWS 13:12–13

EVENING READING

Are you willing to bear the reproach of Jesus and go with Him outside the camp? Christians often find that they are not welcome in the upper reaches of society or the inner circles of secular culture. And yet, should we be surprised when we serve a Savior who suffered outside the gate? An outcast life with Him is far better than a thousand lives of earthly comfort without Him. No suffering can compare with the joy that He offers.

Speaking for an Audience

(EZEKIEL 33:30)

>>>>> ✿ <<<<<

MORNING PRAYER

Lord God, when I speak of Your love and grace, do people listen to me with genuine interest or for entertainment? How encouraged Ezekiel must have felt when people came by his house, eager to hear from You. In turn, how disheartened he must have been when they didn't act on Your messages to them. They appreciated the performance but rejected the reality. Oh Lord, your prophets have been maligned from of old. Onlookers will do the same to me. Let me not speak to garner praise from men, but because You have called me. When I feel the sting of public disapproval, let me draw closer to You. Amen.

> *Pure religion and undefiled before God and the Father is this,*
> *To visit the fatherless and widows in their affliction,*
> *and to keep himself unspotted from the world.*
> JAMES 1:27

EVENING READING

What would you say is pure and undefiled religion? James says that pure religion is visiting the fatherless and widows in their distress and keeping yourself unstained from the world. This is likely not the first answer that we would come up with. And yet, it is what God calls us to. If you aren't caring for those in need, is your heart where it should be? Are you serving God as you ought to serve Him?

DAY 328

Rock-Bottom Truth

(JAMES 2)

>=>>>> ❀ <<<<=<

MORNING PRAYER

Heavenly Father, this chapter jumps out with a commonsense approach to faith. My actions speak louder than my words. When I make an unkind comment, it takes a hundred uplifting words to erase the unkind statement. How I act should match what I say, and both speech and actions should be consistent. May people see Your presence in me before I open my mouth. May I not say one thing today and a different thing tomorrow. When I pray about a problem, may I respond to the need if I'm able to do so. Amen.

Even so faith, if it hath not works, is dead, being alone.
JAMES 2:17

EVENING READING

While good works by no means secure your salvation, they are an excellent barometer regarding your faith. A faith that is not played out in and invigorated by works is a faith that may not be genuine. The God in whom you have faith is a God who daily reaches out to and sustains His people, orchestrating every aspect of their lives. He is a God who is constantly working for our good. If your faith in this God is not similarly accented by working for others, then maybe you do not know your God as you should. Our good works are one of the most obvious ways that we can imitate Christ on this earth and reach others for Him. Let us not be people with a skeletal faith.

Reunited

(EZEKIEL 37:19–28)

≈>)))) ❀ <<<<≈

MORNING PRAYER ·

Lord God, how often I regret the divisions within the church, the walls we put up between us. Though You created one of the first schisms when You split Israel into two nations, You never intended for them to remain separated forever. During the exile, You promised to bring both nations back, to establish them in the land under one Shepherd. Your body, the church, also has one Shepherd. One faith, one Lord, one baptism. If today we work with barriers between us, may the day come when those partitions disappear. You prayed that we would be one in love. Keep us from tearing one another down in hate. Amen.

And shall put my spirit in you, and ye shall live, and I shall
place you in your own land: then shall ye know that I the
Lord have spoken it, and performed it, saith the Lord.
EZEKIEL 37:14

EVENING READING ·

Ezekiel is mostly a very desolate book. God does not treat sin lightly—the punishment for ignoring the law of God is real. The intensity of the book makes the passages about God's redemption stand out all the more vividly. Even when your life feels desolate, God's Spirit remains alive and active within you. He does not abandon His people in the desert. He will bring you into a new and vibrant land. It's the experiences of being drawn out of the desert that cause us to look back and recognize that it is the Lord at work in us.

Wrong Desires

(JAMES 4:1–3)

❧❧❧❧❧ ❀ ❧❧❧❧❧

MORNING PRAYER

My Lord and Father, these verses bring me to my knees, asking You to change my "wanter" to bring my desires in line with Your will. When I want something so badly—simply to satisfy my whims—I invite all kinds of disaster. I'm led to covet others' possessions. Coveting turns into quarrelling and fighting and murderous hatred. What could have been mine by asking has become a root of evil, something I will not receive because I ask amiss. Forgive me when I make the object of my desire more important than You or others. Keep me clear from such covetousness. Amen.

Ye ask, and receive not, because ye ask amiss,
that ye may consume it upon your lusts.
JAMES 4:3

EVENING READING

How often do we ask for something simply for our own comfort or pleasure without regard to how it will fit into God's kingdom plan or how it will affect others? We are masters at molding our idea of God's will to fit perfectly into our preconstructed plan for our lives. Would your prayers sound different if your greatest desire was to be of use to God's kingdom? Would your prayers sound different if your first thought was toward others rather than yourself?

When to Pray

(JAMES 5:13–18)

❧>>>>> ❀ <<<<❧

MORNING PRAYER ·

Lord Jesus, how James's words strike at the heart of prayer. Am I in trouble? Pray. Am I happy? Pray. Am I sick? Pray. There isn't a single situation where prayer isn't appropriate. And as I pray, I become aware of the connection between physical and spiritual wholeness. I don't pray in a vacuum. I am to intercede with and for others. In those prayers I will find healing and forgiveness. What a promise! My prayer can be powerful and effective, like Elijah's, who shut the heavens from raining for three years. I hover between pride and awe at that statement, but as Your answers come, may I return all glory to You. Amen.

Be ye also patient; stablish your hearts:
for the coming of the Lord draweth nigh.

JAMES 5:8

EVENING READING ·

You are to establish your heart to prepare for the coming of Christ. Just as a tree needs water and nutrients for its roots to grow, so you also must feed your heart with the sustenance from God's Word so that your spiritual roots will burrow down into a deeper relationship with Him. Bask in the light of His presence that you may be filled up with His joy.

Wayward Children

(PROVERBS 22:6)

>>>>>> ❀ <<<<<

MORNING PRAYER· ·

Heavenly Father, I lift up this verse on behalf of parents everywhere whose children have wandered from You, starting with my own family. For my grandchildren growing into adulthood, I pray that they will choose the way they were trained. I pray for parents with young children. May they teach Your eternal truth, with understanding of each child's unique gifts and personality. May they not only teach the rules, but also about how to make choices so that their children will have the skills they need to make the right choices. Let them impart not a set of regulations, but a way of life. Amen.

To an inheritance incorruptible, and undefiled, and that fadeth not away, reserved in heaven for you, who are kept by the power of God through faith unto salvation ready to be revealed in the last time.
1 PETER 1:4–5

EVENING READING ·

The kind of inheritance that we should be working for in this life is the one that is being stored up in heaven for us as an incorruptible, undefiled, and everlasting reward. This inheritance has nothing to do with money, ease of life, or status. Our heavenly inheritance is based on what our Father has already done for us and consists of riches beyond our imaginings. Our inheritance is sure because God Himself keeps us by His power and will grant us this inheritance based on no merit of our own.

Spiritual Dialysis

(1 PETER 2:1–3)

❧❧❧❧❧ ❀ ❦❦❦❦❦

MORNING PRAYER· ·

Lord Jesus, I come to You in my unkempt state, my life wrinkled by sinful habits and bad choices, badly in need of a cleansing of my spiritual lifeblood. I thank You for Your forgiveness, instantaneous and irrevocable, when I confess my sins and ask for Your cleansing. I'm asking You to replace ungodly desires with the new. In Your dialysis machine, spin out the past of malice, deceit, hypocrisy, envy, slander. Refill those veins with the milk of Your Word, pure, life sustaining—all I need to grow in You. Let me come to You continuously, seeking to keep my spirit cleansed of the past, that my arteries may remain open and clear. Amen.

But as he which hath called you is holy, so be ye holy in all manner
of conversation; because it is written, Be ye holy; for I am holy.
1 PETER 1:15–16

EVENING READING ·

You are called to be holy just as God is holy. This is a high and daunting calling. You will certainly fall short of it aside from the atoning work of Christ. But sometimes we use an avoidance of legalism as an excuse to not even try to be holy. While we certainly can't muster holiness on our own, this is no excuse not to strive for it in this life. The purity of our lives is one way that God shows Himself to those around us. The brokenness of our lives is how God reminds us of our need for Him. Both our striving for holiness and our admittance of our weakness are important factors in God's work in our lives.

Make Me a Testimony

(1 Peter 2:12–15)

⇢⟩⟩⟩⟩ ❀ ⟨⟨⟨⟨⇠

MORNING PRAYER ·

Dear Lord and Savior, what a daring prayer, to offer my life as a testimony to those who don't know You. May people see evidence in my life of Your ever-reaching and limitless love. May I reveal the truth of Your goodness and seek the good of all without favoritism. Cleanse me; polish the glass of my life, that others may glorify You. Not because of me, but because of You in me. Let me submit to Your authority first and to their benefit next, and not use my freedom to mar my testimony. Amen.

> *Honour all men. Love the brotherhood.*
> *Fear God. Honour the king.*
> 1 PETER 2:17

EVENING READING ·

First Peter 2:17 is a good and simple summation of how we ought to live our lives. Honor all people as image bearers of God, and in so doing, seek to serve them and bring them to Christ. Love your fellow Christians in a self-sacrificial way as Christ has taught us to do by His example. Fear God as the just and holy God who has every right to punish us for our sin but who has mercifully chosen to redeem us instead. Honor those placed in authority over you, and live as an upright and obedient citizen of this temporary home as much as you can while still obeying the law of God as your utmost authority.

EZEKIEL 47–48 ❀ 1 PETER 2:18–3:7 ❀ PROVERBS 23:1–9

Don't Bother the Fool

(PROVERBS 23:9)

⇛⇛》》》 ❀ 《《《⇚⇚

MORNING PRAYER ·

Lord God, hear my plea for discernment. Not everyone will listen to me or heed what I say, whether I'm asking for help or offering advice. Foolish me, when I continue to bang my head against the wall. Give me discernment to differentiate between who will listen and who won't. Perhaps I am trying to take Your place in speaking. Other messengers may reach those who don't listen to me. Keep me from becoming defensive. Let me speak only when moved by You. May I accept words of wisdom when they are spoken to me and not reject them. Amen.

> *It was round about eighteen thousand measures: and the*
> *name of the city from that day shall be, The LORD is there.*
> EZEKIEL 48:35

EVENING READING ·

The city spoken of in Ezekiel was named "The Lord is there." May our lives and homes be worthy of such a name as well. When others look in on your family or your personal life, will they recognize that God dwells with you? Does your life speak of the presence and redeeming work of God?

Praying in a Pickle

(DANIEL 2:17–23)

⋟⋟⋙ ❀ ⋘⋞⋞

MORNING PRAYER ·

Great God of the heavens, You are the answer to every prayer, the "yes" to our every need. Daniel and his friends pleaded for their lives, and You answered. Was this the first time they received an interpretation of dreams? When I receive such clarity, may I, like Daniel, recognize You as the source of the wisdom and the power behind it. Give me the discernment to know when I have heard from You. I trust You for grace when the message is one I don't want to hear or share. I thank You for the example of Daniel's courage to speak Your truth before the king. Amen.

> *Then was the secret revealed unto Daniel in a night vision.*
> *Then Daniel blessed the God of heaven.*
> DANIEL 2:19

EVENING READING ·

Daniel's first reaction to his answered prayer was to praise God. How often do you forget to praise God after He's answered a prayer? How often do you end up attributing the answer to your own intelligence or ability? We should live in an attitude of praise and gratefulness to God as He is constantly answering our prayers and granting us mercies that we didn't even think to pray for. He deserves the credit. Every good thing in our lives is ultimately a gift from Him.

Even If
(DANIEL 3:16–18)

⇒⟩⟩⟩⟩ ❀ ⟨⟨⟨⟨⇐

MORNING PRAYER ·

Lord God, my heart thrills as I read of Shadrach, Meshach, and Abednego's faith, and I pray mine will mirror theirs. They staked their lives on their trust that You would deliver them from the furnace, and the subsequent miracle proved them right. What I treasure is their unwavering commitment to die by the flame—should You choose not to act—rather than worship the idol of gold set up by man and no real god at all. Whatever block is thrust in my way, may I, like them, refuse to give in to fear of man but boldly serve You, even to death. Amen.

> *He answered and said, Lo, I see four men loose,*
> *walking in the midst of the fire, and they have no hurt;*
> *and the form of the fourth is like the Son of God.*
> DANIEL 3:25

EVENING READING ·

The story of Shadrach, Meshach, and Abednego in the fiery furnace is a beautiful illustration of how Christ walks with us through trials. He does not abandon those who have been faithful to proclaim Him. Though we can't always see it, we are never alone. Oh, that God would open our eyes so that we could see that one "like the Son of God" walks by our side when we're in the midst of the fire.

Everything I Need

(2 PETER 1:3–8)

>>>>> ❀ <<<<<

MORNING PRAYER·· ·

Heavenly Lord, You have given me everything I need, and not only in the sense of my daily bread. You call me to godliness, which I can't do on my own. You have already equipped me for transformation through my knowledge of You, calling me to Your glory and goodness. Let me grab hold by building on the foundation of faith a seven-layer-strong structure to make me like You: goodness, knowledge, self-control, perseverance, godliness, mutual affection, love. May I continue to grow in all these areas until at last I am home with You. Amen.

> *And at the end of the days I Nebuchadnezzar lifted up mine eyes unto heaven, and mine understanding returned unto me, and I blessed the most High, and I praised and honoured him that liveth for ever, whose dominion is an everlasting dominion, and his kingdom is from generation to generation.*
>
> DANIEL 4:34

EVENING READING ·

As captives in Babylon, God's people must have felt that God had abandoned them or that He had somehow messed up His plan. They likely thought that maybe God wasn't sovereign after all. But they probably never would have imagined that God would use this very difficult circumstance to bring a pagan king into relationship with Himself. We can never possibly know what it is that God plans to do through the hard circumstances that He puts us in. We must tirelessly trust in His sovereignty and grace and believe that He does have a better plan than ours.

Vision Problems

(PROVERBS 24:1–18)

>>>>>> ❀ <<<<<<

MORNING PRAYER ·

Lord God, I need Your glasses to see others clearly. I'm nearsighted when it comes to seeing their needs. They may be struggling to the point of death, and yet I haven't noticed their pain. At other times, I'm farsighted when I envy the good fortune of the righteous. Just as bad is when I rejoice in the misfortune of my enemies. May I look to others to look for ways to help, but let me focus on living a sober, God-pleasing life. May I consider the weight of my deeds in Your scales and overlook that of others. Amen.

These are wells without water, clouds that are carried with
a tempest; to whom the mist of darkness is reserved for ever.

2 PETER 2:17

EVENING READING ·

False teaching and the warping of God's truth to fit our own lifestyles is a serious offense to God and something that He does not take lightly. He is gracious enough to hate and punish false teaching because to let us adhere to lies would ultimately destroy us. Be careful to test the teaching that you receive against the perfect Word of God. If it doesn't match up, side every time with the Word of God.

The Price of Prayer

(DANIEL 6:1–13)

>>>>> ❀ <<<<<

MORNING PRAYER

God, to have the testimony of Daniel, that the only thing people fault me for is my prayer life. Oh, to have his courage, that he didn't alter his routine when the law said prayer was an offense against his king. I ponder how prayer triggered not only his problem but also the solution, when he turned to You for help in the den of lions. When have I ever been asked to pay a price for prayer? I thank You that I live in a country that practices religious freedom. There are many who suffer persecution, who must pray in secret. I ask that their courage will match Daniel's and that You will protect them if they are brought to trial. Amen.

> *Then said these men, We shall not find any occasion against this Daniel,*
> *except we find it against him concerning the law of his God.*
> DANIEL 6:5

EVENING READING

Daniel's enemies were fully aware that they could bring no accusation against him unless they could somehow use his unwavering faithfulness to God against him. What a testimony that is! Daniel was upright and pure in all his morals and obedience to the good laws of the land. He had no secret sin that could be used against him. He had not slightly bent or ignored any laws that could be brought to light as a witness against him. Could you say the same about yourself? Perhaps even more poignantly, his relationship with God was so well known that his enemies knew that he would never bend in regard to his faithfulness to God. Could you say the same about yourself?

≈ DAY 341 ≈

The Rule of Love

(1 JOHN 1:7–2:17)

≈≈≫≫≫ ❀ ≪≪≪≈≈

MORNING PRAYER· ·

Lord God, may Your Spirit shine Your light on the world around me. May I have the wisdom to discern when my thanksgiving for Your gifts turns into valuing the gift over the Giver. Show me when lust for more things and pride in what I have take Your place on my heart's throne. May I love people, not things. May I love them as You do, giving of myself, placing their needs ahead of my own. May my love point them to You. When I fail, forgive me. I rest in the assurance that You will pardon my sins when I confess them. Let me walk in Your light and love. Amen.

If we say that we have no sin, we deceive ourselves, and the truth
is not in us. If we confess our sins, he is faithful and just to
forgive us our sins, and to cleanse us from all unrighteousness.
1 JOHN 1:8–9

EVENING READING ·

There is no reason not to confess your sins to God. If you don't confess your sins and deny that they exist, then they become witnesses against you that God's truth does not dwell in you. For His truth will inevitably reveal to us how we fail to keep His law. But if you confess your sins, they are guaranteed to be forgiven so that you can live with a clear conscience before God. With this in mind, why would you not daily confess your sins to your faithful Father?

The Great Explorers

(PROVERBS 25:2)

❧❧❧❧❧ ❀ ❦❦❦❦❦

MORNING PRAYER

Oh Lord God, how great Your goodness to cover a multitude of wrongs, to wash away sin stains by the blood of Your Son. You are the final judge who can order my life file to be sealed, only to be opened by You at the final judgment. Only You have the right to cover up misdoings. I pray that people in authority will investigate matters with impartiality and punish the guilty. I also ask that they be people of vision, seeking to discover what is true and noble and of good report, whether in government, the arts, the sciences, or any matter brought to their attention. Amen.

> *Therefore hath the Lord watched upon the evil, and brought*
> *it upon us: for the Lord our God is righteous in all his*
> *works which he doeth: for we obeyed not his voice.*
> DANIEL 9:14

EVENING READING

Because God is righteous and faithful, He must punish sin. If He chose to let an indiscretion slide here or there or simply pretended that He didn't see a sin, He could not be trusted. An unfaithful or fickle god is not one that you would want to put your trust in. It's His very wrath and justice that make Him trustworthy. Because of God's holiness, sin needs to be punished—you ought to be eternally grateful that the punishment fell on Christ instead of you. It was inevitable that the blow would fall, but God is incomprehensibly gracious, having taken the blow onto Himself rather than put it on those who truly deserved it.

Lavished in Love

(1 JOHN 3:1–3)

❧❧❧❧❧ ❀ ❧❧❧❧❧

MORNING PRAYER

Heavenly Father, what honey-coated, life-enhancing, life-giving words these are. You have lavished Your love on me. You spread it extravagantly, not withholding a drop. You called me Your child. I am Yours, in word and deed. In some ways, I am still in a chrysalis. I don't understand what I will one day be, when I am like Christ at His appearing. The more I see of You, the more like You I become. The more I follow You, the more I seek purity. Wrap me in the brilliance of Your light and love until I am changed into the image of Your Son. Amen.

> *Behold, what manner of love the Father hath bestowed upon us,*
> *that we should be called the sons of God: therefore the*
> *world knoweth us not, because it knew him not.*
>
> 1 JOHN 3:1

EVENING READING

You can almost sense the wonder in John's words about the gift of being called a child of God. We should have the same wonder, as well, that the Creator of all things would bestow on us the honor and privilege of being one of His children. He redeemed and justified us so that we would be spared the punishment of sin. But the truly remarkable thing is that He didn't stop there. He went so far as to adopt us. In this adoption He identifies with us and puts the stamp on us that we belong forever to Him. This manner of love is one that is impossible to comprehend.

⤝ DAY 344 ⤜

Fear Can Be Good
(HOSEA 2:20–3:5)

⤝⤞⤞⤞ ❁ ⤝⤝⤝⤜⤜

MORNING PRAYER· ·

Jesus, my Bridegroom, You called me first and second, and You continue calling me. May I reply with swiftest breath. You are my God. You have planted me, watering me with hope so I in turn can point others to You, the source of eternal life. Even when I'm suffering, I take comfort knowing You chasten me to bring me back more in love with You than before. You give me ears more attuned to understanding and accepting Your loving-kindness. Reverence for and fear of You go hand in hand with comprehending Your care. How wonderful, that the greater my fear of You, so also the greater my understanding of Your love. Amen.

> *And I will betroth thee unto me for ever; yea, I will betroth*
> *thee unto me in righteousness, and in judgment, and in*
> *lovingkindness, and in mercies. I will even betroth thee unto*
> *me in faithfulness: and thou shalt know the LORD.*
> HOSEA 2:19–20

EVENING READING ·

In Hosea is depicted a painfully beautiful story that is analogous to God's relationship with us. God has betrothed Himself to us and will therefore continue to seek us out no matter how many times we spit in the face of His faithfulness. We may run from Him. We may muddy His reputation by the worthless and soul-destroying sins that we continue to pursue as though they are more precious to us than our relationship to Him. Even in the face of this heartbreaking betrayal, He lovingly draws us back to Himself. To say that we don't deserve this kind of love is a huge understatement.

Seeking God

(HOSEA 6)

⇒⟩⟩⟩⟩ ❀ ⟨⟨⟨⟨⟨⟵

MORNING PRAYER ·

Seeking God, help me to seek You. Stretch my devotion from predawn dew to a daylong, lifelong affair that will last throughout eternity. Not because I'm steadfast, but because that's how much You love me. I want to know more and more of You. The more I learn, the more I want to know. I live in Your hope. If today I feel cut up and wounded, I wait for You, seeking You, knowing You are near. I acknowledge the little I know of You, and I look forward to the day when I shall see You as You are. What a glorious future is mine. Amen.

> *For whatsoever is born of God overcometh the world: and this is the victory that overcometh the world, even our faith. Who is he that overcometh the world, but he that believeth that Jesus is the Son of God?*
> 1 JOHN 5:4–5

EVENING READING ·

Because of our faith in Christ, we have overcome the world. This means that, being hidden in His wings, nothing on this earth can touch us. There is no power or darkness that could come close to pulling us away from Christ or darkening the light of His presence in our hearts. Christ defeated the powers of this fallen world. Since He lives in us, we have become conquerors as well. Live in light of your victory over the sins and enticements of this world.

Plowing for Righteousness

(HOSEA 10:11–12)

❧❧❧❧❧ ❀ ❧❧❧❧❧

MORNING PRAYER

My True North, keep me centered on You, not whipped around by the hurricane of my own desires. Put a harness on me and put me to work in Your fields. I want to work by Your side, digging in earth that is ready. I'm not sure what a harvest of righteousness looks like, but I trust the crop to You. With Your Spirit moving through me, may I plow straight furrows with right living, acceptance, and rejoicing. Break up the hardness of my heart. Fertilize it with Your unfailing love. Oh Lord, may righteous crops spring forth to Your name. Amen.

> *As a mad man who casteth firebrands, arrows, and death, so is*
> *the man that deceiveth his neighbour, and saith, Am not I in sport?*
> PROVERBS 26:18–19

EVENING READING

The book of Proverbs is fascinating in how accurately it identifies human character. Not much has changed in the way we behave in the centuries since it was written. Do you see yourself in any of the descriptions? For instance, one of Solomon's warnings is against people who are rude and hurtful to someone and then cover themselves by saying, "I was only joking." Solomon compared a person that does this to a madman who casts death. This kind of deception and carelessness is not something to be taken lightly.

Praying for Friends

(3 John)

MORNING PRAYER

Lord God, I love this friendly little letter from John to a Gentile believer. What a Roman-sounding name, Gaius, along with the Greek-sounding Demetrius, testifying to the radical transformation from a primarily Jewish gathering to a very mixed church unified in You. John's prayer for Gaius sounds like my short prayers when I think of friends: *that they may enjoy good health and that all may go well*. Sometimes I castigate myself for such general prayers, but now I discover I am following the apostle's example. I also pray that their souls get along well as they continue to walk in the truth. May I be faithful in praying for my friends in matters large and small. Amen.

Beloved, follow not that which is evil, but that which is good. He that doeth good is of God: but he that doeth evil hath not seen God.

3 John 11

EVENING READING

Follow and imitate what is good. When you do good, you are like God because God is good and only does what is good for His people. Surround yourself with people who are already doing good and working hard for God's kingdom and then imitate these people. By imitating others who are already walking in a way worthy of their God, you are really imitating Christ. The more Christlike you become, the more abhorrent evil will be, and the more wholeheartedly you will strive to do good.

Prayer for Revival

(JOEL 1:14)

⇝⇝⟩⟩⟩ ❀ ⟨⟨⟨⇜⇜

MORNING PRAYER ·

King of kings, I thank You that history doesn't occur in a vacuum, that it began at creation and will continue until everyone bows at Your feet on that great and terrible day of the Lord. I add my voice to those praying for national revival. May a whole host of believers bow before You in repentance. We humbly ask that You will pour out Your Spirit across our nation. Bring back those who have forsaken their roots. May the wonders of Your salvation be heard in every home by listening hearts. Loose the shackles of our preconceptions until we hear as if for the first time, clearly and without excuse. Amen.

Now unto him that is able to keep you from falling, and to present
you faultless before the presence of his glory with exceeding joy,
to the only wise God our Saviour, be glory and majesty,
dominion and power, both now and ever. Amen.
JUDE 24–25

EVENING READING ·

God is able to keep you from falling and to present you faultless before God in glory. This certainly sounds nice, but do you really believe it? Have you let this truth seep into your thoughts about yourself? Under God's care you will not fall. Nothing you can do will mar the perfection of Jesus' robes that you are covered in. Not only will you be blameless at the final judgment, but you will actually be able to stand before the most holy and just God with joy—that is how confident you will be in the work that Christ has accomplished for you. Live in that freedom and confidence here and now.

Forsaking My First Love

(REVELATION 2:1–4)

≈≫⟩⟩⟩ ❀ ⟨⟨⟨⟨≈

MORNING PRAYER

Head of Your body, the church, You walk among us, watching, knowing us, studying our habits. Forgive us for not being aware of Your presence. I confess I am like Ephesus. I don't really remember that first love; I've been a Christian nearly all my life. When I search those pockets of memory, I recall how happy I was to take my place among the body of believers, to have a family that has been more wonderful than I could have ever imagined. I also remember feeling cleansed, renewed, free. May I recall those gifts of family and cleansing always with the rejoicing of a newborn child. Amen.

I am Alpha and Omega, the beginning and the ending, saith the Lord,
which is, and which was, and which is to come, the Almighty.
REVELATION 1:8

EVENING READING

God is the Alpha and the Omega. He is the beginning and the ending of the entire stretch of history. He is the prologue and epilogue to all eternity. He has always and will always exist. Can you imagine anyone better in whom to put your trust? No matter who may disappoint or desert you in this life, your God is present beside you and will remain so throughout eternity. You will never know a day in which your heavenly Father is not caring for you.

Roaring Lion

(Proverbs 28:1)

≫⟩⟩⟩⟩ ❀ ⟨⟨⟨⟨≪

MORNING PRAYER

Lord God, however bullies see themselves, they are made of straw, easily destroyed by wind or fire. I'm supposed to be a lion, my head covered with Your glory, my voice full of powerful praise, that I may lift my countenance to the rising sun and proclaim Your wonders. May I stand up to my enemies, whether humans or circumstances, with the skill of the lioness. May I walk without fear among my peers and instill an appropriate sense of self in my pride, in my family. May I accept the leadership of the Lion of Judah in all areas of my life. Amen.

> *I know thy works, and where thou dwellest, even where*
> *Satan's seat is: and thou holdest fast my name, and hast not*
> *denied my faith, even in those days wherein Antipas was my*
> *faithful martyr, who was slain among you, where Satan dwelleth.*
> REVELATION 2:13

EVENING READING

The Spirit commended the church of Pergamum for holding fast to God's name even though they dwelled where Satan's throne was. Though He goes on to point out some things that the church was not doing well, it remains a beautiful testimony that this faithful church was shining Christ's light into the darkest of places. They stood strong at the very gates of hell. They proclaimed Christ as victor over all the earth, even the parts where Satan's power seemed overwhelming.

Cravings

(AMOS 5:14–15)

>>))))) ❀ (((((<

MORNING PRAYER

Lord God Almighty, thank You for Your Word that shows me that people have always had the same troubles. You offered me a feast of unimaginable riches, but I turned up my nose at it. My hunger has led me to unhealthy, wicked things. I ignore You, when You are my friend—my best friend, in fact. Oh Lord, forgive me. Take what I crave from me, and let me find relief from my withdrawal cravings in You. Continue to mold my heart like Yours, that I will hate evil and love good, shun the one and cling to the other. Amen.

> *Because thou sayest, I am rich, and increased with goods,*
> *and have need of nothing; and knowest not that thou art*
> *wretched, and miserable, and poor, and blind, and naked.*

REVELATION 3:17

EVENING READING

Take an inventory of your true, everlasting riches versus your false, fleeting riches. Sometimes earthly wealth lulls us into thinking that we are safe and secure. But apart from the riches that only come through a personal relationship with Christ, we are wretched, miserable, poor, blind, and naked. Seek the true riches that Christ offers you.

Restored

(AMOS 9:14–15)

❧❧❧❧ ❀ ❧❧❧❧

MORNING PRAYER

My Lord God, You have chastened me, burning away my impurities, and now You swoop in and restore to full beauty and function all that has been destroyed in my life. You don't just replace what was lost; You give me something better. You rebuild ruins, replant gardens, and tend vines in Your vineyard. You've grafted me onto Your vine. The graft has taken; I'm tasting of Your life-giving water. Teach me to depend on You in order for Your Spirit to run through me, strengthening body and soul and spirit to do Your will. Amen.

And the four beasts had each of them six wings about him; and they were full of eyes within: and they rest not day and night, saying, Holy, holy, holy, LORD God Almighty, which was, and is, and is to come.

REVELATION 4:8

EVENING READING

The four living creatures in heaven constantly proclaim, "Holy, holy, holy, LORD God Almighty, which was, and is, and is to come." They do not rest from their praise of their Maker. Though God has put us on this earth for a different purpose than to proclaim His holiness without ceasing, it is still of value to consider how often you praise God. Even if you aren't constantly speaking of His greatness, your life can still proclaim His perfect work in you. And one day we will join in this endless praise, because to encounter the Lord in all His holiness is to inevitably be inspired to praise Him.

Staying Straight

(OBADIAH)

❧❧❧❧ ❀ ❧❧❧❧

MORNING PRAYER ·

Lord God Almighty, whom I'm privileged to call Father, You promise to deliver me, and You do deliver me out of all my troubles. Keep me from repeating the same mistakes. When You rescue me, You offer me so much more. You cleanse me and make me holy, a vessel ready for use. And You will return my inheritance for me to multiply for Your service and glory. May I turn it back into zealous hunger for more of You and for spreading the Gospel. May I accept and act on Your deliverance as a new beginning. Amen.

And I beheld, and, lo, in the midst of the throne and of the four beasts, and in the midst of the elders, stood a Lamb as it had been slain, having seven horns and seven eyes, which are the seven Spirits of God sent forth into all the earth.
REVELATION 5:6

EVENING READING ·

In his vision, John stood weeping because he saw no one who could open the scroll. But then one of the elders assured him that the Lion of Judah had the authority to open the scroll. We look with anticipation to see this Lion, but what does John see by the throne? A slain Lamb. What beautiful imagery that this conquering Lion is displayed in all His power and glory as a sacrificed Lamb. In His completely counterintuitive and glorious plan, God sent His most powerful weapon, a humble sacrifice, to conquer the world, death, and all the powers of darkness.

Where's Dan?

(REVELATION 7:4–8)

>>>>>> ❀ <<<<<<

MORNING PRAYER

Lord God, I read the tribes who are numbered among the 144,000 witnesses and wonder why Dan isn't included. It's another reminder that You are sovereign. I can guess at reasons, but I don't need to know the answer, do I? I only need to trust the who—You! You have appointed the right witnesses to Your truth in that coming future time. Just as today You have placed me in this nursing home while my college roommate teaches the Bible in a public setting. I write stories while my son speaks Your truth to unbelievers. You know how and where we best serve, and I trust Your placement. Amen.

> *But they shall sit every man under his vine and*
> *under his fig tree; and none shall make them afraid:*
> *for the mouth of the LORD of hosts hath spoken it.*
> MICAH 4:4

EVENING READING

What a beautiful picture Micah prophesied, that every person will sit peacefully under their tree with absolutely nothing to make them afraid. Imagine a world in which nothing could make you afraid. This is the world that we get to look forward to in eternity. And even during this life, there is nothing that can make us afraid if we truly grasp the status that we have before God. The Lord of hosts has spoken that you are one of His forever-kept children. With this perspective, fear has no place in your heart or mind.

God's Requirements

(MICAH 6:8)

⇒⇒⟩⟩⟩ ❀ ⟨⟨⟨⟨⟨⟵

MORNING PRAYER ·

Lord God Almighty, how much time do I waste when I ask myself what You want me to do? You have made it abundantly clear over and over again. You don't ask for some terrible sacrifice or even the ordained sacrifices under the Law. Something comes before wondering whom I should marry or what career path I should follow. You mostly want me to make the right daily choices that lead to the bigger choices. It's in how I choose to treat my neighbor and how closely I follow You as my role model. It's in how much credit I claim for myself and how much praise I turn back to You. If I act justly, love mercy, and walk humbly, I will please You. Amen.

Wherewith shall I come before the Lord, and bow myself before the high God? shall I come before him with burnt offerings, with calves of a year old? Will the Lord be pleased with thousands of rams, or with ten thousands of rivers of oil? shall I give my firstborn for my transgression, the fruit of my body for the sin of my soul? He hath shewed thee, O man, what is good; and what doth the Lord require of thee, but to do justly, and to love mercy, and to walk humbly with thy God?
MICAH 6:6–8

EVENING READING ·

Verses 6 and 7 of Micah 6 lay out increasingly costly scenarios of ways to pay for our sins. The last one Micah suggested almost incredulously, as it would be too much to bear—"shall I give my firstborn for my transgression?" And yet, this is exactly what the Lord has done for you. Since He did not desire to ask such a heart-wrenching sacrifice of you, He did it instead. Micah went on to lay out what God requires of us. It is not sacrifices of ten thousand bulls or the surrender of our firstborn. We are simply to do justly, love mercy, and walk humbly with Him—He's done the rest for us.

No In-Between

(NAHUM 1)

>>>>>> ❀ <<<<<<

MORNING PRAYER

God of the heavenly armies, there is no in-between with You. I'm either in Your refuge, protected by the shelter of Your wings, or else I'm against You, with the full fury of Your anger falling on me. How thankful I am that Your goodness falls on me. How great Your goodness! How I rejoice in Your shelter, where You have hidden me during bouts of grief, turmoil, and ill health. You care for me in that You love me. You also take care of me, providing for my every need, keeping me safe from harm in the midst of battle. Amen.

> *Who can stand before his indignation? and who can abide*
> *in the fierceness of his anger? his fury is poured out like fire,*
> *and the rocks are thrown down by him. The LORD is good, a strong*
> *hold in the day of trouble; and he knoweth them that trust in him.*
> NAHUM 1:6–7

EVENING READING

The book of Nahum starts out aggressively depicting God's power and wrath against offending nations. It gives us a good picture of why we ought to fear God. And then verse 6 abruptly switches gears to talk about the goodness of the Lord and how He is a stronghold in the day of trouble. How reassuring in the face of His wrath to be reminded that He knows and cares for those who trust in Him. In the midst of whirling chaos, He is ever your stronghold.

Even When

(HABAKKUK 3:17–19)

>>>))) ❀ (((<<

MORNING PRAYER ·

My Savior and my Lord, I've often camped at Habakkuk's prayer. Your goodness, love, and mercy don't change when my circumstances do. That's why I sing when the things I've planted don't bear fruit. When my surroundings are stripped of signs of life and hope, I still rejoice in You. You are my Savior. You are my strength. You give power to the muscles of my faith so that my quivering soul can climb on mountaintops. From there, I get a better perspective. Whether in the valley or on the heights, may I praise You with everything in me. Amen.

> *Although the fig tree shall not blossom, neither shall fruit be*
> *in the vines; the labour of the olive shall fail, and the fields*
> *shall yield no meat; the flock shall be cut off from the fold,*
> *and there shall be no herd in the stalls: yet I will rejoice*
> *in the LORD, I will joy in the God of my salvation.*
> HABAKKUK 3:17–18

EVENING READING ·

Habakkuk was a man of true resilience. Was this because he was especially powerful or well-off or had a good network of support? No, it was because no matter what the circumstance, he had made the choice to rejoice in the Lord. His was a God-based prosperity, not a circumstance-based prosperity. For this reason, no negative earthly circumstance could touch him because no amount of failed crops or empty stalls would change his opinion of his God. His joy lay in his Savior, not his stuff.

⪻ DAY 358 ⪼

Singing Over Me with Love
(Zephaniah 3:17)

⪻⪼❀⪻⪼

MORNING PRAYER

Lord God, I cannot escape Your presence. You accompany me everywhere I go. You are mighty with the power to save and also a warrior who fights for me. You care about me that much. You take delight in me—in me, as poor as I am! You rejoice over me, singing love melodies and songs of celebration. You are great, and greatly to be praised! With a God like that, I don't need to fear anything. Your powerful presence gives strength to my arms, that I might join the battle at Your side. If that weren't enough, You restore honor and praise to me, although I'm unworthy of either. May all the glory be returned to You, Lord! Amen.

> *The Lord thy God in the midst of thee is mighty;*
> *he will save, he will rejoice over thee with joy; he will*
> *rest in his love, he will joy over thee with singing.*
> Zephaniah 3:17

EVENING READING

The Lord rejoices over you with singing. Can you believe that? Can you imagine that a God who created the universe, constantly sustains it, and listens to the prayers of billions of people every day rejoices over you? Insecurities, self-abasing self-talk, and low self-image have no place in the mind of someone who is rejoiced over by God. People will let you down and make you feel small and worthless, but when this happens, never forget that God continues to rejoice over you with joy and singing. Doesn't His opinion count for so much more than the opinion of anyone else?

On a Continuum

(HAGGAI 2)

⇒⟩⟩⟩⟩ ❀ ⟨⟨⟨⟨⟨

MORNING PRAYER ·

Lord God, Haggai points back to the day the Israelites left Egypt and forward to Jesus' return as Your signet ring. Your promise doesn't change, and in some ways, past and present are the same to You. You're not bound by time; You created it. Whatever I see around me now, a glorious future awaits me in heaven. Eternal peace awaits me. All the gold and silver, everything I strive for now, belongs to You. I pray that I will strive to fill my heavenly accounts with kingdom currency that I may offer at Your feet. May I gladly share the good news of Your salvation, help when there is a need, and spend my life in Your service. Amen.

> *Two things have I required of thee; deny me them not before I die:*
> *remove far from me vanity and lies: give me neither poverty*
> *nor riches; feed me with food convenient for me.*
> PROVERBS 30:7–8

EVENING READING ·

May God be so gracious that He gives us just the right amount of material wealth and comfort so that we continue to rely on and bless Him. May He be gracious enough to grant us contentment no matter what the circumstance. May our lives not be defined by vanity or treachery to get ahead in life, but rather, may they be lives of satisfaction in God alone without regard to material circumstances.

≫ DAY 360 ≪

Praise in Tribulation

(Revelation 15:2–4)

≫≫⟩⟩⟩ ❀ ⟨⟨⟨⟨≪

MORNING PRAYER ·

Lord God Almighty, how much more do I praise You in times of trouble, like the saints of the tribulation? I marvel at Your deeds. They are great and beyond understanding. Your ways steer a straight path, showing no favoritism but delivering a just and fair verdict. You are the ultimate judge of truth. You see all things, even the intents and purposes of the heart. And that's not just true for me and my community, but also for all people in every nation. You alone are holy! No other god worshipped under heaven comes close to measuring up to You. Glory to Your name. Amen.

For who hath despised the day of small things? for they shall rejoice,
and shall see the plummet in the hand of Zerubbabel with those seven;
they are the eyes of the Lord, which run to and fro through the whole earth.
Zechariah 4:10

EVENING READING ·

Do not despise small beginnings. Do you ever have visions of what you want to be or do for God's kingdom? Then when you take stock of your current life, what you're doing seems so insignificant it's almost worthless? God uses small beginnings to make big movements in His kingdom. Who knows how He will use your faithful steps today? Take courage that nothing is wasted in God's economy.

Beyond the Good Old Days

(Zechariah 8)

>>>>> ✿ <<<<<

MORNING PRAYER

Lord God, I read these verses like I'm longing for the good old days, when the elderly stayed at home and children played in the streets. But You promise so much more than restoration. I am one of Your people because You are my God. You are faithful to me. To me! I have done nothing to deserve Your faithfulness, but that's kind of the point. May I respond in ways pleasing to You. May I do the work You have placed in my hands. Let me speak, judge, and live in truth. Forgive me when I tear others down instead of building them up. May I be part of a swelling throng that is gathering before Your throne to praise You. Amen.

> *There be four things which are little upon the earth, but they are exceeding wise: the ants are a people not strong, yet they prepare their meat in the summer; the conies are but a feeble folk, yet make they their houses in the rocks; the locusts have no king, yet go they forth all of them by bands; the spider taketh hold with her hands, and is in kings' palaces.*
> Proverbs 30:24–28

EVENING READING

God's fingerprints are all over His creation. His character can be found in His creativity. Since He is the author of all living things, it makes sense that even the smallest of creatures can speak of His wisdom. Learn from the beautiful creation that He has given us to enjoy.

Hope's Prison

(ZECHARIAH 9:12)

>>>>> ❀ <<<<<

MORNING PRAYER

Oh God who frees me, there's one prison I never want to escape: Your fortress of hope. How blessed I am to dwell in that place where intangible evidence of what is promised is seen as tangible. If I must wear tinted glasses, may they be colored with the golden glory of Your kingdom, blinding me to doubts. Within the walls of my cell, my world expands. I see life through Your eyes, not only today and in my town but also across the miles and through the centuries. You not only restore the past; You also multiply it—twice, ten times, even a hundredfold. Make it so, to Your honor and glory. Amen.

These shall make war with the Lamb, and the Lamb shall
overcome them: for he is Lord of lords, and King of kings:
and they that are with him are called, and chosen, and faithful.
REVELATION 17:14

EVENING READING

Today's reading in Revelation speaks of two things that are inevitable. First, the devil and his armies will wage war against the Lamb. We should not be surprised when we see the attempts of the darkness to overshadow Christ's light. But the second inevitable thing is that the Lamb shall overcome the powers of darkness. Always keep in mind that no matter how hotly the battles are raging, the end is sure.

⊱ DAY 363 ⊰

Raise Up Advocates

(PROVERBS 31:4–9)

⇒⇒⟩⟩⟩ ❀ ⟨⟨⟨⟨⟨⇐

MORNING PRAYER ·

Lord of lords, let this be my passion, that I will speak up for those who can't speak for themselves, especially in the nursing home where I live. There are so many people groups who need advocates. Let each person speak as You lead. I pray for city, state, and national leaders, that they won't disobey the law or deny anyone's rights. When there is a conflict of conscience, give them wisdom to know how and when to fight for change. I pray also for their courage and discernment to defend the poor and judge the needy fairly, without political bias. Amen.

> *Open thy mouth for the dumb in the cause of all*
> *such as are appointed to destruction. Open thy mouth,*
> *judge righteously, and plead the cause of the poor and needy.*
> PROVERBS 31:8–9

EVENING READING ·

We are to be a voice for those who don't have one. We are to be the arms of Christ here on earth to reach out to those who are headed for destruction. We are to speak up against injustice. We are to judge righteously (without regard to social status, economic status, age, race, or gender) just as our heavenly Father does. We are to plead the cause of the poor and needy so that they do not get trampled on. How are you doing with all these things?

Divorce

(MALACHI 2:16)

❄❄❄❄❄ ❀ ❄❄❄❄❄

MORNING PRAYER ·

Lord of hosts, I feel the depth of Your passion when You say, "I hate divorce" (Malachi 2:16 NASB). I hate it too, but I'm a child of divorce and divorced myself. I thank You for Your forgiveness, grace, and second chances. I pray for my son, for friends, and church leaders, that their marriages will be strong. May husbands and wives stand guard against things that will tear their marriages apart. Keep them pure sexually. Let both parties protect their marriage as they would protect their own lives, and together may they raise children who honor You. I also pray for healing for those who are divorced and for their children. Amen.

And he was clothed with a vesture dipped in blood: and his name is
called The Word of God. And the armies which were in heaven followed
him upon white horses, clothed in fine linen, white and clean.
REVELATION 19:13–14

EVENING READING ·

The robe of Christ was marred by the stain of blood as He rode forth into battle. Those who followed after Him, the heavenly armies, were clothed in perfectly clean and white linen. No spot of blood stained their robes. Your robe is perfectly white because He who stands next to you wears a robe that speaks of the bloody sacrifice that earned you your freedom. His bloodstains are your salvation and power. Follow Him into battle boldly, knowing that nothing can mar the white linen He has given you.

Coming Home

(REVELATION 22)

⇒⇒⟩⟩⟩ ❀ ⟨⟨⟨⟨⇐

MORNING PRAYER

Spirit, You called, "Come!" And I have responded, "I am coming." Let me repeat the offer of Your free gift of the water of life to all who thirst. On that day, when the Alpha and Omega closes the door to human history and the bright Morning Star provides all the light needed in His kingdom, I'll be there, by Your grace, because You have made me holy. Just to be there will be glory. Whether my reward is nothing at all or a gold-and-diamond crown, may I throw it at Your feet. Because it's all of You and from You. No more night, no more curse, no more death, no more tears or pain. Hallelujah, amen.

And I heard a great voice out of heaven saying, Behold, the tabernacle of God is with men, and he will dwell with them, and they shall be his people, and God himself shall be with them, and be their God. And God shall wipe away all tears from their eyes; and there shall be no more death, neither sorrow, nor crying, neither shall there be any more pain: for the former things are passed away.

REVELATION 21:3–4

EVENING READING

God will wipe away every tear from your eye with the very hands that are scarred by the nails that were driven in the cross for your sins. Death will be vanquished for all eternity and slowly forgotten as we live in blissful praise of our God, who conquered it for us. There will be no place for crying, sorrow, or pain as all things will finally be made right again. Could there be a more hopeful vision to hold onto in this life? Your struggles, pain, and tears are ephemeral and like a vapor that will be quickly forgotten in the all-encompassing light of God's glory. *Come, Lord Jesus, and make this future our present reality.*

SCRIPTURE INDEX

NEW TESTAMENT